WHERE THE STAR CAME TO REST

BY

GASPAR F. ANCONA

Publisher: Éditions du Signe • B.P. 94 • 67038 Strasbourg Cedex 2 • France
Tel: (33) 3 88 78 91 91 • Fax: (33) 3 88 78 91 99
Publishing director: Christian Riehl
Director of publication: Dr. Claude-Bernard Costecalde
Design and layout : Daniel Muller
ISBN: 2-7468-0317-8
Printed in Italy by Arti Grafiche s.r.l.
Copyright: © 2001 Éditions du Signe
Copyright text: Diocese of Grand Rapids
Copyright illustrations: Margaret Leiber
All rights reserved

To my father and my ancestors
who emigrated from across the seas
and brought their faith with them

TABLE OF CONTENTS

FOREWORD

It is a pleasure to see a good work come to completion. This is especially true when the good work is a long and complicated affair. That is certainly the case with attempting to tell the story of a diocese. In fact, a first attempt was made around the time of the centennial of the Diocese of Grand Rapids in 1982, but somehow the book did not get written. The turn of the millennium has offered another opportunity.

Monsignor Gaspar Ancona has shared his gifts with the Diocese of Grand Rapids in many different ways during his nearly forty years of priestly ministry. He has consistently been called upon to speak for the diocese to the media, whether it be through the written or the spoken word. When plans were being made to produce a "millennial" history of the diocese, it was natural to turn to him to serve as the author. We were very grateful when he agreed to take on this responsibility.

Early on in the planning, the decision was made that this should be a popular history. Our hope was that it would be a book that our people would enjoy reading and re-reading. It was also our hope that teachers of church history in our schools would find it helpful for interesting our young people in the story of the faith that is particular to our own diocese and parishes.

That story is a fascinating one, from the arrival of Father Frederic Baraga to the arrival of the Jubilee Year 2000. Readers of **Where the Star Came to Rest** *will not be disappointed. I have enjoyed it, chapter by chapter, as it came off the computer. I will be happy to read it again, when it comes out in the beautiful edition planned by Editions Du Signe publishers in Strasbourg, France.*

The book has been in process for several years and has involved a large and active group of collaborators. The final section, which includes a page for each parish of the diocese, has been a special project, which called for the cooperation of all of our pastors and their staffs.

I want to express my sincere thanks to all those who have cooperated to make this dream become a reality. In a very special way, I thank Monsignor Gaspar Ancona for the years of work and worry that writing our history has involved. <u>Finis coronat opus!</u>

Robert J. Rose
Bishop of Grand Rapids

Feast of St. Andrew, November 30, 2000

When Bishop Rose commissioned me to write a history of the Diocese of Grand Rapids, I had asked him for a change of assignment after serving as rector for 10 years at the Cathedral of St. Andrew. He mentioned a quiet little parish in the countryside and asked if I would be interested in being pastor there while doing the research and writing for the book. It sounded idyllic.

Idyllic is no exaggeration for St. Sebastian Parish in Byron Center. There is an historic quiet and rustic beauty here. However, new businesses and residents are moving in, and highways are plowing through farmlands. The parish is bustling. Still, its people have provided me a haven for fulfilling the bishop's commission. Usually, the research and writing were done on the run, in between marriages and funerals, power outages and parish meetings, and all the details that make up a community's life together. Always, it was a challenge to emerge from research into one era or another, with all the colorful characters I met along the way, and then try to refocus on the people, the time, and the situation right before me. If some found me with a faraway, distracted look, this project has been my best excuse. I hope the results will in some measure repay the trust and freedom both Bishop Rose and the St. Sebastian parishioners placed in me.

From the beginning I sought out the help of many others. Sister Mona Schwind, OP, was the first person I consulted. She had been professor of church history at Aquinas College in Grand Rapids and archivist for the Grand Rapids Dominican Sisters. She shared with me her experiences in authoring the histories of her Dominican community and the parish of St. Francis de Sales in Norton Shores. Through an introduction from Bishop Breitenbeck, I met Patrick Nugent, who teaches church history at West Catholic High School in Grand Rapids. He showed an interest in the project, having himself authored the parish history of St. Patrick's in Parnell. We brainstormed for a while, trying to give shape to the kind of readable, accessible history that the bishop envisioned. Next Patrick and I met with Mr. Gordon Olson, Grand Rapids city historian, who gave us three hours of his time and much practical advice. That meeting led to further conversations with Bishop Rose to refine our goals. Then I consulted with Dr. James D. Bratt, author and professor of history at Calvin College in Grand Rapids. He encouraged me into thinking that, against my fears, this project was "doable" by a history amateur and active pastor.

I also called upon old friends and new acquaintances to share their talents on an ongoing advisory board. They joined forces in a spirit of adventure and discovery. Calling this "The Magi Project," I wanted to honor those biblical seekers, my own patron among them, who first journeyed into the night, following the heavenly star in order to find where Jesus had been born. They went to pay him honor and present him with their gifts. I felt a kinship with them in this endeavor 2,000 years later.

Those who accepted my invitation have my deepest gratitude. They came from various backgrounds and different parts of the diocese. Some were retired, others in one or more jobs. All had various demands in their lives. Some were able to participate for a time: Thomas Dalton, Louis R. deAlvare, Rebecca Smith-Hoffman, Mauricio Jimenez, Joanne McElwee, Robert Nachtegal, Paul Peterson, Laura Ridout, and Elaine Snyder. Others were with the project to the end, doing research and interviews, editing the parish pages, selecting photographs, tracking down elusive information and details, and offering constructive critiques as we went along: Margaret Audretsch, Bonnie Golder, Joanne Jones, John McNamara, Patrick Nugent, Dr. Allan TenEyck, and Ann Webb.

Throughout these years of meetings we have had the reassuring presence of the diocesan archivist, Father Dennis W. Morrow, who is himself a walking archive of diocesan history. He guided us through the diocesan resources, making them accessible, and connecting us with other people and resources around the community. His colorful stories of people and places in the life of the church whetted our appetites for more. Janet M. Voss from the diocesan administrative office assisted us as secretary for all our meetings and helped keep us on track as the work progressed. Dr. Jeremy Beer provided valuable research during the spring and summer of 2000 and was helpful in evaluating the relative importance of information. William Hebert, of Insightful Imagery, gave of his time and expertise in photographic assistance, and Diane Harwood finalized copy for the parish section in a timely manner. Sue Rose contributed valuable secreterial help and many an emergency solution to baffling computer detours and dead ends. Monroe B. Sullivan generously prepared the manuscript for publication. Joseph Voss and Dr. Gordon Golder contributed careful analysis and helpful critiques as the text neared final form.

Special thanks to Margaret Leiber whose art work graces this book. Not only did she respond unquestioningly with help, but she also intuited the Christian spirit of discovery involved in this effort. She has captured the power and beauty of the people and events whose faith story this book tries to tell.

Most of all, I have been sustained by my family: my mother, sisters, and brother. On dark and unpromising nights and days, when no progress seemed evident, they have unfailingly supported and encouraged me, seeing the breaking dawn, when I thought I lost the star.

Rev. Monsignor Gaspar F. Ancona

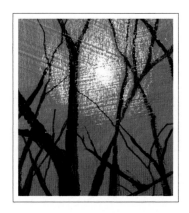

WHEN FORESTS STOOD TALL

1600 - 1835

THE GREAT LAKES ARE WONDERS OF THE WORLD. But then, the whole world and everything in it are wonders of God. By geologic measuring these inland freshwater seas are young, about 11,000 years old.

At that time they emerged from the Ice Age, as did the peninsulas which form the State of Michigan. Great forests covered these territories. The trees became towering and grew together so densely thick that sunlight could barely reach the forest floor. The first inhabitants found themselves a paradise.

They had a deep appreciation of their paradise. They fished the bountiful streams and waters, hunted the deer, bear, and beaver, and clothed themselves with the animal skins and furs.

These first inhabitants, later known as Indians or Native Americans, developed their own communities and tribes. They lived under the leadership of chiefs and councils of elders. They honored the Great Spirit as the source of all the lands and waters and of all the human and animal life around them.

Sometimes they offered a slaughtered dog as a sacrifice to the Sun for the bounty of food. Other times they danced and sang their thanks as well as their needs. They painted and decorated their bodies. In dance and song, they made love, prayed for sun or rain, and signaled friendship or war.

They moved up and down these peninsulas according to the seasons, fishing and hunting as well as seeking their favorite gathering places. When the

1601	1610	1632	1680	1687	1742	1773	1791	1808
Shakespeare writes *Hamlet*	Galileo discovers Jupiter's four moons	Building of Taj Mahal begins	Kateri Tekakwitha dies	Newton publishes *Theory of Gravity*	Handel composes *Messiah*	Boston Tea Party	Mozart composes *Requiem*	Beethoven composes *Fifth Symphony*

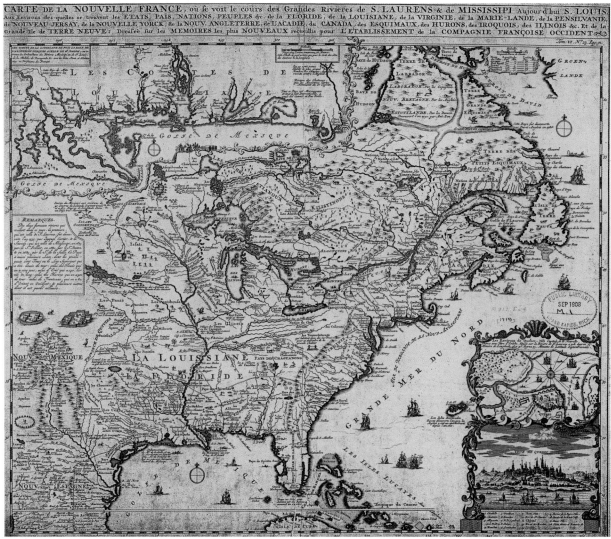

"Map of the New France," including the Great Lakes, from the 1600s.

first Europeans arrived in these territories in the 1600s, the native inhabitants may have numbered fewer than 10,000.

The first Europeans who came to what is now Michigan were adventurers and soldiers, fortune seekers and missionaries. They were Catholic Christians, at least by name and tradition, if not always in practice. They came from France by way of New France, as Canada was then called. Their language, clothes, customs, dwellings, social institutions, and religious beliefs were as strange and alien to the native dwellers as those of the natives were to the Europeans.

Sometimes the natives and the Europeans met in friendly curiosity about one another and with mutual respect. Sometimes they met each other with suspicion and hostility. The first Catholic missionaries in this territory were French Jesuit priests and brothers. They were men of deep religious faith and commitment. They were rigorously trained and highly educated. Their social background in France was often one of means and comfort and sometimes of prominence. Some of the missionaries came from poor, hardworking farming communities, others from cities with already long histories of settlement, commerce, and civic life. They were very disciplined.

The French expeditions along the Great Lakes were in search of a passage to the "Western Sea." When they experienced the grandeur and wonder of the connecting Great Lakes, they thought they were discovering an all-water route to China and Japan. This was the great and coveted prize: an economic boon for the fortune seekers, possible conquest for soldiers and emissaries of the French king, and for the Jesuit missionaries, the prize of spreading the gospel of Jesus Christ to untold numbers.

The roll call of Jesuits in the territory of Michigan includes some revered and famous names: Father Isaac Jogues, Father Charles Raymbaut, Father Jacques Marquette, Father Pierre Charlevoix, Father Henri Nouvel, and Father Claude Allouez.

Father Jogues visited the area of what is now Sault Sainte Marie, Mackinac Island, and Saint Ignace. Later he met a violent end. Having been a captive of the Iroquois once before, he returned to them nevertheless on a peace mission. When the tribe later suffered a long famine and attendant diseases, some of them attributed the presence of the missionaries and the religious articles they left behind as the cause of their misfortunes. Father Jogues and his companions were brutally tomahawked and beheaded. Their deaths, "precious to God," as the Jesuit accounts describe them, took place near the present-day Auriesville, New York, northwest of Albany. A shrine there honors Father Isaac Jogues and his companions as martyrs or witnesses to the faith they professed in Jesus Christ.

Father Jacques Marquette, from an oil portrait of 1937 based on a 17th century outline.

Father Jacques Marquette was a brilliant and engaging young priest with a gift for friendship. He was dedicated to Jesus and to the church. He had a passion for exploration and collecting new information about the places he visited and the people he met. He seemed able to charm everyone, his fellow countrymen as well as the natives he encountered all along his journeys. Mostly, his success with people seemed to come from a personality formed by Christ, one that was welcoming and ready to honor the dignity and customs of others. He was vigorous and athletic, with an air of

friendly but firm authority. He listened long, patiently, and with genuine interest. He learned with respect the languages and courtesies of his native hosts.

It was Father Marquette, along with his friend and fellow explorer Louis Joliet and three other companions who were the first Europeans to navigate by canoe all along the western shores of Lake Michigan, down the Fox River, and eventually through the waters of the Mississippi River. They were guided and assisted in their route of discovery by members of tribes already familiar with the great waters: the Miami, the Maskouten, and the Kikabou.

Along the way Father Marquette shared his religious faith, wrote down his observations, and celebrated the great central act of worship of the Catholic Church, the Holy Mass or Eucharist. It was he who offered the first Mass in what is now downtown Chicago, but then only a clearing by the Chicago River, on his voyage to the Illinois tribes in December 1674.

It was on this journey to his beloved new Christians among the Illinois that Father Marquette became ill, perhaps from dysentery. He persisted in celebrating the grand liturgies of Holy Thursday, Good Friday, and Easter in the open air before thousands. He heard countless confessions, preached movingly in as loud a voice as he could manage, and alone gave the Bread of Life to his vast congregation.

After long and heartfelt farewells, he departed with his two companions. They were very solicitous of him but nothing they could do was able to restore him. They paddled their canoe along the eastern shores of Lake Michigan – the opposite shore of their original trip down – until Father Marquette could no longer bear the journey.

Father Marquette's last journey 1674-1675.

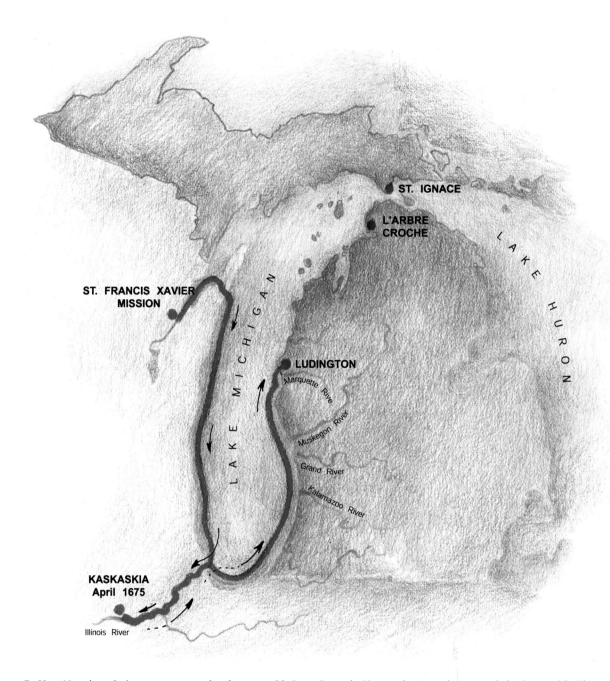

Fr. Henri Nouvel was the first missionary to work in the interior of the Lower Peninsula. He spent the winter of 1675 near the headwaters of the Chippewa River in Mecosta or Isabella County. After his journey down the Mississippi River, Fr. Jacques Marquette wintered at St. Francis Xavier Mission near Green Bay. He then returned in 1675 to the Illinois Indians at Kaskaskia. He died near Ludington en route to St. Ignace in May, 1675.

They landed at a spot south of what is now the city of Ludington, and there in that beautiful place by the shore he died. He was two weeks short of age 38, the 18th of May 1675, having traveled and labored for his Lord seven years along these woods and waters. His companions testified to his sweet and resolute faith in Jesus Christ to the end. Then

and there they buried him with tears and great reverence.

Two years later his devoted Odawa* would return in a flotilla of thirty canoes to carry his bones in honor

*Term currently favored as a more faithful rendition of the former "Ottawa."

to their final resting place at the Jesuit mission in St. Ignace, the mission he himself had established in 1671. The superior of the mission who welcomed back the remains of this hero of faith was Fr. Henri Nouvel.

Years before, during Fr. Marquette's exciting journey of exploration, an elder among the Illinois had voiced his warmth and friendship when he first greeted Père Marquette. Now the priest's grieving brothers and sisters in the faith, receiving him for the last time, could have echoed the sentiment of the Illinois leader: "How beautiful the sun is, O Frenchman, when you come to visit us!"

In the late fall of 1675, the year of Father Marquette's death, a party of Chippewa visited Father Nouvel at the St. Ignace mission and asked him to accompany them on their winter hunt "in the direction of Lake Erie." That invitation was enough for the adventurous missionary to draw up a map with their help and give them a promise to follow them later.

With two Frenchmen as his companions, Father Nouvel set out along the straits and the northeastern shore of the lower peninsula. To his joyful surprise he met some Algonquin women whom he had taught and baptized previously. They all continued the journey south together. November weather along the Great Lakes was just as treacherous then as now, so they took refuge from the cold, fog, and freezing by leaving Lake Huron and entering the Saginaw River. This gave the Saginaw the distinction, as one writer grandly described it, as "the first of all streams in lower Michigan to bear on its water an envoy of the Savior." *

The Savior's envoy, Father Nouvel, had other firsts on this trip. On December 3, 1675, he celebrated the first Mass in the interior of lower Michigan, somewhere between what is now the city of Saginaw and the juncture of the Flint and Shiawasse Rivers. As the band of Chippewa continued their hunt deeper and deeper into the forests, Father Nouvel kept pace, teaching children and adults about Jesus Christ, baptizing them, comforting and praying for their sick, and celebrating the Eucharist every day.

They built him a chapel and a cabin. On December 8, when he observed the feast of the Immaculate Conception, he felt deeply moved by the privilege of being able to share the redeeming Lord in the great sacrament. He remembered fondly the beloved Father Marquette, "who died quite near this spot," as he mistakenly conjectured in his report, but that inspiring example of heroic faith strengthened his own.

When Christmas 1675 drew near, the dark, thick forests of mid-Michigan sheltered the first crèche to commemorate the birth of Jesus. "Having constructed a little crib at the side of our altar, our Christians went thither at midnight and during the day to make these forests resound with their hymns in honor of the new-born Jesus." Father Nouvel does not mention the snow or the cold, the remoteness or the poverty of that place. Only the warmth of faith and the glow of Christ with them.

There, in the northeast corner of Mecosta county or the northwest corner of Isabella, Father Henri Nouvel continued his ministry throughout that winter and into the middle of March 1676. Every day they sang of Christ in those woods and served God's name with love and honor.

Another center of missionary activity was the area known as "L'Arbre Croche" or "The Crooked Tree." It is near the present-day Harbor Springs at Little Traverse Bay. There some of the Odawa had settled. The last of the pioneer Jesuits in what is now Michigan, Father Pierre Du Jaunay, ministered to them from 1761 to 1765. With his departure there was a long lapse of time before the Odawa again saw a missionary. They kept up the practice of their faith as best they could.

In 1799, a priest came by, a Frenchman like the previous missionaries, but not a Jesuit. He was Gabriel Richard. He was based in the Detroit area, but all Michigan was his parish. His English was fractured and his accent and pronunciation very French, but his commitment to Christ overcame the barriers of language as well as of geography.

* Quotations in Chapter 1 are from The Catholic Church in Detroit by George Paré, pp.44ff and The Catholic Church in the Grand River Valley by John W. McGee, pp.31ff.

Midnight Mass in the Michigan forest, December 25, 1675.

Father Gabriel Richard.

Father Richard would later become a famous name in Michigan history as an influential pioneer. He helped found the school which became the University of Michigan. He brought the first printing press to the whole territory, printing the first newspaper and the first books in all the area. He was elected to the United States Congress in 1823 as a non-voting delegate from the Territory of Michigan. In Congress he proposed and helped enact the legislation that created the first road between Detroit and Chicago, opening up the wilderness for settlement. As elected delegate he felt that he could best protect and foster the concerns of Indians in the Territory.

His driving motive was to bring the knowledge and love of Christ to as many as possible, beginning with the Native Americans. It was to these that he would go on long journeys to rekindle their faith or, as he would discover, to evangelize anew, as so many could barely remember the sign of the cross, so long had it been since their last instructions in the rudiments of the faith.

When Father Richard visited L'Arbre Croche in September 1799, he had sailed from Detroit on a government vessel named the *Detroit*, bound for Mackinac Island. All that summer he taught the basics of the Catholic faith, baptized, solemnized marriages, and encouraged Indians and traders alike in the living of the faith. He was even ready to remain in the North, if his superiors would allow, but he was recalled to Detroit.

He was not able to return until 1821. With over twenty years since Catholic Christians in the North had seen a priest, Father Richard knew he would have an enormous challenge ahead of him. He visited many of the centers of trade and settlement, starting with Mackinac Island. When he sailed once more to his cherished L'Arbre Croche, he was frustrated by wild seas and was prevented from landing. Undeterred, he took the opportunity to continue down the Lake Michigan coast, hoping to see for himself the burial place of a hero of his in the faith, Father Jacques Marquette.

He arrived at the mouth of the river already bearing the name of the explorer-missionary, and through the help of ten Odawa families living nearby, he retraced the last steps of Father Marquette. "There I erected a cross…. I placed it directly over the spot where the Indians told me a cross had been standing… until blown down by the winds three years ago. With my pocket knife I carved the following inscription in English: Fr. J H Marquet Died Here 9 May, 1675." His spelling was his own and the date he inscribed incorrect, but his devotion was true and deep. Later Father Richard celebrated the Eucharist there on the shore with a congregation of fifty, some speaking French, some English, and others the language of the Odawa.

Eventually, Father Richard received the assistance of Father Vincent Badin in Detroit, and Father Badin was able to continue the missionary visitations all along the waterways to the north and west on a more frequent basis. The first visit of a bishop, however, did not occur until May of 1829.

The Michigan territory was at that time still under the reponsibility of the bishop of Cincinnati. Edward Fenwick, a Dominican, was the bishop of all Ohio (since 1821) in addition to all of Michigan. He had made his first pastoral visitation outside Ohio to Detroit in 1822, but it was only in 1829 that he went on an extended missionary tour to the far north of his huge diocese.

L'Arbre Croche received the bishop with great solemnity. Chief Assakinac, wearing a large silver cross on his chest, led his tribesmen down to the beach to help the bishop out of his canoe. When the bishop stood, the chief led everyone in kneeling for the bishop's blessing. That fragrant spring evening only the voice of the chief broke the silence of the forest, as he led the tribe in chanting night prayers.

The next day two other chiefs and their tribes joined the festive gathering, Chief Papoisigan and Macatabanis (Blackbird). Chief Blackbird had been educated by the Montreal Sulpicians. As clergy themselves, the Sulpicians were a community founded in France for the education and spiritual formation of candidates to the priesthood. Father Richard had been a Sulpician before his departure from France.

It was Chief Blackbird's own son, William Macatebinessi, that Bishop Fenwick brought back with him to Cincinnati, along with Augustine Hamelin, half Canadian and half Indian. At fifteen years of age, they were placed in Bishop Fenwick's fledgling seminary and three years later (1832) sent to Rome to study for the priesthood at the Pontifical Urban College. Seminarian Hamelin would leave his studies for the priesthood because of poor health, return to Michigan, and become chief of his tribe. Chief Blackbird's son, William, died in Rome a year after his arrival, of complications from an accident he had suffered before he left America.

On his next pastoral visitation to the north in 1831, Bishop Fenwick had a young priest accompanying him. His name was Father Frederic Baraga. In the United States only a little more than six months, the thirty-four year old Slovenian had a gift for languages. In his student days in Vienna, he studied English and Spanish. Yet, in an excess of spiritual fervor, he thought it was all vanity on his part and counted the hours spent on language study as a loss demanding God's forgiveness.

Now in the wilderness of a new world he was learning languages and dialects he never dreamed of.

With zeal he brushed up on his English. With the help of the seminarians, William Macatebinessi and Augustine Hamelin, he delved into the mysteries of the Odawa language and customs. He had first heard about the Indians from Father Frederic Rese, assistant to Bishop Fenwick, when Father Rese was in Europe raising funds for the missions. Bringing the good news of Jesus Christ to the native-born of a new world became the dream of Father Baraga's life. Now, with his adopted bishop, he began living his dream.

During his pastoral visit of May 28, 1831, Bishop Fenwick recounted his personal feelings about L'Arbre Croche and the faith-filled devotion of the Odawa there: "I have never before felt happier and more contented…. Truly I would gladly exchange my place and my honors in Cincinnati for the hut and happiness of the missionary here…. "

As for the young Father Baraga, whom Bishop Fenwick introduced and commissioned to serve at L'Arbre Croche during the same visit, the new missionary wrote fervently: "Happy day which placed me among the Indians with whom I will now remain uninterruptedly to the last breath of my life, if such be the most holy wish of God."

In August of 1832, Father Baraga journeyed via the Lakes from L'Arbre Croche to Detroit. He wanted the help of his friend, Father Gabriel Richard, in having a prayer book printed for his mission. This book would be in the language of the Odawa. Chief Blackbird helped him with the translation. However, as the young scholar-missionary would quickly discover, cholera had broken out in Detroit, carried by new immigrants from Europe. It was a true plague and a swift killer. It spread panic and fear everywhere.

Father Richard was in the midst of his plans for establishing a college; but with the epidemic all around, he went from home to home administering Holy Communion and the last rites of the church. He himself succumbed to the disease, suffering chills and violent cramps over a period of several days, until he died on September 13, 1832. Along with Father Badin, Father Baraga was there to assist Father Richard in his dying and delivered the sermon at his funeral. Bishop Fenwick also fell victim to the disease on his way home to

Cincinnati. He had made another long circuit to the northern missions and passed through Detroit in mid-August to welcome new Redemptorist missionaries from Europe. Less than two weeks after the death of Father Richard, his friend and colleague in the ministry, Bishop Fenwick, himself died.

With his two mentors and friends now gone to the Lord after their earthly labors, Father Baraga returned to his northern mission. His new prayer book in the native language of the First People ("Anishnabeg," as the Odawa refer to themselves), signaled a style of ministry that he would continue and perfect to his own dying day. He would proclaim the gospel of Jesus Christ and the teachings of the church in the idiom of the First People. Whenever possible, he would adapt the Good News to their experience and traditions, just as he expected his hearers, in turn, to adapt their behavior to the requirements of the gospel.

TO THE GRAND

As Father Baraga continued his ministry in the region of L'Arbre Croche, he kept alert for opportunities to bring the Good News of Jesus Christ to other natives of the surrounding regions. He went to Beaver Island, to the Grand Traverse area, and to Manistique in the Upper Peninsula. While he was eager to teach customs and practices from the Christian tradition that were different from the Indian way of life, he became an open admirer of many native characteristics.

"These Indians," he wrote about one of these northern tours, "… possessed a keen faculty of comprehension, a retentive memory, and, what is more precious, a firm resolution to live according to the teachings of the Christian religion…. I cannot praise and admire [them] sufficiently, especially on account of their exceeding great love for prayer. Besides the long beautiful morning and evening prayer which they recite every day, they pray the rosary twice daily and some even three times. During their leisure moments they take their Indian prayer books – which I had printed last summer in Detroit – to pray and sing from them and to learn the catechism attached to it by heart. Most of them already knew how to read, and those who do not are diligently learning."

In the same report to Vienna, Father Baraga described the winter travel for which he became famous. He called mission travel impossible in the winter because "everything is covered with deep snow, and no trace of a path is to be found." He tried to keep up with the Indians anyway and decided, with their help, to go to present-day Mackinaw City. "The Indians," he related, "accustomed to [the snow] from youth, travel with ease and speed with large and heavy snow shoes…. Often I sank in the snow exhausted to rest a little, … and many a time I thought I could go no further. The good Indians who accompanied me had compassion upon me and waited every now and then so that I could follow."

Over his next thirty-five winters on earth Father Frederic Baraga would improve his travel skills. In that regard, as in so many others, he would become an adopted son of those he was adopting into Christ.

When many of his Arbre Croche Christians migrated south in the winter, he of course wanted to know why. They described to him the large gatherings of natives in several villages along the Grand River, how they hunted and farmed, and how their numbers might near a thousand. He remembered that his great mentor, Bishop Fenwick, "this apostolic and zealous man," had urged him to visit that region. So he selected one of the best-trained among the Arbre Croche Odawa Christians, who was going to winter at the Grand River, to go from village to village there and speak in testimony of his Christian faith. His emissary was also instructed to explain that the priest who lives with his tribesmen from the north would come to visit them also.

When that nameless and pioneering native evangelist returned to L'Arbre Croche, he went up to Father Baraga, grasped his hand, and said smiling, "Happy news, my Father, happy news!" Hearing how receptive to the gospel and to his ministry the Anishnabeg would be, Father Baraga without delay prepared to go south to the Grand. Although this would be a journey to explore for himself the potential for a fruitful mission, there was not much doubt that a new phase of his life for Christ was opening before him. Just as certainly, a fresh new chapter in the story of Christianity was about to unfold in the Grand River Valley.

EXPLORING THE GRAND

"On June seventh I set out on a long mission trip that lasted twenty-three days, and that proved successful beyond all my expectations…." With these triumphant words Father Baraga reported his first trip to the Grand River. It was meant to be an exploratory trip. He wanted to see for himself what the possibilities for a mission there would be. "God," he wrote soon after his return, "has called me into a land where so much good can be accomplished…." This enthusiasm came from a missionary who had already, in just the two years he had spent in L'Arbre Croche, baptized 464 Indians.

Louis and Sophie Campau were among the first settlers in Grand Rapids.

He arrived at the Grand River in the area which would become the center of Grand Rapids on June 15, 1833. At the time of his initial visit Father Baraga found several settlements scattered within the beautiful and densely forested wilderness. There were four Indian villages, the largest of them on the west bank of the river. On the east side of the river were the first white settlers, the most numerous being the family of Sophie de Marsac and Louis Campau. Descended from French Canadians, the Campaus were Catholics who gave Father Baraga a warm welcome. They opened their home to him in hospitality and offered him a new house which they had recently built, to use for church services. In this new house Father Baraga celebrated the first Mass in the region, probably on that day of his arrival.

It was not the Campaus, however, who were the first Catholics in the Grand River Valley, but the Anishnabeg themselves, the Odawa who had been evangelized or introduced to Catholicism at L'Arbre Croche or even in New France (Canada). Therefore, when Father Baraga's forerunner had paved the way for the missionary to take up residence at the Grand River, there was already the spark of faith ready to be fanned among the Native Americans and the white Catholic settlers as well.

Among the earliest Catholics of European or Canadian descent were Joseph and Magdaleine LaFramboise. Joseph, from Nova Scotia, was a fur trader who met his half-Chippewa, half-French wife in Grand Haven. They were married in 1804. Her grandfather, Kewinaquot ("Returning Cloud"), was a powerful Odawa Chief. Convent-educated in Montreal, Magdaleine settled with her new husband in the region of Ada, and together they established a trading post there. When Joseph was tragically murdered in 1806, an Indian named Nequat was apprehended for the crime. Magdeleine forgave him and begged for his release. She then assumed responsibility for the trading post herself until 1818, when she sold it to John Jacob Astor's American Fur Company. She left the area for Mackinac Island, settling in a house next to St. Ann Church. There she dedicated her energies and resources to providing education for children in the north. Her daughter married the brother of United States President Franklin Pierce.

When Father Baraga visited the settlements near the rapids of the Grand River, he celebrated Mass each day that summer of 1833 in the house the Campaus put at his disposal. He preached in the mornings and then again in the

Replica of La Framboise trading post on the Flat River near Lowell.

evenings and found that the Indians from the west side of the river "flocked together in multitudes… to listen to and to ponder the teachings of salvation." Before his survey of the area was completed, he baptized 46 Indians in one solemn ceremony at what he called the principal village. He also conducted baptismal ceremonies in three other Indian villages scattered nearby in the forest. In one there were six candidates for baptism, in another 21, and 13 in the third. Father Baraga refers to this missionary trip as taking 23 days from his departure on June 7 from L'Arbre Croche to his return. As he arrived at the rapids of the Grand on June 15, and if he took an equal number of days for his journey back, Father Baraga led into the Catholic Church a grand total of 86 Anishnabeg within only seven days of missionary work.

When he returned to L'Arbre Croche, what had Father Baraga learned from this extraordinary foray? For one thing, he saw for himself how receptive the Anishnabeg were to his ministry. This was revealing,

because a Baptist mission to the Grand River settlement predating Father Baraga's by 10 years had relatively few conversions to Christianity. The difference with Father Baraga's mission was threefold: (1) the L'Arbre Croche connection of acquaintances, friends, and relatives who had already been evangelized and had helped spread the good news to others who wintered at the Grand; (2) Father Baraga was able to communicate easily in the language and dialects of the Anishnabeg; (3) there was a curiosity about the seemingly exotic Catholic ritual, gestures, garments, and symbolism.

In addition, Father Baraga saw that the white settlers had their own need for developing and practicing their religious faith. However, he could already perceive impending dilemmas. The United States government owned all the land on the east side of the river and was opening it up for sale and settlement, while the Anishnabeg had claim to all the lands west and north of the river all the way up to the

19

straits. He noticed early on how white settlers were eager to keep moving across the wilderness and put down roots. While he would list as one of his reasons for setting up a mission in the Grand River Valley the pastoral care of the Catholic white settlers, his heart and his call were with the Anishnabeg. First, there were those who had never before heard of Jesus Christ. Then there were the Anishnabeg who were christened and initiated into the Catholic Church at L'Arbre Croche but who wintered at the Grand. For these reasons, he was ready with his bishop's consent to follow the Odawa to their southern encampments. For them and for their eternal salvation, he was willing to affirm in August, 1833: "I am now ready to leave Arbre Croche to take up my permanent residence in a place assigned to me by Providence and my superior, to establish a new mission." Father Baraga's "permanent residence" in this providential place which had his superior's seal of approval lasted, by his count, just 16 months.

I n later life and after endless journeying for the gospel of Christ by foot, on horseback, by canoe, and steamboat, Frederic Baraga would become legendary as the founding bishop of the Marquette Diocese and the apostle of the Upper Great Lakes. At present, his cause for canonization progresses at the Vatican. In 1833, however, he was pre-legendary, age 36, powerfully gifted, and eager to place all his energies and talents at the service of Christ in ministry to those who did not yet know the Lord or serve him.

In this resolute missionary, there was an unusual combination of capabilities and personal characteristics. He was before priesthood a student of the law, of languages, and of art. Some of his paintings survive, and they demonstrate, according to one author, "skill and delicacy in execution." In all his record-keeping, diaries, and letters as priest and later as bishop, the beauty and elegance of his handwriting are remarkable. So is the perfection of the page for whatever he was recording, even though the leather-bound books look worn and weather-stained from saddle bags. In portraits drawn of him and eventually in photographs, his jaw became firmer and firmer as he aged; his eyes more and more steely. A contemporary of his, a cartographer,

described him as "made of iron. Nothing holds him back and he lives even in places where an Indian would die of starvation."

What this friend of Frederic Baraga was describing was not physical strength ("He is small but sturdy"). Instead, it was the strength of will and character in his friend that he attempted to convey. He also portrayed the, by then, Bishop Baraga as indifferent to food as well as to his surroundings, whether in the forest or at home. This was a man of self-discipline and austerity.

This was the same man and priest in the prime of his earthly life who navigated by canoe down Lake Michigan from present-day Harbor Springs (L'Arbre Croche) in search of his new mission by the Grand on September 8, 1833, the feast of the Nativity of the Blessed Virgin Mary.

THE GRAND: 1833-1835

H e arrived at the mouth of the Grand River at Lake Michigan near today's Grand Haven on September 21 and after a day's rest, continued up the river to the site of the various settlements at the rapids, announcing himself there on the 23rd. He called an assembly of the Indians to present himself to them as their pastor, not just as a visiting missionary. Very quickly strong feelings about Father Baraga and his mission came to the fore: joy and welcome from some, antagonism and hostility from others. These initial conflicting reactions came from powerful and competing personalities. There were also serious economic interests at stake, for the federal government provided financial support for those missions it sanctioned. At the Grand, that meant the already existing Baptist mission. Nevertheless, the Anishnabeg met in council to hear Father Baraga's greetings.

Among the dominant personalities in the area were Chief Noonday (Nawequageezhig), who had become a Baptist, Chief Blackskin (Kewaycooshcum), who affiliated with the Catholic mission, the Baptist missionary, Reverend Leonard Slater, settler Barney Burton, Ada settler and trader Rix Robinson, and pioneer trader at the rapids, the Catholic Louis Campau. Not the least of the strong personalities was Father Frederic Baraga himself.

Notwithstanding the cross-currents of interests but aware of them, Father Baraga proceeded with his commitment to the Anishnabeg. He named his mission at the rapids in honor of the Blessed Virgin Mary, calling it "St. Mary's Mission." One of the Odawa put at Father Baraga's use a log cabin. Immediately Father Baraga set it up as a combined chapel and school. It was on the west side of the Grand where the Anishnabeg settlements were. Twenty-five Native and four settler children were enrolled, the modest and hopeful beginning of formal Catholic education along the Grand in the fall of 1833.

It did not take long before the settlers, in the person of Louis Campau, began to pressure Father Baraga to conduct religious services on the east side of the river. Apparently the argument was made early in his ministry at the Grand, that the land on the west side of the river would soon be taken over by the United States. Therefore, to protect the future of the mission, so the argument went, any buildings and development should be located on the east side. While the new priest was attentive to the spiritual needs of the settlers, he made no secret that his first responsibility and his primary reason for coming to the Grand was the evangelization and pastoral care of the Anishnabeg. The credibility of his service to them might be lost if he set up his mission on the east side. Father Baraga decided to submit the dilemma in a letter to his new bishop in Detroit, Frederic Rese. Before he sent it, he showed the letter, written in French, to Mr. Campau. However, in a private enclosure written in German, he pleaded with his bishop to decide in favor of keeping the mission on the west side. He insisted that whatever the bishop should decide, "I will strictly obey you." The bishop sided with his missionary.

Father Baraga also took unblinking notice of how lukewarm, and in his words, "depraved" the traders could be as so-called Christians. It was the Indians, after all, who showed a great love for prayer and for attendance at the Eucharist. The settler-traders were often indifferent when it came to the rituals of the

church. From Father Baraga's point of view, the zeal for trade and profit was so strong among some pioneer settlers that they made unscrupulous use of alcohol to befuddle the Anishnabeg and swindle them out of precious furs. The missionary complained often and bitterly to the traders themselves for such shameless manipulation of the Indians for their own gain. For his pains, he said, they plied the Natives with even more liquor and slandered the priest in the bargain.

On one occasion, Father Baraga reported, he had to stay in his cabin behind bolted doors, as a crowd of Natives, inflamed by alcohol, surrounded his home and howled threats upon his life. Always after that, he would bar his doors in the dark forest if there was an outbreak of drinking in the settlements.

Among Father Baraga's most satisfying adventures for the faith were his journeys to Maschkigong, the present-day Muskegon. In his exploratory trip the summer of 1833, he had visited there and baptized 21 Odawa, the first known celebration of the sacrament along the lower lakeshore of Michigan. Before his arrival, however, there were fur traders from French Canada at the outlet of Muskegon Lake in the late 1700s and early 1800s.

When Father Baraga arrived again in March, 1834, he revisited the sites in the forest of his previous summer missionary tour. He was deeply moved to find that at one site, where the Odawa were making sugar from maple sap, they had constructed a small chapel for prayer. It was their habit to meet in the chapel twice on Sundays. "I spent three days in this holy wilderness," he wrote, "and read Mass daily in their chapel with unusual emotion and with heartfelt thanks to God…." These were once again the devout Catholic neophytes from L'Arbre Croche.

Further on, he chose a site which the Catholic Odawa wished to have as their center for prayer "on an elevation, offering a beautiful view of the lake and the Maschkigong river." The bluff is thought to be Pigeon Hill in present-day Muskegon, overlooking Muskegon Lake. He decided to name the lakeshore mission after St. Joseph. This mission gave him great joy and consolation because of the deep and sincere religious faith of the Odawa there and the steady

Frederic Baraga as the first bishop of the Diocese of Marquette.

Rendition of the first church in Muskegon. Built by Indians, it overlooked Muskegon Lake at Pigeon Hill and was built in late 1834.

growth in the numbers whom he initiated into the following of Jesus.

At St. Mary's Mission on the Grand River Father Baraga was able to dedicate a new church building on April 20, 1834. It was on the west side of the river. The structure was 50 by 30 feet in size and 12 feet high. He lavished the occasion with the solemn Catholic ritual of a long procession in the woods, led by banners flying. The priest splashed holy water on the log structure in blessing, while the waters of the Grand rushed nearby. Inside the church Father Baraga had arranged for 18 paintings from a noted artist friend in Slovenia to grace the walls. With the imported candelabra, silk vestments, art work, and ceremonies, the spring day of dedication was a stunning celebration of faith for the growing Catholic community.

In less than a year from this high point in his ministry, Father Baraga announced his departure from the Grand. It seemed like such an abrupt and premature development that some have speculated

about a forced reassignment. Was it government sources who pressured Bishop Rese to remove Father Baraga because of his well-known opposition to the government's efforts to acquire Indian lands? There is no record of such pressure. Neither is there evidence that he was forced out because of his open and continual condemnation of the traders' use of alcohol to debase and manipulate the Indians.

Father Baraga's own explanation was that a surprise visit to the Grand by fellow missionary Father Andreas Viszoczky in February 1835, revealed that Father Viszoczky wanted to mission there if Bishop Rese would consent. Further inquiries by Father Baraga revealed that the bishop needed a missionary in the far regions of Lake Superior. Since Father Viszoczky's health was not up to so isolated and harsh an environment, Father Baraga, with his experience in the north, would be an ideal candidate. Intrepid, Father Baraga professed to be overjoyed. His attitude seemed to be, the more remote and pristine the mission, the better. He wanted to serve the gospel to the Indians pure and unhindered.

23

He left the Mission of St. Mary at the Grand by the end of February 1835, never to return. During his 16 months of ministry he had baptized 170 Indians. He also left the thriving Mission of St. Joseph at the Muskegon, having baptized at least 31 there. There are no records of farewells or testimonials upon his departure. However, Frederic Baraga left with the same sense of urgency and high expectation with which he had arrived. He had Good News to share and a bishop who obliged his great desire to carry the gospel north. This he would do faithfully until his dying day, January 19, 1868. He left this earth, venerated and beloved, as the first bishop of Marquette.

The first Catholic chapel at the rapids of the Grand River was built on the Indian (west) side of the river and dedicated April 20, 1834.

WILDERNESS ALL AROUND

1835 - 1882

I F FATHER BARAGA'S SHORT BUT INTENSIVE TIME OF MINISTRY at the Grand left a trail of legends, his successor bestowed a legacy of trail-blazing missionary work and steadfast pastoral care. Father Andreas Viszoczky, like his predecessor, had come from Europe as an ordained priest. He had already served in his home country of Hungary as a parish priest for 12 years. When he came to take Father Baraga's place at the Grand, he was 39 years old. His first stint of service in his newly adopted country was at Cottreville, near Marine City on the St. Clair River. Members of the Cottrell family there were married to members of the Campau family at the Grand.

The mission at Cottreville was frustrating for the new immigrant-pastor. He got off to a bad start by coming down with a fever after a harrowing journey to his post from Cincinnati. There were no signs of welcome for him when he finally arrived, other than an unfurnished room and an empty chapel. He lived on potatoes, peas, and water as his daily diet. Even worse, he found no interest in the practice of the faith by those who were nominally Catholic. When a few did show up for Sunday Mass, he wrote bitterly about their behavior: "They neither sing nor pray; they act as though they were in a saloon and chew tobacco. No one comes to church before the Introit, and they run out at the last Gospel as though they were being driven out by a whip."

He served at Cottreville for only a year. When he came to the Mission of St. Mary's at the Grand River in 1835, he quickly made himself a familiar figure. Native Americans and settlers alike came to know and respect his strict religious standards and

1838	1842	1846	1848	1853	1865	1876	1876	1882
Dickens writes *Oliver Twist*	Ether used as surgical anesthesia	Potato Famine in Ireland	California gold discovered	Verdi composes *La Traviata*	Slavery abolished in USA	Bell invents telephone	Battle of Little Bighorn	Tchaikovsky composes *1812 Overture*

Personally austere, Father Andreas Viszoczky was generous and kind, especially to children.

expectations. Gaunt and severe with himself, he was known for his kindly temperament toward others. Indian children were especially drawn to him, and they counted on receiving the candy treats he would always carry with him.

His dual dedication to both settlers and Indians, however, carried ever-increasing strains. As the number of settlers grew, so did their need and desire for a church and pastor of their own. Louis Campau even built a new church on the east side of the river

Church on east side of Grand River donated to Catholics by Louis Campau and later sold to Congregationalists.

on the southwest corner of the current Monroe Street and Division Avenue for that purpose. Pointedly, however, Mr. Campau did not deed the title of the property to the bishop. Father Viszoczky began offering Mass there nonetheless, while resisting, as Father Baraga had, the callous exploitation of the Natives.

One memorable Sunday in 1839 after his sermon in the Campau church, a sermon evidently denouncing the abuse of the Anishnabeg, Father Viszoczky removed his vestments before the congregation and announced that he would complete the Mass at the old Indian chapel on the west side of the river. Most of the congregation, except for Mr. Campau and his associates, left with their priest, got into canoes to cross the Grand, and finished the Mass

on the Indian site. The Campau church was never again used by Catholics or by anyone else until 1841, when it was sold to the Congregationalists. Madame Therese Campau, the mother of Louis, then held title to the property and insisted that the 25 foot high iron cross which crowned the building not be included in the sale.

It took nearly five years before workmen removed the iron cross from the building. When they did, against their better judgment, it was so heavy and so hard to dislodge that they had to saw it off at the base. It then came loose abruptly and plunged to the ground, carrying one of the workers with it and killing him instantly. The cross still stands today in St. Andrew's cemetery on the corner of Madison Avenue and Prince Street.

Iron cross from Campau church now in St. Andrew's Cemetery where the Campaus, Father Viszoczky, and other pioneers and settlers are buried.

While Father Viszoczky was tending his growing flock at the Grand, he kept pace with new settlements in a wide arc of territory. In Muskegon he would visit two or three times a year, celebrating Mass and the sacraments in the home of William Lasley and conducting religious instructions at his trading post. In Parnell there were by the mid-1840s already 30 Irish families. Father Viszoczky traveled there several times a year, using the home of settlers Michael and Mary Farrell for church services. He also ministered in the areas of Cascade, Bowne, Yankee Springs, Grand Haven, Wright, and Alpine. In each place, it was usually the home of one of the settlers that functioned as church, classroom, and social center, such as that of Patrick Prendergast in Marne (then called Berlin).

The pioneer John Ball described much of the area of West Michigan in 1837 as "primeval forest, undisturbed since creation." The settlements of the

time were clusters of families, scattered at a day's journey or more from one another. He numbered a half dozen settlers at Lyons (with a tavern there kept by Judge Lyons), four families at Portland, a few settlers in the woods near Ionia, with a store, a tavern and a blacksmith shop there, a couple of traders near Ada, several families in Grandville and in the woods south of Grandville. All else was "deep forest to the lake and to the new village of Allegan." The only access to the Grand River settlement was a route from Ionia and one from Kalamazoo. Every other passage was only a trail in the forest, with the major exception of the river itself, giving access to Grand Haven and the lake.

Two treaties changed forever this majestic isolation. These treaties (the Treaty of Washington in 1836 and the Treaty of Detroit in 1855) between the United States and the Indian tribes were the result of long negotiation. The tribes had their say, but only within the confines of what was inevitable: land would be ceded for cash and other goods and services. Already before Father Baraga's arrival there were rumors of such impending developments. In fact, the earlier Chicago Treaty of 1821 had set a precedent for the Odawa, as they had then yielded their lands south of the Grand River to the Kalamazoo River. In exchange, they received small cash annuities and certain specified government services. Included in these services was the provisioning of mission stations. Sometimes this meant that the government supplied livestock, agricultural tools, carpenters, blacksmiths, and farmers to teach the Indians settler-style agriculture. The missionary would then have the responsibility of overseeing the use of government supplies and operations, along with attending to the spiritual needs of those in his care.

Native Americans in neighboring states at the time were already being pressured to leave their territories entirely and take up residence in the west. Such a scheme was being planned for the Indians of Michigan. An overriding goal of the Odawa, however, was to stay in Michigan. When they negotiated the Treaty of Washington in 1836, they achieved this goal. However, they had to give up their title to all lands north of the Grand River, by some accounts amounting to 16 million acres. Where they could stay in Michigan seems somewhat loosely defined. Seventy thousand acres north of the Pere Marquette River were given to them. These areas were around traditional Odawa villages near the Grand Traverse and Little Traverse Bays and along the Manistee River. But the Odawa could also continue to hunt, fish, and farm on any unsold land in their former territory along the Grand.

Naturally, such an agreement was hotly debated among the Odawa before they gave their assent. Leading the effort to persuade them was the Catholic son-in-law of Chief Noonday, Chief Megisinini. With the eventual consent of the tribal councils, the three Odawa signatories to the Treaty of Washington of 1836 were Chief Megisinini, Chief Wabiwidigo, and Chief Mabunagushig.

For the Odawa way of life in the Grand River Valley, the treaty marks the beginning of the end. It also marks the beginning of a radical change in the pastoral life of the Catholic people in the region. Thereafter, the mission to the Indians would never again be primary. The mission to the settlers would come first.

With land, farming, and the lumber of the forests now becoming more available to them, the settlers did, indeed, increase. For Father Viszoczky that meant increased pastoral responsibilty and the need for more space for worship and religious instruction. The community of settlers along the Grand River became incorporated as the village of Grand Rapids in 1838. When Father Viszoczky abandoned the Campau church in favor of conducting services among the Indians on the west side of the river, he and those with him no doubt shared something of the confusion and uncertainty of all the Odawa in the aftermath of the Treaty of Washington.

To accommodate the growing settler community, Father Viszoczky, with the permission of Bishop Lefevere of Detroit, purchased the home of Richard Godfroy, located on the southeast corner of Monroe and Ottawa in the center of Grand Rapids. The

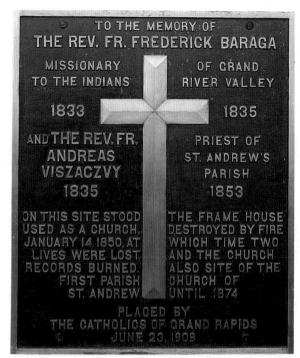

Bronze plaque honoring the two pioneering priests of the Grand River Valley at the site of the first St. Andrew's church and rectory at the corner of Monroe and Ottawa in Grand Rapids.

Godfroy house was meant to serve as a temporary chapel and as a rectory for the priests who would minister to the growing number of missions in the ever-expanding arc of territory where settlers were making their homes and their livelihood. Father Viszoczky began plans for the arrival of an assistant priest and for a permanent church building adjacent to the rectory.

As with many buildings under construction in the 1840s along the Grand, limestone from the river was quarried for the new church. The cornerstone was laid on June 10, 1849, three years after work was first started. Completion of the 90 foot long and 50 foot wide building neared, when tragedy struck on January 14, 1850.

In a Latin "Notice to my Successors" Father Viszoczky summed up the horror of that night: "There broke out in the residence of the Mission a fire caused either by wanton malice or by negligence, I know not which, more probably by ashes, and by four o'clock (in the morning) it had destroyed the entire house together with its contents, and the mother and sister of my assistant, the Rev. Lawrence Kilroy, and part of the newly finished [and adjacent] church building. There perished likewise all the Baptismal, Matrimonial, and Death Records, and the Church Census, which had dated from the month of June, 1833, and had been begun, and kept for a time, by the Rev. Frederic Baraga, now the very zealous missioner at the station on Superior."

Father Kilroy had been at the mission of St. Patrick in Parnell for Sunday Mass when the fire occurred. A nephew of his, also staying at the rectory, tried to help Father Viszoczky rescue the bed-ridden Mrs. Kilroy and her

A monument in memory of Father Viszoczky was erected in 1860 in St. Andrew's Cemetery.

daughter, but the flames were too intense. Bystanders in the cold January night were later criticized for not helping to put out the fire until they were shamed into action by women who formed lines from the site at Monroe and Ottawa to the river to get water.

Always beloved in his priesthood from the beginning to a ripe old age, Father Kilroy was to carry this night's grief in his heart as a permanent wound. The entire community mourned with him, as Father Viszoczky conducted the funeral Mass in the home of Mr. and Mrs. Henry O'Grady. Protestant and Catholic alike filled all the rooms of the house and all the adjacent streets during the sad ceremonies.

It would take several months before the new church could be first restored and then completed. Bishop LeFevere came from Detroit to consecrate the building on August 11, 1850. St. Mary's Mission, now a parish, began to carry the name of St. Andrew the Apostle, after the patron of the revered pastor, Father Andreas Viszoczky. The church building was the largest structure in the town of 2,886 inhabitants. The parish counted 160 Catholic families.

Worn out by all his labors and by a developing case of pneumonia, Father Viszoczky celebrated his last

Christmas in 1852. On Sunday, January 2, 1853, he insisted on celebrating two Masses. He thereupon collapsed, had to be carried to bed, and died later that day at the age of 57. The pioneer pastor and missionary at the Grand River for 17 years left this world quietly. He was memorialized in a stone monument in St. Andrew's Cemetery with inscriptions in English, French, German, and Latin. He had usually preached his sermons in the first three languages plus Odawa. For posterity he was described as a "holy pastor… when all around was wilderness."

EXODUS

After Father Viszoczky there would still be many years of pioneering in West Michigan and in all the state. For the Anishnabeg, however, their days in the Grand River Valley and their way of life in Michigan were undergoing radical change. To block a move to relocate them to the prairies of Kansas, they successfully negotiated the 1836 Treaty of Washington. The cost to them was high, as the concession to the United States of their favored lands, streams, and forests from the Grand River to the Pere Marquette River indicated.

However, many of the Odawa made no move to go north. Among those who persisted in staying were the Catholic Anishnabeg with their Chief Megisinini. They assimilated somewhat to the settler style of farming, schooling, and working for wages. When they purchased land, however, they used it communally, as was their custom, for farming, fishing, and hunting. They sold their food and game to the settlers and shared in the profits, again in keeping with their tradition. They even decided that their best protection was to become citizens of Michigan, recognized as such by the state.

Still, as more and more settlers were arriving and eager to purchase land, the title to the lands they were still inhabiting was in the possession of the United States after the Treaty of Washington in 1836. The Anishnabeg knew they had to enter into another treaty to salvage what they could and preserve their right to stay in Michigan.

In 1855 the Treaty of Detroit was signed. One of the leading negotiators with the United States government was Chief Cobmoosa, who lived in the Lowell area. Chief Cobmoosa was shrewd and eloquent. He revered the ancient ways of his people and wanted to preserve them. Always abstaining from any use of alcohol, he was majestic in his leadership during a severely trying time for his people.

The new treaty set aside four adjoining townships in Oceana and Mason Counties for Indian ownership of land. Individuals received 40 acres and heads of families were given 80 acres for their use and ownership. All were allowed five years from the date of the signing of the treaty to leave the Grand River Valley. It was this timetable and compromise that led to what some have called the depopulation, others the exodus, still others the removal of the Native Americans from the Grand River Valley. While this was no forced military operation but rather a negotiated agreement, it still carries the odor of the ethnic cleansing of a later era, or of an expulsion.

In the spring of 1859, hundreds, some use the word "thousands," of Odawa went by canoe on the Grand River to Lake Michigan. Along the banks of the river they moved their livestock. At Grand Haven the government provided steamboats to take the women and children to their destination at Pentwater. Most of the men rode by horseback along the shore.

Chief Cobmoosa himself would always thereafter walk at least once a year from Pentwater to Grand Rapids to visit friends and see the old places. Before his death he became a Catholic. A chapel serving the relocated Odawa was built in Elbridge. Priests came from L'Arbre Croche to provide pastoral care and celebrate the sacraments.

The era of evangelizing the Native Americans as the first priority of the church in the lower peninsula of Michigan was coming to a close by the mid-1800s, but the frontier nature of life was not yet over. Father Frederic Baraga wrote in 1834, "It is not easy for one to imagine how difficult a journey is through the primeval forests of North America." Missionaries like Father Baraga were not rhapsodic about the beauties of nature all around them in Michigan. Rather, they viewed the Great Lakes for how navigable they were for part of the year, how dangerous at other times for their sudden and fierce storms, and how unusable during the winters. The terrain was likewise not a subject for their poetic observations. Instead, it represented to them and to many a settler the struggle to eke out a living, even as it was threatening and inhospitable.

It took a special spirit of courage and determination for settler and missionary alike, the famed "*frontier spirit,*" to cope with life on the edges of human civilization. When the newly married Irish immigrant, Patrick Savage, arrived in Big Rapids around 1855 with his wife Margaret, he came to settle on 160 acres he had purchased on an earlier trip there. The site was nearly all hardwood forest, several miles northwest of the present city. As other Catholics arrived, they began receiving occasional visits from Father Matthias Marco, the first pastor of St. Mary's Parish in Grand Rapids. Father Marco's visits were so infrequent and unpredictable that Mr. Savage was delegated by the scattered Catholics of the area to appeal to Bishop Lefevere in Detroit for a resident priest. Patrick Savage set out on foot to Detroit. He was able to secure a donation of $50 from the bishop himself for the building of a church as well as the promise of regular pastoral visitations from Grand Rapids. Father Henry Beerhorst arrived to fulfill this promise in 1864 on a cold and rainy night in November. He had to be guided on foot by lantern's light from the town of Big Rapids into the deep forests where Patrick and Margaret Savage lived.

Fifteen miles northwest of Grand Rapids, Henry and Louise Host and their two sons were also living in the dense woods, near Wright. When they arrived from Ohio in 1846, they simply drove their ox and wagon as far into the forest as they could penetrate. In the winter Henry walked to Grand Rapids, where he worked six days of the week as a wagon maker. To find his way home, he marked trees along his path through the forest. Louise, alone all week with their young children, planted potatoes and corn when the snow melted. Until then, she made do with the corn flour Henry brought home on the weekend. Once several Indians came into their clearing and motioned to Louise for food. She shared bread, which was all she had, with the Indian children. Several days later the Indians returned with half a deer to give her in gratitude.

Fr. Edward Van Paemel, pastor of St. Andrew's Parish, Grand Rapids (1853-1857) from which he helped found the parishes of St. Mary's, Grand Rapids and St. Mary's, Muskegon.

In the 1850s, when the Belgian-born priest, Father Edward Van Paemel, journeyed to the Muskegon area four times a year from Grand Rapids to minister along the lakeshore, he, like most others except for the Indians, found travel through the forests very difficult. On one occasion he was summoned urgently to administer the last rites to a man who lived near Grand Haven. By the time Father Van Paemel arrived in all due haste, the man had fully recovered and was working in the fields.

The French commentator, Alexis de Tocqueville, described one kind of frontier spirit when he wrote in 1838, "They owe nothing to any man, they expect nothing from any man, they acquire the habit of considering themselves as standing alone, and they are apt to imagine that their whole destiny is in their own hands." The famous observer of the American scene of that time perceived much, but the Christian faith and human compassion many times tempered the rough edges of this frontier spirit.

As settlers bravely faced the challenges of the untamed lands, the country at large faced its greatest challenge since the revolution had brought it into existence. Slavery and the Union were the overwhelming issues of the era and were engulfing the nation in bitter division. While the East and the South, along with the border states, were committing men and treasure to the upheaval, Michigan itself was also impassioned. Out of a population in 1860 of 749,104 people in Michigan, the state sent 87,364 men to the Civil War. Strongly pro-Union, Michigan was not so united on whether to free the slaves or what status blacks should have in the nation. In the state there were only 6,800 blacks. In that number there is no known record of black Catholics. Interracial marriages were forbidden by law, and blacks were excluded from the militia and from the right to vote. In this racist, white-supremacist climate, there was still a vigorous underground railroad extending across the south of the state from Covert to Detroit, in an effort to speed blacks to freedom across the border to Canada.

Bishop Lefevere, the Catholic leader of all of Michigan, took a public stand in favor of recruiting soldiers for the war in defense of the Union. Patriotic rallies were numerous throughout the state. One Catholic priest from the western side of the state volunteered to be a chaplain, no less than the pastor of Saint Andrew's Parish, Father Thomas Brady. Catholics, however, as a community, had no cohesive stand on the war. As an institution the Catholic Church was officially neutral. In Michigan there was no Catholic newspaper to galvanize opinion within the church. With most of its clergy foreign-born and its membership dependent on settlers from other states or other countries, the Catholic Church in Michigan in the 1860s mainly concerned itself with its internal growth and organizational stability.

Just before the war, the ratio of priest to Catholics in Michigan was one to 2,000. After the war, there was one priest for every 1,500 Catholics. The war had witnessed a decline in Michigan of immigration, yet

River drivers on the Muskegon River in the late 1800s.

part of the decline in numbers of Catholics as well as of the general population surely was due to the carnage of the war. For of the 87, 364 Michigan soldiers who went to battle, 14, 700 lost their lives – most of them from secondary infections after being wounded or from the contamination of food and water supplies. Father Brady, by one report, was among those who succumbed to "disease contracted while in service." In the infantry, cavalry, and artillery batteries for which West Michigan provided troops, 841 died in battle and 2, 403 of disease. Thousands of families, therefore, were in mourning in West Michigan, hundreds of them Catholic families.

One such family which suffered the loss of their loved one was the Hefferan family of Cannon Township. James Hefferan, born in Ireland, had volunteered for service in the war, leaving behind his wife, Anne, and their family. He died in Bowling Green, Kentucky, in 1863, at the age of 56. He was buried in Tennessee. His sons, Daniel and George, traveled all the way south by team and wagon to return their father home for burial in St. Patrick's Cemetery, Parnell.

With the joyous relief of war's end came the fresh wound of an assassination. President Abraham Lincoln, revered and reviled, was killed. His death prolonged the divisive agony which gripped the country. Grief, for whatever personal, national, or political reasons, pervaded homes everywhere.

As the country began to resume normal life after the Civil War, the natural resources of Michigan lured immigrants once more. In the Upper Peninsula, iron ore and copper supplies were considered inexhaustible. Throughout the state, lumber was thought of in the same way. One historian, Bruce Catton, describes the frenzy in pursuit of these resources as a repeat on an even grander scale of John Jacob Astor's earlier approach to the fur trade: "Take what there is, take all of it, and take it as fast as you can, and let tomorrow's people handle tomorrow's problem."

When Chicago experienced its disastrous and famous fire of 1871, which destroyed most of the city, it was as if a spark from there ignited the forests of

Michigan. For in order to rebuild itself, Chicago needed enormous supplies of lumber, which Michigan was ready and willing to supply. Coming together at that time were all the elements needed for huge economic productivity: large numbers of immigrants and new settlers, development of railroads in the southern part of the state and into Chicago as well as into the forests of the lower peninsula, schooners and steamers plying the Great Lakes, and lumbering. Each element fed the other, making the lakeshore communities like Muskegon, Ludington, and Manistee wealthy and teeming with sawmills and workers, and towns like Big Rapids, Greenville, and Grand Rapids centers for shipping or rafting logs and finished lumber along their rivers. Staggering estimates of log footage reveal the profligate production in the 1870s and 1880s: almost two billion feet of logs handled by the Ottawa County Booming Company, and 47 sawmills in Muskegon alone at the height of the lumber boom, qualifying that city as the "Lumber Queen of the World."

With such increasing immigration and industry, a new influx of Catholics continually flowed into the state. The clergy were still in the 1870s mostly foreign-born, with English as their second language. While they gallantly struggled to communicate with their multi-language flock in the tradition of Father Baraga and Father Viszoczky, it was not easy for either speakers or listeners. Even Father Baraga in the 1830s had to start out with an interpreter at his side. "I preach in French," he wrote to his sister, "and when I have said a few sentences, I remain silent, and the interpreter, who stands some distance away from me, says it in the Ottawa language. I also hear confession through this interpreter," he writes matter-of-factly and with the assurance that his interpreter "is an excellent Christian and at the same time very well instructed." Even more surprising was the statement by the missionary in the southern part of the state, Father Stephen Badin: "During my absence they wanted to confess to my interpreter, who is a very pious lady."

When Father Patrick Joseph McManus became pastor first of St. Patrick's parish in Parnell in 1866 and then of St. Andrew's parish in 1872, he was among the first Catholic pastors in what now constitutes the Diocese of Grand Rapids to speak English as his first language. Others at the time were

Father Patrick Joseph McManus, pastor of St. Patrick's Church, Parnell, and then of St. Andrew's in Grand Rapids from 1872 to 1885.

Father James C. Pulcher and Father Thomas Brady, the Civil War chaplain and, preceding Father McManus in Parnell, Father William Quigly.

The bustling postwar times found a worthy match in the dynamic Father McManus. Born in Ireland, he came to this country as a 12-year-old, studied at the seminary in Bardstown, Kentucky, and at the Grand Seminaire in Montreal, Canada, and was ordained for the diocese of Detroit in 1865. His first assignment was as pastor of St. Patrick's Church in Parnell. There he won the hearts of his fellow Irish settlers by his charm, zeal, and personable spirit. He had a way of accomplishing much and winning support and cooperation for his goals. The strength of his leadership was tested during his first building project: the expansion of St. Patrick's church. During construction the entire building burned down. The whole project was begun over again, this time as a completely new building. The parishioners showed as much zeal and determination as their pastor.

Seasoned by his experience at Parnell, "Father Mac," as he was affectionately known, was assigned to St. Andrew's Church in downtown Grand Rapids. The city had been changing rapidly, especially after the Civil War. Early Irish immigrants had arrived in the 1830s and 1840s, fleeing the devastating potato famine back home. In the 1870s they were taking advantage of the schooners and steamships on the Great Lakes and of the new railroads to go west and find land and work. The lumber industry especially needed as many workers as it could find.

Many Germans had also been arriving in West Michigan in the 1840s and 1850s, settling in and around the village of Grand Rapids and in the areas of Alpine, Wright, Byron Center, and New Salem, as well as Marne, Miriam, Portland and Pewamo. They welcomed the occasional and, at best, monthly pastoral visits of priests from St. Andrew's. Pioneer hospitality continued to prevail, as Mass was celebrated in homes that could accommodate neighbors for worship and religious instruction. Eventually small log churches were built, even if a resident pastor was still not possible.

When Father McManus came to St. Andrew's, Father James Pulcher had already been both the founding pastor of St. James Parish in Grand Rapids (1870) as well as the pastor of St. Andrew's. Earlier, Father Edward Van Paemel had assisted in the founding of St. Mary's Parish in Grand Rapids (1855) while pastor at St. Andrew's. St. Mary's received its own pastor in 1857, Father Mathias Marco from the Diocese of Strasbourg in France. Father Van Paemel also helped formalize into a parish the original Father Baraga mission of St. Mary in Muskegon in 1855. Within this expansion Father McManus would add his own restless energy and propel the Catholic community of Grand Rapids into the additional mission of providing formal religious education for the young. This became the first of his two great goals almost as soon as he began his pastorate at St. Andrew's Church. The second goal was to build a new church for a community that was outgrowing the space of their beloved stone church in the middle of town.

Steamboats at Haire's Landing, Grand River, Ottawa County, 1879.

The religious education and formation of children had been a priority from the beginning days of the Catholic mission at the Grand River, with parents and clergy alike working to bring the young into the knowledge and practice of the faith. Before Father McManus added his efforts and vision, there was a short-lived "St. Andrew's Academy," administered and taught by a former seminarian, Peter G. Koch. It lasted for the years 1853-54 and then had to close for lack of finances. In 1858 Father Francis Van Erp of St. Andrew's was able to secure the use of a house on the southeast corner of Ionia Avenue and Fulton Street as a school. The house belonged to the Michael Hughes family. The first teachers were Kate Berry and Kate King, both of whom later became nuns. They were followed by two Brigidine Sisters from Ireland, Sister Mary Angela McKay and Sister Mary Ann Foran, the first nuns to serve in West Michigan. With their arrival in Grand Rapids in 1860, enthusiasm for the school they came to lead captured public attention.

An excursion on the Grand River was planned as a fund-raiser, and Bishop Lefevere was invited to attend. He duly arrived from Detroit, and the gala event took place June 11, 1860. According to the *Grand Rapids Daily Eagle*, "A brass band met the group and accompanied them on their way, greeting them and providing sweet music on the trip…. The excursion the other morning was cool and enchanting. At eight o'clock the procession started to the boat…. There were 350 aboard. A short distance below Lamont, the boat landed, and the excursionists had a pleasant time rambling through the forest. An hour was spent there, and then later another stop was made farther down the river. At 6 1/2 [sic] the excursion returned. There were no accidents, and everyone enjoyed himself."

The Brigidine Sisters were to teach in Grand Rapids for six years. Then, because of a dispute about their lack of authorization from their convent of origin in Ireland, they left the city. Father McManus inquired far and wide for a teaching staff of sisters to replace them. After a fruitless search with several religious communities, he received the asssent of the Sisters of Mercy, founded by Catherine McAuley in Dublin. Coming to Grand Rapids were Mother Mary Joseph Lynch, Sister Mary Agnes Boland, Sister Ada O'Brien,

and Sister Mary Brady, who died within three years of her ministry at St. Andrew's.

The valiant sisters quickly set about organizing the school and opened for classes within a week of their arrival in late September 1873. A barn, also described as a stable and as a "small brown frame building," housed the school on land just behind the present school at Maple Street and Sheldon Avenue. Meanwhile construction of the permanent school building was already underway, as Father McManus wished to lose no time either for a proper structure for education or for temporary space within it for the Catholic community to worship, while he simultaneously spurred on the construction of a new church. Besides adapting quickly to their new surroundings and challenges, the sisters not only established a school but also provided private instruction in voice, music, and needlework. In addition, after the school day was over they visited the sick.

Srs. Mary Gregoria and Mary Gabriella Eardley entered the Brigidine Order in 1862 and are believed to be the first vocations from the Grand Rapids area.

Before long there were incompatible differences of vision for the ministry of religious education between Mother Mary Joseph Lynch and Father Patrick McManus. Given the strong personalities of both, the conflicts came soon rather than late. Mother Lynch was no stranger to controversy and dispute. Before arriving in Grand Rapids, she had served in the Crimean War, providing nursing care in collaboration with Florence Nightingale and several Sisters of Mercy. Their working arrangement was not always congenial. Sister Lynch also had some testy confrontations with the bishops of Brooklyn and Rochester. Bishop Caspar Borgess of Detroit, under whose jurisdiction Grand Rapids was at the time the Sisters of Mercy arrived, would join that list. It was Bishop Borgess who complained to Father McManus that Mother Lynch "appeared to consider asking permission of ecclesiastical superiors as a mere formality." She also, he wrote, objected to any questioning of her own judgment, even by a bishop.

Mother Mary Joseph Lynch established the Sisters of Mercy in Grand Rapids.

In frontier and pioneering times, not to mention the occasional contemporary example, bishops were often faced with free-wheeling, independent-minded priests and sisters, who, in turn, were faced with decisions which had to be made when consultation and permission could take months if not years to obtain. The same was true regarding the bishops themselves and their collaboration with the pope and his advisors. The length of time for travel and communication required a certain independence of initiative and decision-making.

Still, Mother Lynch seems to have had more than an assertive style of leadership. It appears to have been a style both blunt and confrontational. She also, not unlike Father McManus, had a sense of urgency which her contemporaries among the Sisters of Mercy described as enabling her to "do more work in a day than many could do in a week."

The rift between Mother Lynch and Father McManus came over a proposed private academy for girls, a long-held dream of Mother Lynch. She, along with wealthy parishioners who thought the "barn-school" quite inadequate, went forward with plans for a "convent school" despite the vehement objections of Father McManus. Both were deeply concerned about finances: Father McManus for the support of the newly opened St. Andrew's School and Mother Lynch for the support of the pioneering Sisters of Mercy. As was her custom, Mother Lynch proceeded with her plans anyway, and the Academy of Our Lady of Mercy opened in 1877 on the corner of Goodrich Street and Division Avenue in Grand Rapids, not far from the parochial school the sisters were also staffing a couple of blocks away.

Her academy lasted a year. Then, because of the worrisome debts accumulating, Father McManus as well as Bishop Borgess became alarmed, so much so that the bishop challenged the very status of the sisters as a lawfully constituted convent of the Sisters of Mercy. Not until the sisters removed all debts and proved their capability to sustain themselves financially, the bishop wrote, would he recognize their community in Grand Rapids.

However, without a contract, they were not given the opportunity to work their way out of their debts. They were terminated, and the Sisters of Charity replaced them. It was a hurtful blow to the sisters and to the Catholic community in the bustling young city on the Grand.

The pastor of St. Mary's Church in Big Rapids heard of these trying developments and saw an opportunity for his own far-flung parish and its needs. Father Andrew Herbstret was a member of the Congregation of the Precious Blood. Under his

Logging at Slocum's Grove, Muskegon County, c. 1890.

pastoral care were 13 missions and "stations" requiring periodic visitations. Especially urgent was the spiritual and physical care of the loggers then laboring in the forests all across Michigan. Logging could be hazardous for both body and soul. It was Father Herbstret's dream to establish a hospital to serve the injured and ailing lumbermen.

Aware of Mother Lynch's past nursing experience, Father Herbstret invited the Sisters to travel the 60 miles north and help build and staff a hospital. They saw the hand of providence in his invitation and followed hopefully. Bishop Borgess in Detroit at first suspected only further unsanctioned schemes, as he distrusted Father Herbstret's past fundraising activities, in addition to being exasperated with Mother Lynch.

This time, immediately upon their arrival in Big Rapids in the fall of 1878, the Sisters of Mercy opened an academy. A parochial school planned by Father Herbstret would have to wait. Girls were welcomed at the academy as boarders or day students. Plans also went ahead for a hospital with the purchase of 40 acres by the Sisters of Mercy. Construction of the building and fund-raising occurred simultaneously.

The great lumber boom in Michigan spanned the years of the early 1840s to around 1910. It swept into its vortex speculators, capitalists, surveyors, timber cruisers, blacksmiths, axe-men, sawyers, teamsters, camp bosses, cooks, river-men, horses, and oxen. Nurses, doctors, morticians, and grave-diggers, of necessity, were not far behind, for logging was no recreational activity but extremely strenuous and dangerous work.

When logging first began in earnest, teams of a dozen or so would go into the forests and set up camp near a river or stream. Winter and early spring were the best times for accomplishing their work, since the loggers had to slide the huge logs on ice with the help of chains, horses, and oxen to the nearest and best means of transporting the timber, which was a waterway. The first lumber camps have been described as primitive and repellent. A windowless log shanty housed the entire crew. In its earthen floor was a makeshift fire pit for heat and cooking, with a hole in the roof to carry smoke away. Pine boughs or hay covered the platform pole bunk beds. As the number of workers grew, the cabins improved, with chimneys, stoves, and wood floors.

Mercy Hospital, Big Rapids in the early 1900s.

From November to April, from dawn to dark, the life of the lumberjack was outdoors under white pines that climbed as high as 125 to 175 feet straight up. At every point of the work-process there were dangers to life and limb, from axes, chains, and saws to falling trees, slipping, run-away tons of logs, jams in rivers choked by avalanches of timber, and the continual battle with cold, snow, and clothes that never dried.

The very idea of a hospital was, therefore, God-sent. Mother Lynch and her sisters started their building with only wood-burning stoves for heat and no running water, but the atmosphere of love and care they created was several rungs above the hard life in the woods. In their hospital the sisters even instilled a community-minded spirit among the patients themselves by insisting that those who could move about should come to a common meal, and those who were able should assist in sweeping floors, making beds, and carrying water for those who could not.

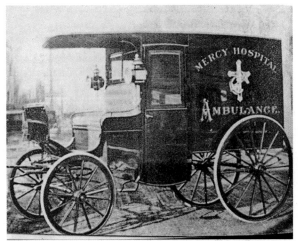

Mercy Hospital ambulance purchased in early 1900s for $ 500.

They also were in the lead with an innovative method of payment for the care they provided. They issued certificates or tickets which they sold to lumberjacks for five dollars. The card, valid for a year, would entitle the bearer to hospital care and a bed in a ward, one of the first forms of health-care and hospitalization insurance.

As demand for lumber increased, tracks were laid closer to the forests so that railroads eliminated the need for waterways to transport timber. The numbers of loggers multiplied, as did their physical injuries and fatalities. Their spiritual condition as well was tested by their isolation and rigorous life in the camps. Come spring, with their work cycle over and paycheck in hand, they were free to return home if they had one, or patronize the bars and brothels that proliferated in the newly prosperous lumber towns along the lakeshores, rivers, and streams of the Lower Peninsula such as Manistee, Ludington, Saginaw, Bay City, Muskegon, and Grand Rapids.

Bishop Borgess eventually lent his support to the mission and funding of the Big Rapids hospital and urged his clergy to do likewise, but Mother Mary Joseph Lynch had to move on. She was granted permission to seek a mission in Minnesota, where she labored for seventeen years, and then in Oregon, where she established a fourth Sisters of Mercy foundation in 1896. She died in 1898, holding the candle she had received when she first became a Sister of Mercy 54 years earlier with the crucifix nearby, blessed by Pope Pius IX for her work in the Crimean War.

Exterior of St. Andrew's Church in 1876.

Interior of the new St. Andrew's Church, Grand Rapids, early 1880s.

Father McManus, for his part, fulfilled the second phase of his dream in Grand Rapids by completing the construction of the new St. Andrew's church on Sheldon Avenue at Maple Street. While St. James Church was being built on the west side, he and Father Pulcher lived and worked at the old stone church downtown "like veritable brothers," as Father Pulcher warmly described those days. With the blessing and dedication of St. Andrew's on December 19, 1876, Father McManus set himself to strengthening the resettled and continually growing parish community.

Restless, energetic, and always the man in a hurry, he remained generous in friendship and in charities, even donating significantly to the hospital of the Mercy Sisters in Big Rapids, the building of which he had thought misguided and doomed to fail. Then, on the Sunday evening of December 27, 1885, Father McManus rushed out of his neighbor's horse-drawn carriage across from the St. Andrew's rectory and in the dark ran toward the rectory entrance and headlong into a hitching post. Though he recovered enough to leave for dinner, he fainted at the home of his hosts, the architect of the new church, John Grady and his wife. In a little more than a day, he died of peritonitis at the age of 45.

MANY FOUNDERS ONE CHURCH

1883 - 1918

As the Brigidine Sisters were reluctantly departing St. Andrew's School in Grand Rapids, another congregation of women religious sent three teachers to St. Mary's Church on the west side of the river to begin their mission at that parish's fledgling school. Answering the invitation of the pastor, Father Henry Beerhorst, the School Sisters of Notre Dame arrived from Milwaukee on August 6, 1866. They became the forerunners of many others from their congregation to follow, whose influence through their teaching ministry spread into many faith communities in West Michigan.

In 1879 one of the sisters, the principal of St. Mary's School in Grand Rapids, became an advocate for the Polish members of the largely German parish and school. Of Polish ancestry herself, Sister Mary

Tita Hutsch encouraged and assisted them in their dream of establishing their own church and school. Those efforts would result in the founding of St. Adalbert's Church and School. She did not realize it at the time, but Sister Tita's love for serving her people would lead to her becoming the first of the Notre Dame Sisters (after the Felician Sisters had left in 1892) to become principal of the St. Adalbert School, and later the first principal of St. Isidore School (1901), and still later (1916) a substitute teacher at Sacred Heart School, all in Grand Rapids.

In any era of the church's existence in the United States, dedicated and competent staffing or personnel have been the key for bringing about and sustaining the work of Christ. Another continual challenge for Catholic communities has been to attain the financial

1884	1895	1902	1903	1912	1914	1917	1918
Twain writes *Huckleberry Finn*	Marconi invents radio	Elgar composes *Pomp and Circumstance*	Wright brothers fly first airplane	*Titanic* sinks on her maiden voyage	Panama Canal opens	Bolsheviks seize power in Russia	Worldwide flu epidemic

means to sustain a particular ministry. As the mission of the church began to bear fruit in the mid-1800s and as the number and needs of Catholics increased, so did a variety of methods emerge for raising revenues. In Muskegon, it was the women parishioners of St. Mary's Church who spearheaded a fund-raising drive to establish their new school. In the early summer of 1870 they held a "Fair and Festival" at the Opera House. Their efforts enabled the parish to build the school the following year and invite three Sisters of the Immaculate Heart of Mary from Monroe, Michigan, as the teaching staff.

St. Mary's School, Muskegon, 1909, first and second grades.

The rental of pews in the church was at this time the common method of raising ordinary revenues. At the end of 1863 the church committee of St. Mary's Church, Grand Rapids, in union with their pastor, Father Ferdinand Allgeyer, issued "Rules and Regulations Governing the Rental of Pews." With clear detail, the rules specified that a pew, once rented, could not be sublet. A pew could be rented whole and entire or just for "a single sitting." Pews along the middle aisles were more expensive than those on the sides. A name plate on the pew was to indicate whether the pew was rented only for that individual or family or whether others, also to be named, could use that pew. As there were German-speaking Catholics attending St. Mary's from the mission in Alpine, one half of the income from their pew fees paid to St. Mary's would be returned to Alpine. Anyone from whichever congregation who entered a pew "not rented by them, will be asked to vacate the same."

A strong reminder was also given as part of the regulations that the Catholic school was a mission of the whole parish and not just a private institution for those enrolled. Therefore, all were alerted to be faithful to fulfilling their pew fees in support of both their parish and their school. In succeeding years such appeals would be continual and urgent, even as the particular method of financial support varied. St. Joseph Church at Wright, for example, charged higher rates for seats in the back of the church, as those were deemed the most desirable. St. Alphonsus Church, Grand Rapids, announced that no pew would continue to be reserved "after the Gloria of the Mass has commenced." The rules went on to declare, "In all well-regulated parishes, offerings of pennies are accepted from children only."

Church boards and parish organizations were expected to work hand-in-hand with their pastor and under his authority to accomplish the mission of Christ in their designated territory or community. In the Catholic Church, however, bishops have the special responsibility of overseeing the entire flock of Christ entrusted to them. They are assigned an area over which by church law they have the call and the duty to exercise the ministry of an apostle. The assigned area is called a diocese, from a Greek word referring to administering or "keeping house." Bishops are pastors of a community of many communities. In the mid-1800s, the bishop of Detroit served the entire state until the Upper Peninsula was designated as the diocese of Sault Sainte Marie (later Marquette) in 1853. He was keenly aware of the increase of Catholics in Michigan and therefore of the growing number of parishes, schools, hospitals, and organizations sprouting up all across the state. By

1881, the archbishop of Cincinnati was the leader ("metropolitan") of eight bishops in surrounding dioceses ("suffragan sees" or supporting seats of authority). They included the states of Michigan (except for the Diocese of Marquette, which at the time was aligned with the archdiocese of Milwaukee), Ohio, Kentucky, Indiana, and Tennessee.

When the bishops of these dioceses met as the "Province of Cincinnati" in July, 1881, Bishop Caspar Borgess of Detroit urged them to support a petition to the pope to divide his vast diocese in Michigan – all the Lower Peninsula – and form a new territory with its own bishop. His fellow bishops studied his request, and when they met again in

Map of the newly-formed Grand Rapids diocese in 1882.

November they agreed with him unanimously. The pope's offices in Rome ("the Holy See") ratified the request. On May 19, 1882, Pope Leo XIII issued the decree formally establishing the Diocese of Grand Rapids. Its territory covered 39 counties, with the southernmost being Kent and Ottawa and the rest reaching from the Lake Michigan shore to the Straits of Mackinac to the north, the Lake Huron coast on the east to the Saginaw Bay on the south, and across the middle of the Lower Peninsula. The rest of the Lower Peninsula comprised the Diocese of Detroit. In this huge expanse of territory (22, 561 square miles) for the new diocese, the city where the bishop would reside and have his cathedral and offices was in the extreme southwest corner.

As the second most populous center in the state of Michigan, Grand Rapids was a natural choice for the see city. Yet its location in relationship to the rest of the diocese would present many a challenge for the shepherding and community-building ministry of the new bishop and his successors.

Bishop Henry Joseph Richter, founding bishop of the Diocese of Grand Rapids.

The first bishop of the Diocese of Grand Rapids was Henry Joseph Richter. He was a priest of the Archdiocese of Cincinnati. Born in northwest Germany in the town of Neuenkirchen in 1838, he immigrated to America when he was 16 years old. While all his preparatory seminary training was in the United States, he completed his studies for the priesthood at the recently established North American College in Rome. As a priest, he served on the faculty of Mount St. Mary's Seminary of the West in Cincinnati and as pastor of St. Lawrence Parish in the same city. Nearly a year after the diocese was established, he was consecrated bishop of Grand Rapids on April 22, 1883, in the Cathedral of St. Andrew, the church Father McManus had built on the corner of Sheldon Avenue and Maple Street. He had just turned 45.

Bishop Richter was a man of medium height, with blue-gray eyes, and personal warmth, but with great public reserve. In his long ministry as bishop in Grand Rapids (33 years, until 1916), he became well known for his courtesy and pastoral attentiveness. His extensive hand-written correspondence displays brevity, avoidance of pomposity or inflated language, a passion for order and detail, and blunt to-the-point attention to the question at hand. To one of his priests in Alpena he wrote in his straightforward manner: "As your hearing is defective, we exhort you in the Lord and burden your conscience to invite from time to time a priest to hear the confessions of those who prefer not to make their confession to you." Despite having spent nearly half his formative life in Europe, Bishop Richter was said to speak English with no detectable accent. Though poorly audible in his cathedral and not captivating as a speaker, he was generally held in respect and admiration for his integrity and dedication.

When he came to shepherd his new diocese, there were about 45,000 Catholics in a total population of 475,000. Only three cities had more than one parish: Grand Rapids (four), Bay City (four), and Saginaw (three). As widely separated as they were geographically and as far-flung as the diocesan territory was, the new bishop arrived just as the lumber-boom was at its peak and when the rail system was reaching efficiently across the state into the burgeoning mill towns. He developed a pattern of travel by train to every corner of the diocese on weekends for pastoral visitations, returning to his offices in Grand Rapids for the weekdays.

During his tenure Bishop Richter was able to fulfill several major goals to a remarkable degree. They were not goals he arrived with when he began his ministry, but rather needs he identified and set himself to meet as he pastored his flock . When the Catholic bishops nationally issued a call in 1884 at the Third Plenary Council of Baltimore for a Catholic education for children of the church, Bishop Richter resolved to establish a Catholic school in every parish. Sixty-six of them were put into operation during his years of service. During his pastoral visits to the parishes, he would make a point of stopping in at the schools and visiting the students in their individual classrooms, listening to their recitations and speaking with them.

When he was in Rome in 1905 to give an official report to the pope on the state of the diocese, he was impressed by the encouragement Pope Pius X (later canonized a saint) gave him to start a seminary. With his silver jubilee as a bishop approaching, many proposed taking up an offering as a gift to him, but he refused. He did allow an offering for the proposed seminary, however, and by 1909 he was able to witness its opening. St. Joseph Seminary began in a frame house south of the cathedral with 32 students. The faculty members were Fathers Anthony Volkert, Michael Gallagher, Salvatore Cianci, Andrew Narloch, and John Schmitt. Among the first class of students were the future Fathers T. Raymond Dark and Theodore Liebek, and Doctor Frank Doran.

Through the years Bishop Richter had several close co-workers among the clergy. Some of them, along with the cathedral priests, lived with him in a kind of monastic community in the large house and offices he built in 1889 south of the cathedral. There he led the breviary prayers throughout the day, summoning his household with a little hand bell he himself rang. One of his closest friends and co-workers, Father Joseph Benning, came to the new diocese with him from Cincinnati. As vicar general, Father Benning

administered the diocese when Bishop Richter was in Rome or otherwise away from his office. In 1900 he left for Wisconsin to become a member of the Capuchin Fathers. Other vicars were Father Cornelius Roche, who died in a drowning accident, Father Joseph Schrembs, and Father Michael Gallagher.

Bishop Joseph Schrembs, coadjutor bishop of Grand Rapids and first bishop of Toledo, Ohio.

Father Schrembs, like Bishop Richter, was born in Germany. He left his Bavarian home town of Ratisbon (also called Regensburg) in 1887 when he was 21 years old to come to America. His eventual home diocese as a priest came to know about his birthplace not only because of him but even more so because it is the birthplace of the Grand Rapids Dominican Sisters. Father Schrembs followed Father Benning as the pastor of St. Mary's Church, Grand Rapids, and then as vicar general. He was the first priest to be named a monsignor in the Diocese of Grand Rapids. Much in demand as a speaker for eulogies, anniversaries, and welcoming addresses, Monsignor Schrembs was chosen as the first auxiliary bishop of the diocese. In fact, when the silver jubilee honoring the consecration anniversary of Bishop Richter as well as the founding of the diocese took place in 1908, Father Thomas Whalen spoke at the banquet following the jubilee Mass. He presented the bishop with a gift of $28,000 from all the priests for the establishment of a diocesan seminary. Then, speaking openly on behalf of the priests, he suggested that for the strengthening of the diocese and the health of the bishop, Monsignor Schrembs should be selected as coadjutor bishop, that is, bishop with the right of succession to Bishop Richter. The priests, Father Whalen urged, would like Bishop Richter to request Rome for this appointment.

Though it took a few years, Rome acceded to the request, and Joseph Schrembs was consecrated bishop in the Cathedral of St. Andrew on February 22, 1911. He was a few weeks short of his 45th birthday.

The previous autumn had witnessed a breakout of friction within the all-important furniture industry of Grand Rapids. Within the city there were 59 furniture factories with 7, 500 employees. Grand Rapids was known as the "furniture city" and "the furniture capital of the world." The honors and titles, and more importantly, the success and profits from such an industry were built upon the skills and hard labor of a largely Polish, Lithuanian, and Dutch immigrant work force. Workers averaged 10 hour days and 60 hour weeks with average wages of $11.27 per week or $2.05 a day.

What the workers demanded in October 1910, was a nine-hour day, a 10 percent increase in wages, and the abolishing of piecework, which had proved abusive and punishing to the workers. Management refused any collective bargaining or arbitration, but consented to a fact-finding commission. Named to the five-man commission were the Rev. Alfred W. Wishart of Fountain Street Baptist Church and the Most Rev. Joseph Schrembs. They issued their report in April 1911. While conceding the reasonableness of the workers' grievances, the report (authored by Rev. Wishart) deferred local points of contention to national furniture industry boards and standards. Therefore, it was claimed, local factory owners were not in a position to grant any worker demands. Moreover, the report gave assurances that the local Furniture Manufacturers Association could be counted on to provide for the workers' well-being. In essence, unions should have no place in the industry.

Within two days of the report, the strike was on. Five thousand workers left their jobs, forcing the closure of every furniture plant in the city. Rev. Wishart, whose congregation included several leading furniture executives, fanned the discontent by issuing an open letter rebuking the strikers. Bishop Schrembs, assisted by Father Michael Gallagher, put out an open letter of his own, urging the manufacturers and owners to take the lead in ending the strike by acceding to the just demands of the workers and communicating with organized labor.

It was not to be. Factory owners first began transporting non-strikers into the plants (approximately 2,000 of the 7,500 workers did not join the strike). Strikers subjected them to harassment, while some owners, including Harry and William Widdicomb, taunted the pickets and brandished firearms. Then scab laborers were imported, and the owners unilaterally declared the strike ended. Crowds gathered at the Widdicomb factory on the west side of the Grand River, eventually numbering some 2,000. A melee broke out, with the mayor appealing for calm and the police and firefighters joining in to keep order. Rocks went flying, fire hoses streaming, and warning shots filled the air. By nightfall all the windows of the Widdicomb plant were smashed.

The strike lasted a total of 17 weeks. None of the workers' demands were met. In addition to their bitter defeat, the employees as well as many in the city at large were engulfed in the divisiveness that accompanied the strike. Famously, a staff member (Viva Flaherty) of Fountain Street Baptist Church publicly dissented from her minister's stance in the strike. Leaders of the Christian Reformed Church had been sympathetic to the strikers' cause, especially since large numbers of the workers and pickets were Dutch. Eventually, however, suspicions over unions won out, and the Christian Reformed leadership turned against the strike. Within their ranks, too, another vigorous exception in defense of the strikers was the Rev. John Groen of the Eastern Avenue Christian Reformed Church.

Bishop Schrembs was forthright in bringing the teachings of Pope Leo XIII to the factories and streets of Grand Rapids. The Pope had defended the rights of workers in his encyclical letter *Rerum Novarum* in 1891. According to the *Rerum Novarum* pope's teaching, justice is the foundation of social order, and the forces of capital and labor have the responsibility of working together to shape a just social order. After the strike the newly named and consecrated bishop was called the "Angel of the Workers" in some quarters for his public and steadfast commitment to them and their cause. What he was called in other circles is not recorded. He was, however, very soon named as the first bishop of the newly created diocese of Toledo in Ohio. The appointment came on August 11, 1911. The strike ended August 18.

Joseph Schrembs would go on to be the bishop of Cleveland, with the personal title of archbishop. He died November 2, 1945.

If there was increasing strain in politics and in the working place between management and labor or between a prosperous civic elite and a struggling, poor underclass, the church experienced its own stresses and strains in the late 1800s and early 1900s. Sometimes these pressures arose from differing customs and traditions among the various immigrant groups now making their home in America, as well as from mutual suspicions carried over from the old country. In the United States the Catholic experience within the church itself often included disputes over ownership of church property and ultimately over the authority of the bishop versus the authority of parish lay groups. In addition, there were opposing views regarding the assimilation of new immigrants into mainstream American society (the "melting pot" approach) versus retaining and cherishing the mother language, European customs, and old traditions.

The new Diocese of Grand Rapids began with a German-born bishop coming to a territory with a large Irish-born constituency already well settled and a German-born membership not as large but very devoted. In addition, the early years of Bishop Richter's ministry witnessed new waves of immigration from Poland, Italy, the Netherlands, and Lithuania, as well as an influx of French Canadians to such coastal towns as Muskegon, Ludington, Manistee, and Cheboygan.

When the differences of nationalities, languages, and customs were added to differences of expectation with regard to such matters as church governance, church ownership, and styles of worship, there were the makings for misunderstanding and conflict.

Bishop Richter seems to have steered as steady and impartial a course as could be expected in such a zesty mix of people as his young diocese was quickly becoming. Even before his arrival as bishop of Grand Rapids, a celebrated challenge to the authority of Bishop John Foley of Detroit was brewing in North Dorr, just over the southwestern limits of Kent County. Those county boundaries were the demarcation line between the new diocese of Grand Rapids and that of Detroit. Parishioners of North Dorr were used to worshipping interchangeably at Saint Sebastian Church in Byron Center or Saint Mary's Church, New Salem, or in their own church of the Visitation. After their church burned down in 1896, they were instructed that nearby Saint Sebastian Church, just a mile and a

Visitation Church, North Dorr.

half away, would be receiving its first resident pastor. Thus Catholics who lived on the Kent County side of the line were expected thereafter to attend Saint Sebastian Church as their proper parish.

The ruling failed to take note that many in that area's German farming community were interrelated. Neither did it acknowledge the depth of attachment that people had for their home of religious birth and nurture, not to mention the hard-earned money and personal labor invested in their church. Nor were there considerations given for the reverence and care for the cemetery grounds where their loved ones were laid to rest. Catholics on both sides of the diocesan boundaries rebelled.

When the remains of one deceased parishioner from North Dorr were being disinterred in March, 1898, to be reburied in Grand Rapids, a riot broke out. Bishop Foley, the pastor, and all authorities were heartily cursed, including the local health officer certifying the proceedings.

No matter how many legal rulings the bishops of Detroit and Grand Rapids eventually received in their favor, from the Vatican to the Michigan Supreme Court, Catholic laity on both sides of diocesan lines conducted and led their own services. To the great embarrassment of Father John Schmitt, rector of St. Andrew's Cathedral in Grand Rapids and close friend of Bishop Richter, it was his uncle, Philip Schmitt, who was leading most of the services. When they proceeded to build their own church, they received an interdict from Bishop Foley. They were excommunicated for setting foot in it.

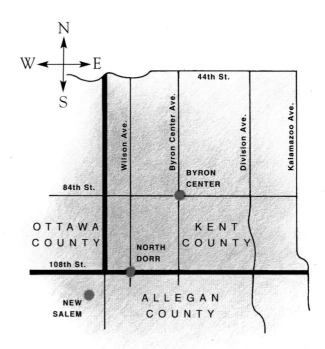

North Dorr area where southwest boundaires of Kent County meet county lines of Ottawa and Allegan.

Finally, in 1917, Bishop Gallagher of Grand Rapids arranged for their official recognition and inclusion in his diocese by conceding a parish in Birch Run near Saginaw to the Detroit diocese in exchange for the steadfastly faithful, if independent-minded parishioners of North Dorr. At the height of the conflict, when their loyalty to Bishop Foley was being questioned, Anton Schneider of North Dorr wrote the bishop: "That is false…. We pray for our Holy Father the Pope, for the Bishops, for all Pastors of souls… we pray to Almighty God to enlighten the heart of our Bishop, that he may some day greet us with a good pastor that will remain with us a long time…."

The time span of the fracas in North Dorr involved first the jurisdiction of an Irish-American bishop in Detroit, then the jurisdiction of a German-American bishop in Grand Rapids, and finally the leadership of another Irish-American bishop in Grand Rapids. Evidently national origins were not the central issue of the confrontation. At issue was the question of authority: that of a bishop versus that of the laity. Sometimes the authority question was obscured by ethnic feelings or expectations. Bishop Richter came under increasing suspicion by some ethnic groups for not being accommodating to them. However, it would seem that Bishop Richter's stance had everything to do with his concept of his own authority and responsibility and had little or nothing to do with the ethnicity of the people involved.

In the fall of 1892, the bishop had a run-in with the Ancient Order of Hibernians. As a growing fraternal lay organization both nationally and locally, they conducted an increasing number of benefits and bazaars, organized a ladies auxiliary, and built a hall in downtown Grand Rapids. As other ethnic groups would do, the Hibernians formed their own marching band, brought in notable speakers, and in various ways sought to advance the well-being of Irish-Americans.

Bishop Richter laid down the rule that bazaars and fairs could not be held in the Diocese of Grand Rapids without his explicit permission. As the bazaar in the fall of 1892 was scheduled without his permission, he had his vicar general, Father Joseph Benning, announce at Mass in the cathedral that parishioners were not allowed to attend the bazaar. If they attended or promoted it, they incurred excommunication. Later, those who took part in the event anyway and who wished to be received back into the good graces of the church, were instructed to stand up publicly before the congregation and express repentance.

The harshness of the penalty reveals the priority Bishop Richter placed on his authority as chief shepherd in matters of good order and governance. It also reveals the bishop's commitment to the assimilation of ethnic groups into a common American identity and his great uneasiness with any movements, groups, or individuals emphasizing ethnic distinctiveness or separateness. Nowhere was this more painfully evident than in his dealings with Catholics of Polish ancestry.

The parish of St. Adalbert, founded in 1881 in Grand Rapids, had difficulty in finding a pastor. Their first choice, a priest in Poland, proved unable to come. Their second choice, Father Casimir Jablonowski, arrived in their midst in May of 1883, with tales of being an exile from Siberia and descended from a wealthy and noble family in Poland. All too quickly he proved overbearing and aggressive, with the inevitable response of resistance from parishioners. As he pressed his own plans for a school and for finances to support such a venture, his people rebelled. Death threats ensued, rotten potatoes were hurled into his bedroom window, and eventually, before dawn on February 2, 1884, two gun shots rang out in his study.

Ancient Order of Hibernians, St. Patrick's Day Parade, 1914, Grand Rapids.

Arrests were made and a trial arranged within days of the troublesome events. During the four-day trial Father Jablonowski tendered his resignation to Bishop Richter. The five defendants presented alibis, and questions arose whether the shots came from outside the study or inside. The accused were found not guilty. The bishop accepted Father Jablonowski's resignation, and, as the newspaper then reported, "he will leave for other parts of the Lord's vineyard."

Into this maelstrom stepped a cooperative and reconciling Father Marianus Matkowski. After a becalming two years at St. Adalbert's parish, he was succeeded by Father Simon Ponganis, whose father was Lithuanian and whose mother was Polish. Father Ponganis had been a seminarian in Rome at the Polish College when Bishop Richter made his first visit to Rome (in 1885) as the new shepherd of the Grand Rapids Diocese. It was at the college that the two first met, as Bishop Richter was purposely there to recruit priests to serve the burgeoning Polish immigrant population in his diocese. He accepted seminarian Ponganis for his diocese and ordained him in Grand Rapids on December 28, 1885. Father Ponganis lived in the bishop's household until March of 1886, when he became the pastor of St. Adalbert Church. He would prove to be energetic, talented, and combative. He also would sorely test the equanimity and impartiality of Bishop Richter.

Bishop's house, chancery, cathedral rectory, and later convent 1889-1997.

Among the developments in the Polish population, as in the Irish, was a flowering of benevolent and fraternal societies and organizations. They assisted new immigrants, helped the struggling to find their rightful place in American life, and fostered a social and cultural network hospitable to those whose language and customs were different from the majority population. Father Ponganis was suspicious of lay-led and lay-organized groups. He disliked their independence from church authority. He himself, however, enjoyed acting independently in his own political endorsements and in approving clubs and associations of his choice, to the chagrin both of some of his parishioners as well as of his bishop. His freedom and dynamism of spirit enabled him to help found the parishes of St. Isidore and SS. Peter and Paul in Grand Rapids, and St. Michael in Muskegon. The same spirit led him to oppose the founding of Sacred Heart parish, as being too close geographically to his own.

In the founding of St. Isidore parish on the eastern limits of Grand Rapids, in an area known as the Brickyard ("*Cegielnia*" in Polish), there had been several societies formed under Father Ponganis' direction to lay the groundwork and organizational structure for a future parish. Named by Father Ponganis after the Spanish farmer-saint, the St. Isidore Society of Fraternal Help (1892) was one of the earliest. As the years went on, however, two policies of Bishop Richter came into conflict with the emerging plans for a new parish. One was his inflexible and uncompromising financial requirement for any foundation or construction in his diocese: nothing was allowed to proceed unless the total amount of money needed was already raised and in hand. The other ruling by Bishop Richter was that no saints' names particular to national or ethnic groups should be given to churches with parishioners of that group. Instead, saints who were universally honored should be chosen as patrons. Both policies of Bishop Richter affected the new parish planned for the east side of the city.

The bishop's inflexible financial rule came with him when he left Cincinnati to become bishop of Grand Rapids. In that archdiocese where he had been a priest, a huge financial scandal swamped the church.

Father Simon Ponganis, pastor of St. Adalbert Church, Grand Rapids.

origin. This approach of his would antagonize various immigrant groups, the largest among whom were the Poles. It also ran up against an assumption on the part of some parishioners that they should be the ones to choose their own patron, an assumption Father Ponganis encouraged, as long as he led the choice.

Thus it was that, during the years of preparing financially and organizationally for the establishment of a new parish, Father Ponganis used the name St. Stanislaus, bishop and martyr, as the patron of choice. A meeting of the parishioners in 1897 ratified the choice as theirs.

When the day arrived for the blessing of the cornerstone and crowds were gathered for the festivity on September 5, 1897, Bishop Richter intoned the prayer, reading out the name of St. Isidore. Father Ponganis corrected him, saying, "Bishop, this is not St. Isidore's but St. Stanislaus." Bishop Richter, after a pause, replied, "It is the bishop who gives the name of the church." Then, according to one report, Father Ponganis left in mid-ceremony.

When banks repeatedly failed in the mid-1800s, people began depositing their savings in the care of the archdiocese. When creditors sought payment during difficult financial times, there was a run on the deposits. The value of church property was assigned for repayments, but even that proved insufficient. Years of litigation ensued from 1878 to 1892, with the church nationally being asked for help and Rome stepping in with the naming of a coadjutor bishop to govern the archdiocese. From this great loss and shame came Bishop Richter's resolve and ruling for his own administration, even if work must stop in mid-construction until sufficient funds were on hand to complete the project. Thus, plans for a new church on the east side of Grand Rapids, as for many another parish in the diocese, would move apace only as funds were raised.

Bishop Richter's ruling on saints' names was nearly as inflexible as that for finances. His reasoning seems to have been in keeping with his aim to help immigrant groups assimilate and Americanize. In his vision the country of the future, and the church with it, would not be characterized by lines of national

Though sensitivities were bruised, this tussle paled next to a prolonged agony called "The Bay City Church War." Father Marianus Matkowski, who had brought harmony to St. Adalbert Church in Grand Rapids, was sent by Bishop Richter as pastor in 1886 to do the same at St. Stanislaus Kostka Parish in Bay City. His ministry was achieving the desired effect until the arrival of a newly ordained assistant priest, Father Stanislaus Turski, in 1895. The young man soon gave public notice of his dissatisfaction with both pastor and housekeeper and began an open campaign defaming Father Matkowski. It would lead to charges by a 14-year-old girl that the pastor had made sexual advances against her. The parish was in such a tumult and so polarized by the escalating accusations, that Bishop Richter closed down the church and placed it under interdict from April to October 1896.

Father Matkowski was arrested in May 1896. By June all charges were dropped and rejected. It would be seven years later, however, when the plaintiff lay dying, that she confessed in a sworn deposition that she had perjured herself in her previous testimony.

Father Marianus Matkowski, pastor of St. Adalbert and St. Isidore Parishes in Grand Rapids and St. Stanislaus Kostka Parish in Bay City.

With amazing resiliency and grace, Father Matkowski continued in effective and respected ministry within the diocese as pastor of several churches, including the first pastorate of St. Isidore's in Grand Rapids. Father Turski, for his part, soon after the court proceedings, publicly renounced and deplored the scandal he had given. Two years after these events, he was committed to a mental care facility where he spent the rest of his 55 years of life.

As if the scale of this human and religious tragedy were not large enough, the wounded and fractured parish community in Bay City continued to be at odds with itself after the departure of Father Matkowski. The next pastor allied himself with one faction, infuriating the other, until actual rioting and violence broke out in January 1897. In the face of such open rebellion and bloodshed, Bishop Richter once more shut down the church, placed it under interdict, and kept it closed for 17 months. Parishioners had to go elsewhere for the sacraments.

In the heat of such tumultuous events, the naming of a parish takes on even greater significance than it might otherwise have. As immigrants faced daily

hurdles of language, customs, societal rules, livelihood, misunderstanding, ridicule, and rejection, they and their pastors hoped that their church would not itself be one more hurdle. Rather, they looked to their church to validate them and their cherished heroes in the faith. Furthermore, the alienation frequently at the surface in the immigrant communities was ready to erupt into divisiveness and violence. With those concerns 14 priests of Polish ancestry formulated an official document dated February 13, 1900, at St. Joseph Parish, Manistee, which they sent to Bishop Richter, to the archbishop of Cincinnati, and to the pope's representative in Washington, D.C. In a series of resolutions, they requested a change in Bishop Richter's policy for naming churches.

The letter had some effect. Though Bishop Richter felt that encouraging the development of national parishes was already an accommodation until such time **as immigrants could be assimilated, he went further after 1900 in his willingness to allow national saints' names for parishes. Still by way of exception, eight new parishes of Polish, Slovak, and Bohemian membership began carrying the names of such saints as Hyacinth, Hedwig, Cyril and Methodius, and Wenceslaus.**

St. John's Home on Leonard St. in Grand Rapids, dedicated August 25, 1889.

It was no doubt a pleasurable relief for Bishop Richter, even in the midst of these broiling tensions in the Catholic community, to welcome and work with newly arriving women religious in the diocese. The Dominican Sisters began their ministry in Traverse City on October 23, 1877, before the formation of the Diocese of Grand Rapids. Six of them, under the leadership of Sister Mary Aquinata Fiegler, arrived from Brooklyn, New York. They had been recruited by Father George Ziegler, pastor of St. Francis parish, to staff the school there. Their ministry would rapidly become fruitful and in demand in many parts of the state, with Traverse City serving as a center. When the Diocese of Grand Rapids was formed and Bishop Richter evolved his ministry with a goal of a school in every parish, the need for the Dominican Sisters only magnified.

The bishop found in Mother Aquinata a **kindred spirit. From the Saxony or north-central area of Germany, she, like the bishop, was devoted to detail, precision, cleanliness, and order. Especially endearing to Bishop Richter was how she and her sisters combined their natural talents with deep faith and a readiness to endure hardships. It was just**

Sister Mary Aquinata Fiegler, OP, at her profession and (inset) at her 50ᵗʰ anniversary.

such a spirit of adventure, infused with meticulous attention to planning and prayer, that he wished for his new venture, an orphanage in Grand Rapids. The wealthy lumberman, John Clancy, had bequeathed $60,000 and a farm for the orphanage on eight acres at the corner of Lafayette Avenue and Leonard Street in the northeast section of town.

Coming to Grand Rapids in May 1889, for the foundation of the orphanage were Mother Aquinata herself and two other sisters from Traverse City. In July they were joined by another sister, Mary Agatha McCauley from Adrian, who would spend 47 years in the new ministry. The dedication of St. John's Home (named in honor of the benefactor's patron) was a grand civic as well as religious event, with many city officials and dignitaries present. During the speech given by Redemptorist Father Theodore Lamy of St. Alphonsus Church (also beginning at the same time and near the orphanage), "hats and collection boxes were passed in the crowd and the clinks of the

Little Sisters of the Poor Building, now razed and the site of the Peter M. Wege Center for Health and Learning at St. Mary's Mercy Medical Center, Grand Rapids.

temporal aid for the orphans mingled with the spiritual words which flowed from the lips of the preacher."

With this introduction to Grand Rapids, the Dominican Sisters had little time for settling in. The demand for their ministry kept expanding, as St. Alphonsus parish needed them for a new school. So, too, did the newly forming St. Joseph Church for Catholic Dutch immigrants on the southwest side of Grand Rapids. From Wright to Mount Pleasant, from Muskegon to Bay City and Essexville, sisters were continually sent forth to staff or open new schools and academies. Their base at Saint John's Home became their center and motherhouse after 1894.

The Little Sisters of the Poor were the first congregation of women religious whom Bishop Richter invited into the Grand Rapids Diocese. Six of them arrived May 1, 1884. Serving the elderly poor, as was their mission, they themselves lived in poverty. To help them get started, many neighbors, Catholic, Protestant,

and Jewish, provided them with food, furniture, and monetary offerings. By the 1890s they located their ministry on the site now occupied by Saint Mary's Hospital-Peter M. Wege Center for Health and Learning in Grand Rapids. They became well known and beloved for their deep Christian faith and their trusting reliance on the generosity of earthly benefactors as they went on begging missions. They also relied on heavenly benefactors, as they prayed often for the help of St. Joseph. His statue in the main hall of the Lafayette Avenue building was turned face against the wall until special needs they were praying for were met.

Two other communities of consecrated women religious who came to the young Diocese of Grand Rapids at Bishop Richter's invitation were the Sisters of the Good Shepherd and the Discalced Carmelite Sisters of Our Lady of Guadalupe. The Good Shepherd Sisters from Carthage, Ohio, had as their mission the care and education of troubled girls in their teens. The Sisters provided a residence for them as well as private schooling and technical training in such areas as secretarial skills and dressmaking. It was an era when few public opportunities were available for preventing delinquency among teens, especially for girls. The site where the Sisters established their mission in 1904, called Villa Maria, was on Walker Avenue on the west side of Grand Rapids.

In a little more than a decade they would be welcoming new immigrant sisters who eventually became their neighbors across the road. These Mexican sisters were as dedicated to the Lord and the work of Christ as the Good Shepherd Sisters were, but their origins and mission were quite different. "Discalced" means "without shoes," and the word begins to reveal the austere style of living that the Carmelite Sisters embrace. They choose to live cloistered lives, literally walled off from the outside world, so as to devote themselves entirely to prayer and contemplation. Tracing their roots to the 1200s in Europe and even to the spirit of prayer shown by the prophet Elijah on Mount Carmel, the Grand Rapids Carmelites came here by way of their communities in Mexico. Theirs is the much-venerated tradition of spiritual reform and prayer espoused by St. Teresa of Avila, Spain, in the 1500s. In Mexico or New Spain, they flourished until the persecutions of Christians during the mid-1800s and the early 1900s.

I t was during those persecutions that priests, religious, and others publicly identifiable as Catholics were routinely rounded up, jailed, and executed by firing squads. The Carmelite Sisters had to live in hiding, disbursed in private homes, and disguised with civilian clothes over their distinctive religious garb, even in the heat. When Mother Mary Elias was out on the streets to beg, she often saw scattered everywhere the vestments, chalices, and statues from ransacked churches. The vandalism so sickened her, that she went about gathering them up and challenged the governor to restrain his soldiers and have them cease and desist from their sacrilegious behavior. Her boldness so impressed the governor that he issued the order.

This, however, was only a momentary reprieve. Soon the sisters would be exiled from their country. In the course of many anxious separations, Mother Mary Elias and a companion sister were imprisoned and sentenced to be executed. In her prayer Mother Mary Elias turned for intercession to the recently deceased young Carmelite, Therese of Lisieux.

The sisters were bound. They knelt but refused the blindfold. Six soldiers shot at them. They were left for dead. They awoke before dawn, conscious that they were still in this world. When a guard burst in, Mother Mary Elias shouted, "Don't shoot at us. Our Blessed Mother will punish you if you do!" She so startled him, that he showed them the way out. Once in the fields and not knowing where to go, they saw a horse galloping toward them. When the rider challenged them, they told the truth about their escape. The rider revealed that he was a priest who came every night to pray with those in the prison who were to be executed. He gave them his horse, and the horse knew the way to the train station.

From Mexico City to New Orleans to Chicago, the displaced and fugitive Carmelites wandered until they found the providential invitation and welcome of Bishop Richter. An equal welcome and hospitality were provided when eight of the Carmelites finally arrived in Grand Rapids in 1915. The Good Shepherd Sisters, the Sisters of Mercy, the Dominican Sisters, the School Sisters of Notre Dame, and the Little Sisters of the Poor – all provided them with accommodations, food, and clothing.

Valeria Lipczynski and husband John were charter members of both St. Adalbert's and St. Isidore's, and promoters of religious and civic life in Grand Rapids.

55

Each bell of the cathedral was anointed with oil and dedicated to its patron saint at the afternoon ceremony of the blessing of the bells.

When Mother Mary Elias and her sister companion first met Bishop Richter and began to tell him of their spiritual odyssey, he asked them to return for a visit the next day and to bring with them their rule and constitutions. As they were leaving, he said, "I tell you what the disciples told our Lord on the way to Emmaus: 'stay with us for the day is now far spent!'" Bishop Richter was in his 32nd and next to last year as chief shepherd.

As various congregations of religious women were arriving in West Michigan to take up the work of Christ according to the special mission of their founding traditions, a husband and wife offered their own considerable talents and deep Catholic faith to a wide variety of services. Valeria and John Lipczynski left their native Poland and arrived in Grand Rapids in 1869. They attracted others from home to make the same journey and helped them get

settled by seeking out employment for them, as well as places to live. They became charter members of two churches by assisting the founding, first of St. Adalbert's and then of St. Isidore's in Grand Rapids.

Accomplished and cultured, they encouraged the arts at the same time they were helping their fellow immigrants meet basic needs through the establishment of mutual aid societies. Without planning to be so, they became politically influential, since they often acted as intermediaries between their people and the civic, judicial, or law enforcement officials. Valeria was at the forefront of promoting women's rights, first within Polish societies and then within the wider civic and even national community. All the while, John and Valeria Lipczynski remained fully engaged as participating members of their parish and in the Catholic community, John until his death in 1917 and Valeria until hers in 1930.

Their gifted nephew had a rockier path as a Catholic. Stanley B. Lipczynski, his wife Victoria, and their six children were all devout members of St. Isidore Church, with Stanley as the first organist there. He is said to have become increasingly alienated by Bishop Richter's policy on the naming of patron saints for ethnic churches, until he left the church to become a member of Wealthy Street Baptist Church. His family remained active parishioners at St. Isidore's. Not until his deathbed in 1943 was Stanley reconciled to the Catholic Church.

The priest Bishop Richter invited to come from Italy to serve the Italian community in Grand Rapids found himself immersed in many of the same activities as Valeria and John Lipczynski. With one

St. Andrew's Cathedral bells were the only complete set of bells in any church in the state when they were blessed on Easter Sunday, April 11, 1909. Note heights of bells next to standing man.

doctorate in theology and another in church and civil law, the brilliant Father Salvatore Cianci arrived in his late twenties in 1908, and in short order not only began pastoring his fellow immigrants in matters religious but representing and defending them at city commission meetings, in the courts, and at city hall. An Americanizer like Bishop Richter, Father Cianci was at the same time fiery in his insistence that the Italian community take pride in their faith and their traditions. At a celebration of the Italian-American brotherhood in Grand Rapids in September 1916, David Cavera, as president of the organization, introduced Father Cianci to deliver the banquet address. "Because Italy is your mother country," declared Father Cianci, "you should reverence her flag, [but] you must be good citizens of your adopted country. To be a good citizen, you must be honest, learn the English language, and give your children a good education…." Then he blessed with holy water the

Consecration of Bishop Michael J. Gallagher, September 8, 1915.

Father Salvatore Cianci with eighth grade graduates, 1931. Back row: Antoinette Annerino, Maria Antoinette Mancuso, Grace Naimo, Dena Zanella. Front row: Rose Pellerito, Father Cianci, Catherine Zanella.

Italian and American flags, equally large, which were prominently displayed near the speakers.

Father Cianci celebrated Mass and the other sacraments and held religious instruction for his parishioners and their children in the basement of the cathedral from the time of his arrival until 1921. Never shy about his convictions or political leanings, he enlightened, entreated, scolded, inspired, and excoriated in Italian and English, often within the same sermon or the same conversation.

As Bishop Richter advanced in years, the constant round of pastoral visitations across the expansive territory of his diocese, the administration of the multiplying institutions and agencies, and the contending needs of so diverse a flock took their toll. When he had sought and then received Rome's assistance with the appointment of a coadjutor bishop in February of 1911, he found only short-lived relief, as his intended successor, Bishop Joseph Schrembs, was so quickly named the first bishop of Toledo in August of the same year. In 1915 Rome announced that another coadjutor would be appointed to the Grand Rapids Diocese. He was Father Michael J. Gallagher.

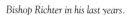

Bishop Richter in his last years.

58

Father Gallagher was born of Irish immigrant parents in Auburn, Michigan, in 1865 and completed seminary training for the priesthood in Ireland and Austria. Ordained a priest in Innsbruck in 1893 and returning home in 1895, he served parishes briefly in the Saginaw area before becoming assistant priest at St. Andrew's Cathedral in Grand Rapids and secretary to Bishop Richter. In succession he served also as chancellor and as vicar general, taking on many special tasks entrusted to him by Bishop Richter, such as chaplain to St. John's Home, spiritual director for the Dominican Sisters, and editor of the first Catholic publication in the diocese, a monthly called *The Light of Truth*.

In his years as a priest of the diocese he was invariably described as bright, talented with literary gifts, a man with kindly blue eyes and a gracious manner, warm, and fatherly. On September 8, 1915, he was consecrated coadjutor bishop with right of succession to Bishop Richter. He proved conscientious about fulfilling his role with due deference to his long-time patron, the aging bishop. In his letters to Bishop Richter, apprising him of various personnel problems or the condition of parishes, Bishop Gallagher always signed himself, "Yours obediently in Christ" (using the Greek abbreviation "*in Xpto*").

It was in May of the same year, 1915, that the Catholic community, not only of the city of Grand Rapids but of the widespread diocese, lost one of its towering spiritual leaders. Mother Mary Aquinata Fiegler had led the Dominican sisters since their first mission in Traverse City in 1877. She guided and fostered their expansion into ministries throughout much of the lower peninsula of Michigan. With strong faith and in close collaboration with Bishop Richter, Mother Aquinata forged her sisters into a diocesan congregation while maintaining ties with the wider Dominican order. So well respected had she been that the congregation of Dominican sisters in New York, where the Grand Rapids Dominicans originated, elected her as their prioress or leader while she was already serving in that capacity in Grand Rapids. At Bishop Richter's insistence she opted to stay with the Grand Rapids Dominicans, serving as their elected leader for three six-year terms until her death from cancer at Saint John's Home, May 1, 1915. The previous year had witnessed an outpouring of respect and appreciation over her 50th anniversary as a Dominican sister. At her funeral Bishop Richter wept openly before her casket.

The Grand Rapids Dominicans then numbered nearly 400 sisters in 42 parochial schools, 2 academies, 1 orphanage, and 2 high schools.

Henry Joseph Richter, the founding bishop of the Grand Rapids Diocese, became ill on December 24, 1916, and died on the first day of Christmas in the early afternoon. His close friends and protegés, Bishop Schrembs and Bishop Gallagher, were at his bedside in St. Mary's Hospital, as were many sisters and priests who were praying the rosary. At his death he was frequently and publicly described as saintly, venerable, revered, and wise. He was 78 years old.

Dedicating one church and school after another in his 33 years as bishop, he took greatest satisfaction in his legacy of Catholic education and the training of candidates for the priesthood in his cherished seminary. Remarkably and according to his wish, every church and institution in the diocese was paid for when he died. During his years of ministry the number of priests went from 34 to 161; Catholic school pupils from 2,867 to 18,300; churches with resident priests from 33 to 108; missions, stations, and chapels from 74 to 156; and Catholics from 45,000 to 140,000. The total population in the 39 counties comprising the diocese had grown from 475,000 to 925,000.

Among the thousands with whom he shared the Holy Spirit through his ministry, there are still alive today at the beginning of the new millennium witnesses to Christ whom he anointed in the sacrament of confirmation.

Above: Bishop Richter, second from left, at blessing of St. Joseph's in Elbridge, September, 1915.

WAR, PESTILENCE AND PROSPERITY

1 9 1 8 ‑ 1 9 2 6

WHILE THE NATIONS OF EUROPE sank into the violence and terror of war with one another beginning in 1914, America stayed largely uninvolved. The ethnic groups in the United States, however, became personally affected by the war's impact on their relatives and friends in their homelands. At the same time recently settled immigrants and new citizens were eager to prove their allegiance as Americans. Sometimes these efforts took the form of downplaying use of their ancestral language in parochial schools, especially among German-speaking Catholics, though this did not happen until later in the war and affected Dutch and German-speaking Protestants as well. As suspicions grew and patriotism was challenged, protective measures were taken, with a town like Berlin, 10 miles west of Grand Rapids, changing its name to Marne. In the United States Catholic leaders at first remained neutral or urged peace efforts during the early years of the war, as Pope Benedict XV had pleaded. The Paulist editor, Father John Burke, declared in a national Catholic magazine, "War is by no means a Christian tradition. Indeed, our very profession of Christian means that we are pacifists." While Bishop Gallagher would not go that far, he went on record urging citizens to petition their congressmen "to keep Americans out of the war zones and thus save us from the unspeakable horrors and stupendous cost of war…."

However, once the United States entered the war in April, 1917, by an act of Congress, church leaders like Cardinal Gibbons of Baltimore spoke forcefully about the responsibility of Catholics to support their

1919	1920	1920	1922	1923	1924	1926
Prohibition amendment	U.S. women win vote. League of Nations established	Gandhi leads non-violence movement	Insulin first used for diabetes	Gershwin composes *Rhapsody in Blue*	Knute Rockne Notre Dame coach	Hemingway writes *The Sun Also Rises*

country. "The members of both houses of Congress are the instruments of God in guiding us in our civic duties," he stated. Others quickly took up the cause with passionate language. The pastor of the parishes in Belding and Miriam, Father John M. Zindler, said, "Soon the best young men of our country… will be fighting for humanity… suffering and dying to rescue the Sacrament of liberty from those who would despoil it and deny it to humanity." That April after the declaration of war, Bishop Gallagher changed his position with a ringing call "to support the government, whenever and in whatsoever it commands, with our property and our lives in defense of the flag we love." Then he made a remarkable pledge: "In spite of the great scarcity of priests the diocese will detach a sufficient number to safeguard the spiritual and moral welfare of our co-religionists in the ranks." Thus began a direct and formal involvement of Catholics in the Diocese of Grand Rapids in World War I.

By war's end Bishop Gallagher estimated that 10,000 Catholic young men from the diocese were in military service. In keeping to his pledge, the bishop allowed eight of his priests to serve as chaplains, most working overseas. Four were pastors of parishes in Big Rapids, Alma, Mancelona, and Grand Rapids. The remainder were associate priests in Muskegon and Grand Rapids, with two of them leaving for the war from St. Andrew's Cathedral. One of the pastors who volunteered, Father Joseph Kaminski of Sacred Heart parish in Grand Rapids, had two brothers already in the service. Father Aloysius M. Fitzpatrick, D.D., left his assignments as an assistant at St. James parish in Grand Rapids and associate editor of *The Light of Truth*. Other priests volunteered but were not called to duty.

For their part, women who graduated from the nursing program at St. Mary's Hospital in Grand Rapids also supported the war effort with 42 of them "in their country's service." Parish Young Ladies Sodalities held special meetings at which bandages were made for the Red Cross. Women around the state were even asked "to sign and live up" to a pledge coming to the assistance of their country's food supply needs in the midst of "the pressing military necessity." The pledge stated, "I will use only those amounts of foods required for adequate nourishment: I will endeavor to control the waste in all kinds of materials in the household, and to live simply. I will begin now."

A massive and ambitious program was developed by the Knights of Columbus to aid the war effort. Funds were raised nationally with the approval and backing of the hierarchy for the purpose of constructing and staffing recreational centers at military camps both in the United States and in Europe. Bishop Gallagher was lavish in his praise for the spiritual, social, and physical assistance which the Knights thus made possible for soldiers during the war. He also escalated his rhetoric about the patriotism of Catholics in America by assuring his listeners in the cathedral that, if the time should ever come, "the Catholic churches would be sold and the chalices melted" to ensure the successful conclusion to the war. For this sentiment he was widely quoted and praised both within the Catholic Church and outside it in West Michigan.

Father Kyran J. Whalen, pastor of St. Mary's, Muskegon.

As forceful as was the bishop, it would be hard to outdo the soaring emotion of Father Kyran J. Whalen, who had succeeded his own brother as pastor of St. Mary's Church, Muskegon. In April 1918, on the occasion of a farewell parade there for troops leaving for the war, thousands turned out in jubilant spirit as bands played, banners flew, and recruits marched. At the Occidental Hotel, hundreds paused to hear Father Whalen exhort and command: "I charge you never to return until you can return carrying the emblem of freedom and democracy…. There can be no failure. You must drive back the enemy, and it is your duty to succeed or to die in the attempt…. Go, march on, but never return until success is yours. Death must come before failure." His address was interrupted several times by deafening applause.

K of C trucks and autos line up at the Grande Place before the Hôtel de Ville, Paris, France, for inspection by Overseas Comissioner Edward L. Hearn, World War I.

Two laymen from the diocese were prominent in the state and nation for their work with the Knights of Columbus, Luke Leonard and Martin Carmody. Mr. Leonard revealed the inter-faith cooperation taking place in the midst of the war effort. Echoing the observations of a rabbi, he described how the Y.M.C.A., the Young Men's Hebrew Association, and the Knights of Columbus were all "helping one another, planning to conserve all that is good in every soldier. They are building up a fence…. Every dollar given to the Knights of Columbus fund helps construct that fence separating the soldier boy from vice and temptation."

The centers established by the Knights were more than places for recreation. They also provided chapel areas for worship and financial support of the volunteer chaplains. The buildings became well known for their "Everybody Welcome" signs. So successful was the campaign, that a year after this country entered the war, 99 buildings had been established, with another 41 under way in training camps at home. Abroad the Knights had set up another 20.

As brutal and lethal as the war was, Americans experienced its sorrows for the relatively short time of 19 months. As it was coming to a close in 1918, a strange and terrifying new enemy stalked, first American soldiers and then the world. In recent times medical historians have traced the beginnings of the erroneously named "Spanish Influenza" to a military camp in Kansas. The influenza virus literally traveled with our troops, spreading first in this country, then in Europe, and then around the world. Before it was spent, it claimed the lives of up to 40 million people, of whom some 675,000 were American, more dead than in all our major foreign wars combined. The manner of dying was as terrifying as the death itself. The virus struck down more among the young and the strong than it did the elderly or the infirm. The first symptoms of severe aching in the eyes or joints were often swiftly followed by a filling of the lungs with fluid and bleeding from the nose, with discoloration spreading throughout the body.

Medical and civic authorities of the time realized that this was an infectious disease, but the methods of combating it were far more limited than those for the great war. Quarantines for the sick were declared. Public or community gatherings were limited or banned entirely. Churches were closed. Since there was no vaccine against the disease, all that could be prescribed was good hygiene, staying away from crowds, and as one large advertisement bluntly if cruelly put it, "Avoid visiting the sick."

The first ones to break that rule were the loved ones of the sick and nurses. As so many of the nurses had left their hospitals to serve in the military camps, it was left to the women religious, the sisters, to do much of the nursing themselves on the home front. Such was the case in the Diocese of

Grand Rapids. In St. Mary's Hospital, Grand Rapids, the Mercy Sisters were taking the place of their 42 nurses who had left for Camp Grant, Illinois. Those nurses had been contacted by Father Aloysius M. Fitzpatrick from St. James, Grand Rapids, who was chaplain at the camp. He wrote back home to tell Mother Gertrude Bertrand at St. Mary's "how proud I am of [your] nurses… they are doing heroic, noble work." However, the work they were doing was not with battlefield casualties but with victims of the dreaded influenza. Father Fitzpatrick added, "We had 116 deaths yesterday and 47 up to noon today."

In Grayling, where they had built another hospital, the Sisters of Mercy went from house to house taking care of the stricken, as there were often entire families sick, with no one else to care for them. Eventually there were so many emergencies that a hotel was requisitioned as a temporary hospital. In Bay City the teaching Sisters of Charity, with their schools closed because of the emergency, joined the Sisters of Mercy in the care of the sick. In Saginaw a private club gave the use of its building as an emergency hospital and the teaching Sisters of St. Dominic joined the Sisters of Mercy in attending to the sick and the dying. The Sisters of Mercy in Parnell, Ludington, and Pinconning also nursed the sick in their homes. Not only was an entire floor at St. Mary's Hospital in Grand Rapids given over to influenza patients, but 12 sisters from Mount Mercy also went every day to visit the sick in their homes from early morning to early evening.

There were some casualties, but very few, among the sisters and the clergy. Among the Dominicans, Sister Julia Chesney died in Lake Leelanau, as did Sister Mechtildis Weigl in Suttons Bay and Sister Irmina Latuszek at the motherhouse in St. John's Home. At least one priest died of the disease, Father J. Arthur Houle, pastor of St. Ann's Church and missions, Harrisville. He was a native of Cheboygan and 31 years old at the time of his death. His illness had lasted a week. He was described as "in the prime of his life, strong, robust, and in the vigor of manhood… kind and gentle… courteous and affable… he won many to the faith that otherwise might have remained estranged from the faith. Catholic and non-Catholic respected him.…"

As the pandemic "worse than the seven plagues of Egypt" abated, testimonies of gratitude poured in for the brave and selfless ministry of the women religious. In January 1919, the health officer of Grand Rapids, C.C. Slemons, M.D., wrote to the Sisters of Mercy: "I wish … to express to you my sincere appreciation of the valuable assistance rendered by the Sisters of Mercy during the recent influenza epidemic.… If at any time you can use my services in any capacity, kindly call upon me as I feel under deep obligations to you all for the splendid manner in which you responded to a general call for help."

Bishop Michael J. Gallagher, second bishop of Grand Rapids, left in 1918 to become bishop of Detroit.

In the midst of the turmoil of the war and the epidemic, Bishop Gallagher was named as the new bishop of Detroit. That diocese had been administered for 10 months since the death of Bishop Foley by its highly respected auxiliary bishop, Edward D. Kelly. It came as something of a surprise, both in Detroit and in Grand Rapids, that Michael J. Gallagher should receive the appointment. Bishop Gallagher had served only a year and seven months in Grand Rapids since the death of Bishop Richter. He was seen as carrying on the legacy of the founding bishop with his own special warmth and force, along with a detailed knowledge of the diocese and its people, gained through decades of close collaboration with Bishop Richter. In Detroit Bishop Kelly was viewed in a similar way, having spent most of his priestly ministry in the Ann Arbor-Detroit area.

The installation of Bishop Gallagher in Detroit was postponed by the restrictions against large gatherings during the influenza epidemic. Though the announcement had been made in July of 1918, he was not able to leave Grand Rapids until November. He left with the love and affection of many. He retained his own fondness for many of his old friends, returning often in the years ahead to visit the western side of the state. A later historian would describe the man previously known for his genial, witty, and affable nature as abrasive, impetuous, and stubbornly independent. Apparently the pressures of his years of service in Detroit, especially with the explosive expansion of population and industry there, took a toll on Bishop Gallagher's health. Church buildings, new institutions, and personnel were in ever greater demand. A growing source of contention and public controversy was Bishop Gallagher's unwavering defense of his friend, Father Charles Coughlin, the phenomenally charismatic radio priest with an adoring national following of nearly 40 million listeners. Even when Father Coughlin descended into Fascist-leaning (though not yet anti-Semitic) pronouncements while espousing social justice, Bishop Gallagher never publicly disavowed him nor restricted his high public profile. Father Coughlin reciprocated by adorning the great granite tower of his new Shrine of the Little Flower in Royal Oak with "the figure of the Archangel Michael bearing the unmistakable features of Bishop Michael Gallagher." When he died in 1937, Bishop Gallagher left a diocese with a greatly expanded church structure, splendid new buildings, and an enormous financial debt.

Edward Dionysius Kelly was born on the southwestern side of the state near Watervliet in 1860. As a boy, he grew up in a farmhouse that served for many years as the gathering place for Mass whenever a visiting priest came to minister to the area's Catholics. Ordained a priest in 1885 for the Diocese of Detroit, he served first in parishes and in 1887 at the newly established and short-lived seminary at Monroe, where Bishop Foley sought to

Bishop Edward D. Kelly, third bishop of Grand Rapids, 1919-1926.

train candidates for the priesthood. In 1891 he began his ministry as pastor at St. Thomas parish, Ann Arbor, where he would remain for 27 years. While there he was consecrated auxiliary bishop in 1911 and named administrator of the Detroit Diocese upon the death of Bishop John Foley in January 1918. In February of 1919 he was appointed the new bishop of Grand Rapids. At the time of the announcement, he was on sabbatical at a sanatorium in California. He was apparently recouping from the stresses of his 10-month administration of Detroit and, some have felt, from the shock of not being confirmed in that post after so effective a ministry for the diocese both in the last years of the ailing Bishop Foley and then as administrator.

The handsome, sophisticated bishop received a glittering welcome in his new diocese, a welcome made all the more public and ecumenical because some ministers in the city of Grand Rapids had urged civic officials to boycott the festivities in the name of separation of church and state. Instead, such dignitaries as the governor of the state (a friend of the bishop), the mayor of the city and other state and local officials, the president of the Y.M.C.A, and the rector of Grace Episcopal Church attended. Arthur H. Vandenberg, publisher of *The Grand Rapids Herald* and later distinguished senator from Michigan, organized the gathering and gave a stirring address emphasizing the patriotism shared by Americans of all creeds during the recent war. Capitalizing on the proven patriotism of American Catholics during the great war, Bishop Kelly spoke eloquently in his first public address as bishop of Grand Rapids about an "apostolate of optimism" as the "need of the hour" and of how the variety of political, industrial, civic, and church institutions could all play their part in the advancement and health of society. "There is room for healthy competition… competition is the very pulse of our national life; but there is no room for bigotry…." Reports of that evening state that he was constantly interrupted by loud applause.

The post-war years would test the unity of American citizens in the bloom of their triumph upon returning to normal life. In Michigan in the 1920s three major issues confronted the citizenry, each one a challenge to the moral values and beliefs of its people and their way of life. One was a proposed school amendment, brought before the people for a vote in 1920 and 1924, with an attempt in 1922 failing to achieve enough names to be placed on the ballot. The second major issue was women's suffrage, and the third, prohibition. While citizens struggled with the passions and convictions on either or all sides of these issues, a boom in industry was taking place, with the expansion of cities and their supporting physical and social institutions. Detroit was at the center of this boom nationally, led by Henry Ford and his assembly-line approach to automotive production. Other sections of the state were also impacted, though not to the degree of the motor city. The Catholic Church, along with other communities of believers, likewise tried to keep pace with the religious, educational, and social service needs of its expanding membership. Bishop Kelly's inaugural plea for optimism as an apostolic need and for healthy competition would call for concerted energy and imagination.

Concerted energy and determination were needed in abundance and over a period of several years to defeat the proposed school amendment. The first time it came before the voters of Michigan was in 1920. The proponent of the legislation, James Hamilton of Detroit, couched the debate in terms of religious hysteria: Catholic parochial education, he charged, advocated the "yellow banner of the pope" rather than the Stars and Stripes. This, coming after the sacrifice of many Catholics for their country in a world war just ended, gained little credibility. In fact, at one rally in a Baptist Church in Lansing the debate aroused only laughter, hissing, and catcalls.

The contention revolved around the proposal that "all residents of the State of Michigan between the ages of five years and 16 years shall attend the public school in their respective districts until they have graduated from the eighth grade." This would have meant the end of the parochial school system so boldly and generously established by hard-working Catholics in the Grand Rapids Diocese and their far-sighted founding bishop, Henry J. Richter. Other religious communities like the Lutherans and the Reformed had the same objections to the amendment. A similar amendment had been passed in Oregon and then declared unconstitutional by a federal court.

Bishop Kelly, however, took no chances on a solely optimistic view of the good will of the electorate. He, on the west side of the state, and Bishop Gallagher on the east, mobilized the Catholic community with informational and motivational assemblies, articles in the press, and orders to pastors to divide up their parishes block by block for voter registration. Many pastors took the ballot form into the pulpit to explain to parishioners how to fill it out. As this threat to the very existence of parochial schools coincided with the movement for women's suffrage, Bishop Kelly actively sought the vote of women by addressing the convention of the Catholic Women's League in August 1924, and urging them to register for the vote. He also encouraged all nuns and women religious to cast the first votes of their lives against the proposed amendment. As one commentator slyly observes, for a bishop then to "encourage" sisters to vote was tantamount to an order requiring religious obedience.

The repeated effort to defeat the proposal not only brought gratifying support and praise for the Catholic schools, but also drew out of the shadows the bigotry that had surfaced briefly at Bishop Kelly's inaugural ceremonies. In Grand Rapids the Rev. Alfred W. Wishart of Fountain Street Baptist Church, who had deserted the furniture workers during the strike of 1911, presented a series of widely reported sermons describing parochial schools as a "relic of the past" whose dominant motive "is not citizenship but sectarianism…." The Ku Klux Klan also weighed in with a campaign of its own in Michigan to pass the amendment. They gathered in the Big Rapids and Mecosta area in 1923, claiming to be 255 strong. Where the French missionary, Father Nouvel, had celebrated the first Mass in the woods of mid-Michigan, where devout founding families like the Minkels, Wernettes, and Wendlings hosted Mass in their homes or led prayers themselves in the absence of a priest, there the KKK lit a huge bonfire for a meeting with 500 citizens. The voters of Michigan defeated the amendment resoundingly by margins of two to one both times it appeared on the ballot in 1920 and 1924. Besides these legislative defeats in Michigan, the Supreme Court of the United States struck down the similar Oregon law in 1925, and the issue died.

A byproduct of the school amendment battle was a concession the bishops of Michigan made in 1921 to support the passage of the Dacey Law, enacted that year. It required all private schools in the state to come under the jurisdiction of the state superintendent of public instruction. Therefore, teachers in private or parochial schools would be held to the same standards as those in the public schools. This meant that all parochial teachers needed certification.

What began as a reluctant concession in order to gain support for the major battle against the contested amendment developed into the pioneering graduate education of women religious on a large scale. Since it was the sisters who were staffing all the parochial schools in the diocese and the state, they were the ones who became the largest group of professional women and graduate-trained teachers in the state. Already in the summer of 1917 Grand Rapids Dominican Sisters began attending the Sisters Summer School at the Catholic University of America in Washington, D.C. and in the next summer the University of Notre Dame as well. With the Dacey Law, however, the Sisters began attending summer schools at public institutions with fellow lay students in 1921. By 1927 the Grand Rapids Dominican Sisters already counted 255 in the community with life certificates from the state colleges in Mt. Pleasant and Kalamazoo, 56 sisters with baccalaureate degrees, and 9 with master of arts degrees.

St. James' School graduation class, Grand Rapids, c. 1920.

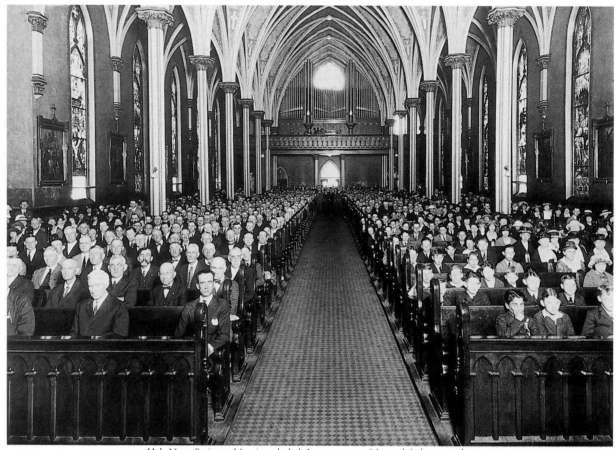

Holy Name Society at Mass in cathedral, June 11, 1922. Men on left, boys on right.

Compared to the intense involvement of Catholics in Michigan and in the Diocese of Grand Rapids at all levels with the school amendment proposal, the national issues of women's suffrage and of prohibition did not capture nearly the same degree of energy or concern. Even though the National Suffrage Convention was held in Grand Rapids in 1899, a woman's right to vote represented a long and often lonely struggle on the part of brave and determined visionaries. Nationally there were Catholic laywomen deeply committed to the cause, but few among the hierarchy. A notable exception was from the Midwest, Bishop Austin Dowling of Des Moines (later, archbishop of Saint Paul). Catholics, in general, were assumed to be opposed to a woman's right to vote. Cardinal Gibbons, in fact, voiced the fears of many of his fellow American bishops when he ventured the opinion that woman suffrage "will tend to increase the searing, social evil, divorce… and bring about moral looseness, discord, and dishonor in the sacred family circle." Yet, when that right was affirmed by Congress in the Nineteenth Amendment in 1920, leaders of the hierarchy encouraged women to exercise their right in the hope that it would be women who showed men how to use the vote for constructive purposes. Perhaps unknowingly, they were echoing the view of Susan B. Anthony: "Give woman her rights, and she will lift up the world into a nobler and purer atmosphere." It was in that spirit that Bishop Kelly seized upon the newly gained voting rights of women in order to develop support for defeating the Michigan school amendment.

For different reasons, the Eighteenth Amendment to prohibit the manufacture, transportation, and sale of alcoholic beverages likewise did not engage the interest or support of most Catholics. Some segments of the church had long encouraged total abstinence from alcohol, and there were societies and leagues to foster temperance. Yet, because of the many ethnic and cultural traditions of American Catholics, alcohol use was viewed more as a matter of custom than of law. Cardinal Gibbons of Baltimore, so often a national spokesman for Catholics, thought the passage of the amendment would be a national catastrophe because, among other reasons, of the impossibility of policing prohibition. He described himself as "a temperate man, but not a temperance man." Prohibition, however, went into effect nationally in 1920. Michigan had anticipated the amendment in 1916 and began experiencing before the rest of the nation what new criminal problems bootlegging brought in its wake. Prohibition was repealed in 1933.

The country's involvement with social reforms did not lessen people's continued attention to the restoration of Europe after the war. Since the war experience was brought home through American soldiers, nurses, and chaplains, the sacrifices which war brings were personally felt by many in America. Also, such necessities as fuel became scarce at home, so that St. James School in Grand Rapids, for example, had to announce on January 13, 1918, that school would be closed for the entire week. Even the church could be heated only six hours a week. After the war, the schools raised funds to send to the needy children of Europe. St. Mary's School children in Grand Rapids raised $100, including money originally saved to buy gifts for Christmas. The diocese itself joined a nationwide Catholic campaign to raise $15,000,000 for those European children wounded in the war or still suffering from hunger. On the home front the Knights of Columbus in Grand Rapids extended their assistance to servicemen by offering free evening school classes to the returning military, with courses in auto mechanics, welding, bookkeeping, and electrical work.

After the World War it was a time of rapid growth in dioceses across the country. In the large eastern Archdiocese of Philadelphia the cardinal archbishop, Dennis Dougherty, took to calling himself "God's bricklayer" for all the churches, schools, and institutions whose beginnings he presided over from the time he became bishop there in 1918. In the Diocese of Grand Rapids Bishop Kelly in the same time period became known as the "Builder Bishop." Historian Father John W. McGee lists over 100 churches, schools, convents, rectories, halls, and gymnasiums either newly built or remodeled during Bishop Kelly's relatively short administration of seven years. Most of these endeavors were the hard-won fruit

of committed parishioners, zealous pastors, and dedicated women religious. Bishop Kelly, however, through his administration facilitated, encouraged, and sometimes initiated the efforts that would lead to these structures and communities, many of which still support and express the faith-life of the Catholic people.

Among the institutions with far-reaching influence which came into being or expanded in Bishop Kelly's time were Mount Mercy Academy, the Catholic Central High Schools, St. Joseph Seminary, and Sacred Heart College, all in Grand Rapids.

The Sisters of Mercy were well established since the late 1870s in Big Rapids with a school, academy, convent, and combination mother house-hospital-novitiate or training school for new candidates for the sisterhood. With such a fruitful ministry they were in much demand around the state. They had more than their share of sorrows as well, since their hospital in Big Rapids was destroyed twice by fire. After the second fire in 1908, ten other cities, by their count, invited them to relocate their headquarters elsewhere. The sisters maintained their allegiance to Big Rapids, but with serious misgivings about the city's abilities to provide adequate fire protection at that time. As the numbers of sisters grew, they sought a mother house and novitiate separate from their hospital. This time, looking to a city with better fire protection, they found a site, the Harrison estate, in Grand Rapids on a beautiful hilltop just west of the city. They moved there in July 1914. Two special Pere Marquette railroad coaches were requisitioned for the transfer of 94 sisters to their new home. Sadly, their reasoning for the move was borne out again in 1919 with a third fire at their hospital in Big Rapids, this time with the loss not only of the building but of five lives as well.

On their new serene hilltop then outside of Grand Rapids they established an academy for girls. The first structure went up in 1918. By 1920 they were adding a chapel and auditorium as well as student dining halls and recreational facilities. Already in 1925 they acquired accreditation from the North Central Association for high schools and colleges. From this academy would come new generations of women leaders in family, civic, and religious life throughout the city and west Michigan.

St. Mary's Hospital Nurses, Class of 1926, Grand Rapids.

It was also during Bishop Kelly's administration that the Sisters of Mercy initiated a major expansion of St. Mary's Hospital in Grand Rapids. Already in 1893 four Sisters of Mercy had taken up residence in Grand Rapids to begin establishing a hospital there at the express invitation of Bishop Richter. They were provided with the two-story McNamara residence at 145 Lafayette Avenue S.E. which had been given to the bishop for a hospital. Named St. Mary's in honor of Mrs. Mary McNamara, the home-turned-hospital was supported by donations, door-to-door begging by the Mercy Sisters, and fees of $1.00 a day for the wards and $10 to $20 a week for private rooms. Included in the fee was the cost of medicines. The Sisters themselves were the nurses. By the early 1920s there had been several additions and expansions and still people were being turned away for lack of space. In spite of some misgivings on the part of the Sisters, a new campaign drive was begun in November of 1924 to raise $350,000. Within one week pledges totaled $384,316. The Sisters of Mercy were able to proceed with their new building and have a grand public viewing in October 1926. It would prove to be one in a long series of expansions, transformations, and

satellite clinics even into the next millennium in order to serve the health care needs of a growing population in the religious spirit of their congregation.

As other institutions within the diocese joined the roll call of construction or renovation, it was clear that Bishop Kelly had modified the policy of Bishop Richter. Whereas the founding bishop would allow a project to proceed only when and if all the monies required were on hand, Bishop Kelly allowed for some borrowing and scheduling of debt repayment. He was criticized for taking what some considered a riskier approach than his predecessor, but he was still more cautious and fiscally conservative than his counterpart in Detroit, Bishop Gallagher.

On the corner of Ransom Avenue and Fountain Street in Grand Rapids the Dominican Sisters purchased an estate in 1899 and converted the residence into a girls' academy, opening it for classes in 1900. They had the guiding spirit of Bishop Richter supporting them, so much so that he used to spend an hour or two every week giving instruction himself in religion and visiting during the recreation hour, even to within a week prior to his death in 1916. When the student numbers outgrew these accommodations, the academy moved to the west wing of the new Marywood building. With the encouragement and financial assistance of Bishop Kelly, the Dominican Sisters had proceeded in 1921, after much delay, with the construction of Marywood on the eastern outskirts of Grand Rapids known as Fulton Heights. Described lyrically as situated in shady, leafy groves, the spacious acreage and center housed not only the mother house but what had by then become the Sacred Heart College and Academy. It was dedicated with great fanfare in 1923 before hundreds of guests, alumnae, sisters from throughout the Midwest, Bishop Kelly, and the Dominican guest preacher, Archbishop John T. McNicholas of Cincinnati.

Dedication of Marywood, 1923.

The cherished project of Bishop Richter, the diocesan seminary, was also close to the heart of Bishop Kelly. If Bishop Richter was well known for insisting on a school in every parish, Bishop Kelly, with his 27 years at St. Thomas Church in Ann Arbor, was keenly attuned to higher education. The University of Michigan was nearby, and many students and faculty were members of St. Thomas parish. Bishop Kelly was sensitive to the needs of their religious faith as well as to their pastoral care in a secular academic culture. While at Ann Arbor he had even been described as a latter-day Father Gabriel Richard. Later in Grand Rapids it was in character for him to welcome opportunities to further Catholic education and formation at all levels. When St. Joseph Seminary outgrew even the expanded first facilities south of the cathedral, Bishop Kelly selected a site in June 1919, for a new seminary south of Grand Rapids in an area still somewhat rural at the corner of Burton Street and Union Boulevard. The cornerstone was laid in November 1919, and the building completed and blessed January 12, 1921. Reports at that time acclaiming the structure take pains to relate that, while carefully equipped, "luxury and superfluity have been avoided." Monsignor Anthony Volkert had led the fledgling seminary since its founding in 1909 but resigned those duties in 1919 in favor of becoming

the spiritual director of the much expanded institution. The new rector, Father Charles D. White, D.D., became the bishop of Spokane in Washington in 1926, the first in a distinguished line of faculty and alumni in the course of the seminary's 72-year history to be named to the hierarchy.

In the early 1900s there were four parish high schools in Grand Rapids, one in Muskegon, and a handful of others around the diocese. Even though universal high school education was not yet common, the pooling of students, teachers, and resources already was a concern of Bishop Richter and several of his priest advisers. In Grand Rapids the Dominican Sisters consented to opening up their Sacred Heart Academy for all Catholic girls of high school age around the city, beginning in 1906. The Sisters of Charity, who staffed the cathedral parish school, made room in that building for all Catholic boys of high school age from the city parishes. Together the girls and boys numbered 250 at the opening of their first classes. Three years later the girls' program separated off from the Sacred Heart Academy and relocated twice, with the remodeled former seminary building south of the cathedral becoming the central high school for 300 girls. The Sisters of Charity left the diocese in 1914, and the Dominican Sisters took responsibility for the boys' high school as well.

To house the sisters staffing the new central schools and cathedral grade school, Bishop Kelly in 1922 turned over his large residence and chancery office (built by Bishop Richter in 1889) immediately south of the cathedral. A new rectory was built that

Faculty and students of St. Joseph Seminary 1926. Front row middle is former rector, Bishop Charles White of Spokane, flanked on left by Thomas Noa, later bishop of Marquette, and on right by founding rector Anthony Volkert. Seminarians Joseph Shaw and Thomas Martin are in third row from top on right. On right pedestal are Louis Verreau and Julius Amman.

year for the cathedral parish, eventually with an addition for diocesan offices on its north side. Bishop Kelly purchased a private residence for himself on the east side of Grand Rapids.

The pressures of leading such an expanding faith community with multiplying public demands took a toll on the bishop's health. It did not help that there was a troublesome spirit between the bishops of Detroit and Grand Rapids during times which called for collaboration on important social and church issues, such as the state school amendment. Vatican officials had even lodged their concern privately so that the church could have a united gospel witness. Whatever misgivings Bishop Gallagher may have had in his estimation of his successor in Grand Rapids and vice versa, most people who

had come to know Bishop Kelly thought he was a prince of a man and were glad to work with him.

He suffered an attack of bleeding ulcers March 19, 1926. There was great concern but not alarm. A week later at his home, after days of much improvement, he suddenly grew faint and weak, dying quickly of a blood clot. He was 67 years old. He had served the church of Grand Rapids for seven years. One of his youngest priests, Rev. Speer Strahan, eulogized Bishop Kelly as a "man of swift and generous sympathies, of magnificent enthusiasms [and] exceptional qualities of head and heart… transforming a pioneer diocese into one of the best organized and best administered in the country."

Stained glass window in St. Joseph Seminary Chapel. The Latin inscription reads: "Come after me and I will make you fishers of people."

CHAPTER FIVE

Hard times

1 9 2 6 - 1 9 4 0

THE MAN WHOM PROVIDENCE PLACED AS CHIEF TEACHER and shepherd of the Catholic community in the Grand Rapids Diocese after Bishop Kelly could not have been more different from his predecessor in personality and style of leadership. Neither could the times and social climate have differed more in the late 1920s and 1930s from the era during which Bishop Kelly had served.

Joseph Gabriel Pinten was ordained a priest for the Diocese of Marquette. Born in 1867 in Rockland, Michigan, in the western reaches of the upper peninsula, he grew up in copper country further north in Calumet in the Keweenaw peninsula. After seminary training in Milwaukee, he continued his preparation for priesthood at the Pontifical Urban College for the Propagation of the Faith in Rome. It was the same seminary where Chief Blackbird's son, William Macatebinessi, and his friend, Augustine

Hamelin, both from L'Arbre Croche, had studied 53 years earlier. As a young priest, Father Pinten utilized his facility in the Italian language by ministering to Italian immigrants around Iron Mountain. Later he was pastor at St. Peter's Cathedral in Marquette and served as chancellor and vicar general of the Marquette Diocese. Named as bishop of Superior, Wisconsin, at the western point of Lake Superior, he served there from 1921 until he was named to succeed Bishop Kelly in 1926.

Described as quiet and retiring, Bishop Pinten shunned any civic gathering or public celebration to welcome him other than the cathedral ceremony formally installing him as bishop of Grand Rapids. What quickly became a signal to the clergy was his insistence that the ritual at St. Andrew's be called an "enthronization," not an "installation." Except with a few close friends among the priests, he was guarded,

1927	1928	1929	1933	1934	1935	1939	1940
Lindbergh crosses Atlantic	Penicillin discovered	U.S. stock market crashes	Hitler German Chancellor	U.S. adopts Social Security Act	Amelia Earhart lost on Pacific flight	*The Wizard of Oz* produced	Churchill England's Prime Minister

Bishop Joseph G. Pinten, fourth bishop of Grand Rapids, 1926-1940.

cautious, and, as later years would reveal, suspicious about the motives of others. He was not at ease socially. Personal or public approval was never anything he seemed to seek, desire, or even appreciate.

As pastor of the diocese, he was intent on restoring the strict and exacting financial rules of the kind that the founding bishop, Henry J. Richter, had required before allowing for the construction of any new buildings or the purchase of properties. These directives slowed down the expansion of the church and its institutions which had been fostered under the leadership of Bishop Kelly. Remarkably, they came at a time just a few years before the nation would undergo the long ordeal of the Great Depression, the deep economic slide that would put more than 25 per cent or 13 million of its workers on the streets in breadlines and job seeking. Bishop Pinten's stringent financial requirements with the resulting cutback in church projects also came shortly after the time (1924) when the United States Congress enacted a restrictive quota system with the deliberate goal of cutting back the rate of immigration into this country, especially from

southern and eastern Europe. By 1930 limitations were extended to Mexican immigrants as well, with hundreds of thousands of them forcibly returned to their country even if they had become American citizens. One Protestant historian observed that the concern was widespread across the country that America "would go Catholic by immigration" unless preventive steps were taken.

In any case, dioceses did not face the sometimes overwhelming flood of new members who would need pastoral service, so the consolidating efforts of Bishop Pinten proved timely. What they faced instead was a climate of mixed signals from the society around them. In the late 1920s Catholics across the United States became newly aware of themselves as an identifiable community with its own gifts and potential to contribute to the good of society and to the cultural climate. In Chicago there was an extraordinary public witness of the Catholic presence in the nation when the International Eucharistic Congress took place in June of 1926. What the country saw in photographs and printed news reports was an assembly of 150,000 Catholics openly gathering for Mass in Soldier Field, and nearly half a million Catholics from all around the country and even the world on the spacious grounds of the rural seminary north of Chicago, hosted by that city's dynamic bishop, Cardinal Mundelein. Equally important was the realization among Catholics themselves, observing one another giving witness to their faith in full public view, that they were a united community coming into their own in the nation.

Yet this heady experience of recognition and solidarity was soon followed by the blatant hostility and open prejudice against them during the presidential campaign of the Catholic candidate, Al Smith, in 1928. Chastened and wary, Catholics may have returned to their barricades but not to full isolation. There was a feeling that the time was right to continue to step forward. In Rome itself, after all, the papacy had come to an accommodation with Italy, ending its own exile within the confines of the Vatican. The Lateran Treaty of 1929 gave formal recognition to the independence of the Vatican City State. Fifty-nine years had passed since Italy had become a nation. The popes, in protest of the seizure of papal lands and buildings throughout Italy in the forming of the nation, had refused to leave the small territory around St. Peter's Basilica. With their mutual recognition, the Vatican and Italy began a new relationship. Two brilliant young seminarians from Grand Rapids were students at the Lateran University in Rome at the time and sent reports back home to their friends at St. Joseph's Seminary. Mr. Joseph E. Shaw wrote about the surprise dawn visit which the Holy Father, Pope Pius XI, made to the Basilica of St. John Lateran on December 20, 1929. That basilica, the cathedral of Rome, had also been the church where Pope Pius had been ordained a priest 50 years earlier. Now, for the first time since 1870 the bishop of Rome was coming to reclaim his seat of authority. "Somehow the church seemed small for him," Mr. Shaw wrote, "and one almost doubted that what he was seeing were really so...."

Mr. Thomas O. Martin continued the report with fresh, precise details. "We went to night prayers as usual at 9:15 and were ready to file out when the rector began to speak in a low voice.... On the morrow we were to come to morning prayers in... festive soutane with cloak and surplice, because the Holy Father was to say Mass in St. John's.... No one save the Chapter of St. John's, of which we are considered a part, knew it.... The spiritual director came from the passage behind the altar, which leads to St. John's, and beckoned us. We went around the altar and lined up in the sacristy.... The rector told me to take the processional cross.... It was dark, even though a few electric lights shone along the wall. There was a stir down near the portone (gateway) of the palace, and a car drove in and stopped. His Holiness the Pope

Pope Pius XI.

alighted. The monsignori advanced and kissed his ring... the procession formed. A papal master of ceremonies took my cross and carried it ahead of the pope. I had nothing else to do, so I folded my hands and trailed along a couple of yards behind the pope...."

After describing the ceremonies, which Mr. Shaw felt were like "some dream of the ages of persecution... some secret Mass in the catacombs, while the unknowing world swirled around outside on its ordinary round of business," Mr. Martin wryly records the aftermath: "The Holy Father returned to the room where he had left his cloak and had breakfast. We were not allowed to pass. Some Swiss Guards in civilian clothes did their usual work of shutting doors in people's faces.... I got a look at [the pope's] car and found it was a Graham-Paige some Americans had given him not long before.... The pope, however, was back in the Vatican at work when Rome learned of his trip."

Even as the economic distress increased back home and financial constraints tightened around families as well as around larger communities like the church, the churches themselves do not appear to have bound together in coordinated action to alleviate the ravages of unemployment. Nationally, Catholic leaders did petition President Hoover as early as 1930 to initiate a program of public works "to stabilize business and relieve unemployment"; but the president, like many others at the time, believed local or regional efforts among employers and workers would be enough to help them through what many predicted would be only a temporary, perhaps year-long economic slump.

In the absence of any federal assistance local officials like City Manager George Welsh of Grand Rapids initiated a bold and innovative program of work relief with payment through scrip rather than cash, with the scrip certificates redeemable at a "city store" well provisioned with groceries and sundries. Work projects such as snow removal were offered to unemployed married men. At 50 cents an hour the men shoveled snow downtown and on weekends around every church and synagogue throughout the city, a significant project in the "city of churches." Even on other days, when weddings, funerals, or other events were scheduled, they would come to shovel snow on request.

The organization through which American Catholic bishops and Catholic associations first worked together nationally began in the midst of World War I and was called the National Catholic War Council (NCWC). Bishop Schrembs, formerly of Grand Rapids, then in Toledo at the time of the NCWC founding, had been an important influence in its structuring and in securing for the organization the pope's recognition and approval. In the early years of the depression the NCWC provided the pastors of Michigan and of several other states in the Midwest informational materials on parish credit unions. It was an attempt to share with Catholic parishes the experiences of their counterparts in the northeast states and the province of Quebec. In 1930 Quebec already had 122 parish credit unions. They touted the benefits of thrift and reasonable rates of interest for people

of small means, which included most Catholics of that time. It would be at least another generation, however, before church credit unions would be formed in the Grand Rapids Diocese.

Perhaps more than most parishes of the diocese in the early 1930s, St. James parish in Grand Rapids endured extreme financial distress with an indebtedness of $178,000 from school construction. The distinguished and beloved pastor, Monsignor Edward A. Lefebvre, worried himself sick over how to reduce the debt. But with so many parishioners out of work, the parish income for all of 1933 was only $17, 697. The pastor, twice named adminsistrator of the diocese when it was without a bishop, and vicar general as well, resigned in March of 1933 because of ill health at age 64 and retired to his home in Saginaw. (Five years later he was called out of retirement to be the first vicar general of the new Saginaw diocese, so highly was he held in esteem.)

In his place at St. James was assigned a young and vigorous Father T. Raymond Dark. He was able to renegotiate the debt, almost halving the indebtedness. He also greatly lifted the morale of his parishioners by connecting those who were skilled workers with contacts in the business community, as well as inviting them to work for some compensation on improving the parish grounds and buildings.

Often, in place of parish or church-organized

Two pastors of St. James Parish, Grand Rapids, during the Great Depression. Top: Msgr. Edward A. Lefebvre. Bottom: Father T. Raymond Dark.

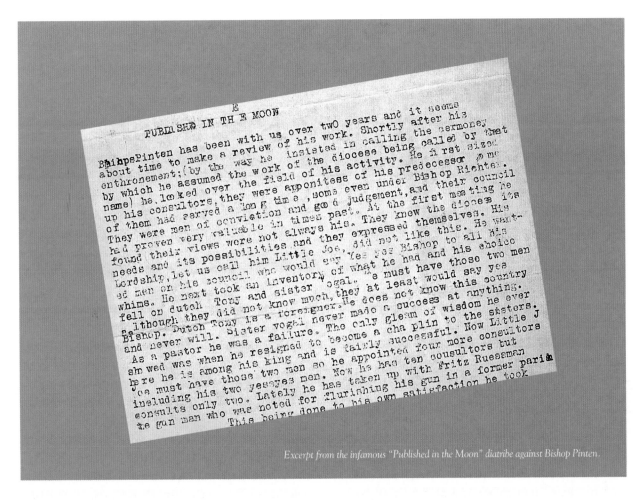

Excerpt from the infamous "Published in the Moon" diatribe against Bishop Pinten.

assistance to the struggling or the poor during the depression, extended families or caring individuals watched out for one another. Quiet deeds of charity or neighborliness seemed the norm for the Catholic people to work their way through the fears and privations of unemployment. Mary Helen Rose remembered at the end of the millennium how a woman had approached her at her father's wake in 1967 and asked, "Are you Mr. Gogulski's daughter?" When she answered that she was the eldest of his three children, the inquirer continued, "I've never forgotten him. During the depression we lived in a small upstairs apartment on Second Street [in Grand Rapids]. My husband could only find small, part-time jobs to work at, and I was pregnant. We would buy coal from your father when we could pay for it; but at times we had no money, so we went without. Several times in the cold of winter we would find a bushel of coal outside our door. We knew Mr. Gogulski had left it. There was never a bill nor did he ever mention it to us. He seemed to know when we needed it most. I've never forgotten his doing this."

Stanley Gogulski owned the Republic Coal Company on the west side of Grand Rapids. Born in Poland, educated in Germany, he came to this country when he was 22 years old. Though they knew he was a generous man, no one of his family had ever heard of these deeds of Christian love until his death.

Rather early in the administration of Bishop Pinten it was evident that it would be challenging and difficult to work with him. He was usually described as frugal and ascetic, qualities which would prove to be a blessing for the Catholic community during the depression years. Others considered him miserly. He is said to have come from a wealthy family with considerable iron and copper investments. However he himself lived without many of life's comforts, as did the majority of his flock. Joseph D. Cavera, just beginning his service on church boards in the 1930s, remembered over 60 years later a winter's meeting in the bishop's house (located since Bishop Kelly's time on Lake Drive near Cherry) with a group of other Catholic laymen and Bishop Pinten. There was no heat in the house. It was so cold that the committee members kept their scarves and coats on all during the meeting.

During the already burdensome depression years, the weight of Bishop Pinten's authority fell particularly heavily on his clergy. Only two years after his arrival an anonymous underground letter circulated among the clergy, poking fun at the bishop but then, more seriously, holding him, his policies, and his three closest priest advisers up to ridicule. It enraged Bishop Pinten. He was determined to find the typewriter which had produced the document and thus the author. Celebrated in clergy lore for generations after, the letter was titled *Published in the Moon,* though often remembered as *The Letter to the Moon.* The typewriter is said to be at the bottom of the Pere Marquette River.

The Sisters of St. Dominic were not immune from misunderstandings with Bishop Pinten. Their previous relationships with Bishops Richter, Gallagher, and Kelly had been so warm and agreeable that it seemed particularly unsettling for them to contend with the new bishop's efforts to bring them more exclusively under his authority. Not until 1936, when the Sacred Congregation of Religious in Rome ruled on the status of the Dominican Sisters as a pontifical, rather than a diocesan community, did Bishop Pinten accept that he was not the lawful and immediate superior of the sisters. In the meantime, his decisions in their affairs often seemed to them arbitrary and intrusive. These included denying permission to take out loans for new mission projects or refusing permission to send sisters out of the diocese for new apostolates or conferences. Already in late 1928 the sisters were receiving rumors that the bishop was about to resign. Quite aware of the growing clergy disgruntlement with their bishop, Mother Eveline Mackey wrote privately of the bishop's unfavorable rulings, "… it is very hard to

work under such strain…. He is looking poorly himself, and maybe sometime in the near future he might leave us." Then, perhaps not trusting to be able to distinguish wish from prophecy, she added, "… it is just as positive that he might be here for the next twenty years…." By the mid 1930s they could not even establish a channel of communication with him or his officials.

Even a priest from the Detroit Diocese could receive stern disciplinary rulings from the Grand Rapids bishop, at least when he proposed to exercise his ministry within Bishop Pinten's jurisdiction. Father James B. Fitzpatrick requested permission to offer Mass every few months a year in the home of his parents, who lived in Clare. His father, he explained, "is and has been very sick, and is not able to attend Mass at his parish church." The bishop's prompt reply on April 2, 1927, conveyed by a secretary, explained tersely that "he is unable to grant you permission…. He feels that this privilege is reserved only to missionaries…." Perhaps Father Fitzpatrick had been emboldened to make the request by the example of a fellow Detroit priest whose mother had been gravely ill in the spring of 1925. Then, just ordained in Rome, Father Allen J. Babcock rushed back to his family home and celebrated Mass at his mother's bedside. His first Solemn Mass a week later was his mother's requiem.

A perfectly composed and beautifully handwritten letter of February 9, 1927, by a senior high school student at St. Mary's School, Muskegon, respectfully and politely requested "with the permission of our principal and the knowledge of our pastor… a first favor for our school, a great favor." President of the class of 15 students, Robert Hanson invited Bishop Pinten to give an address at the graduation service in St. Mary's Church June 12. "If you are not free on this date we can fit ourselves to any evening of that week. Please do not refuse us…."

The refusal came nearly three months later. "He is sorry if he

Mother Eveline Mackey, prioress of the Grand Rapids Dominican Sisters, 1927-1936.

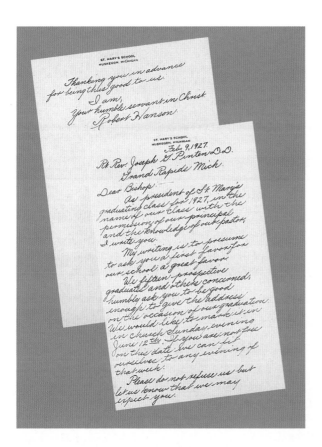

Sister Jane Marie Murray, OP.

disappoints you," the secretary wrote, "but it is unavoidable." The delay in responding was because plans had to be completed "for a contemplated trip to Europe… he will be away on the day when you planned to have him address you and the graduating class."

Though the church climate may have been restrictive and the economic climate depressing, there were still bold initiatives taking place in the faith community. In the late 1920s the Grand Rapids Dominican Sisters began studies in the liturgy at St. John's Abbey, Collegeville, Minnesota. Under the leadership of the Benedictines, especially Father Virgil Michel, Sister Jane Marie Murray and Sister Estelle Hackett immersed themselves in the principles of active, participative liturgy. They also experienced the power and the beauty of such liturgies and were full of enthusiasm to share what they were learning.

Their goal was to educate children in the liturgy. They secured the equal enthusiasm of Mother Eveline Mackey, who committed another 16 sisters to their first summer school in liturgical studies at Collegeville in 1929.

Sister Estelle Hackett, OP.

Before they knew it, Sister Jane Marie and Sister Estelle were writing meditations on the liturgy for children in the national magazine *Orate Fratres*, which led to creating the eight-volume *Christ Life Series*

Catholic Junior College in downtown Grand Rapids in the 1930s. It evolved into Aquinas College.

published by the Macmillan Company in 1933-1934 for the religious education of children in the elementary grades. These initiatives led the sisters into the revival of Gregorian chant, culminating in a Mass at St. Andrew's Cathedral on April 25, 1933, with a thousand children from the parochial schools of Grand Rapids chanting the *Missa de Angelis*.

At the start of this surprising journey, Sister Hackett had exclaimed, "But truly the liturgy is worth all this if only Bishop Pinten doesn't learn of it."

One Dominican project Bishop Pinten not only learned of but eventually supported was the founding of the co-educational Catholic Junior

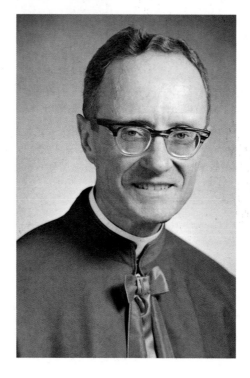

College, formed out of what had been a women's school, Marywood (also known as Sacred Heart) College. Located in downtown Grand Rapids at 69 Ransom Avenue, it opened its doors for classes with 73 students in September 1931. In five years its enrollment rose to 200. When the first dean, Doctor Burton Confrey, left in 1934, Bishop Pinten appointed Father Arthur F. Bukowski as chaplain and dean of the college. He became its president in 1937, and remained in that office when the institution evolved into Aquinas College in 1940. Yet, even with the bishop's basic support, the Dominican Sisters continually sought to clarify with diocesan

Msgr. Arthur F. Bukowski, president of Catholic Junior College and first president of Aquinas College.

leaders that the college was their mission and ultimately their responsibility, not the diocese's.

Just as sisters in the religious life were developing creative methods and materials for the religious education of the young in the 1920s and 30s, so were laywomen. Concerned over the loss of faith and the practice of the faith among children, a teacher in Detroit, Josephine VanDyke Brownson, formed a group of catechists who helped her create a training program for lay teachers. By 1938 they became the Catholic Instruction League. A co-worker in the original group was Mary Kay Kirby. She shared her experience with members of the Grand Rapids League of Catholic Women in September of 1934. Moving to Grand Rapids, she was invited, after her presentation to the League, by St. Alphonsus Church to put her experiences to work there. She was joined by Marge Boucher, Loyola Kirchhoff, and Mary Miller. Together they held their first classes with 32 children on November 11, 1934. With no texts as yet, they used visual aids "to excite the children's imagination." Their efforts mark the beginning of the first organized lay catechetical program in the Grand Rapids Diocese. A year later they extended the scope of their mission to adults by forming the Baraga Rental Library, named after the pioneering missionary to the Grand River Valley of a century before.

Seminarian Charles Brophy, crossbearer. Acolytes Aloysius Homan (left) and Willliam Flohe. They lead the 1933 anniversary procession at St. Joseph Seminary.

Anniversary celebration at St. Joseph Seminary, Grand Rapids, June, 1933: 100 years since Father Baraga's first Mass at the Grand, 50 since Bishop Richter's consecration, 25 since beginning of St. Joseph Seminary.

In the nation at large a new effort to influence not only the moral behavior of Catholics but even of the country took the form of an annual pledge. It has been called "the most far-reaching Catholic venture in public morality," at least up to that time. Since the silent movies became "talkies" in 1927, the influence of movies was becoming pervasive. By 1934 Cardinal Dougherty of Philadelphia was calling them "perhaps the greatest menace to faith and morals in America today." The pledge was the creation of the National Legion of Decency. Under the direction of the bishops, the Legion classified all movies as "morally unobjectionable" for all or for adults, or "objectionable in part," or "condemned." In every parish once a year Catholics were asked to stand at Mass and take the pledge to abide by the ratings. The ratings were first formed in 1933 and became more widely publicized in1934.They became a staple of parish life and religious instruction for the next 30 years.

It was in 1933 as well that the Diocese of Grand Rapids celebrated with the full pageantry of bands, processions, flags, and speeches the 100th anniversary of Father Baraga's first Mass at the Grand River. Held on the grounds of St. Joseph Seminary, the celebration also commemorated the 50th anniversary of Henry J. Richter's arrival and consecration as the first bishop, as well as the seminary's 25th anniversary. Reports state that 35,000 people were in attendance at the Mass. This would mark the largest Catholic gathering in the state of Michigan, perhaps until the pope would come to the Detroit area in 1987. In another Depression era cost-saving effort, St. Joseph Seminary expanded its enrollment policy to include the two years of philosophy on the Burton Street premises, thus housing students for the full term of both high school and college rather than sending them to other cities for their philosophy studies.

International events did not much press in on American life in the late '20s and early '30s. With enough to face at home in economic distress, Americans of all religious backgrounds seemed vaguely aware of disturbing developments overseas,

but they were like distant storm clouds off and away on the horizon. The threat of communism was much discussed in the Catholic press, especially with the events unfolding in the Spanish Civil War. There were rumblings about the crudities of the Fascists and Nazis and their dictatorial leaders, Mussolini and Hitler. Yet the horrors of Kristallnacht on November 9-10,1938, when Nazi thugs set fire to synagogues, smashed the windows of Jewish-owned stores, and attacked Jews on the streets of German cities and towns, did not command the general attention or response of Catholic Americans.

Seminarians Joseph Cieslukowski and Francis Flynn in mid-1930s.

In Rome itself during the middle 1930s another two gifted seminarians from the Grand Rapids diocese were completing their studies for priesthood at the famed Pontifical Urban College for the Propagation of the Faith. Francis Flynn and Joseph Cieslukowski had a front row seat on the early stirrings of Fascism and Nazism in the streets of the eternal city. In his personal diary for the date of April 21, 1935, seminarian Flynn wrote: "2,500 German youths, half in blue uniforms, half in white came down in 100 buses. They stood just in front of the barriers (in St. Peter's square). Their deep 'Heil, Heil' in the midst of the cheering of the piazza was like the bass in an orchestra. At each 'Heil,' the Hitlerian salute." Two years later, in the same diary, he records without comment for January 31: "Mussolini is having a review for other troops returned from Abyssinia. They camped out behind our college – over near Villa Pamfili."

For February 18, 1937, Frank Flynn continued his observations of the eerie preparations unfolding before the very eyes of the international student body of seminarians: "At 6:25p.m. all the lights of Rome were switched off for about 15 minutes for anti-air practice. The first aid 'red cross' and firemen were getting practice at running thru the streets in the dark. Twas interesting to see the city waking up again. Lights began blinking out of the darkness, now here now there. Soon the trams along the Tiber lit up, were boarded, and the busy life of the city began anew. The Vatican called up 4 times to tell us to put out every light in the sem. for they could see candles in some rooms. The Vice [Rector] tried to make us stay in our rooms, but we knew he couldn't distinguish us in the dark, so as soon as he went to another cam ["camera," i.e., room], we all slid out into the corridor again."

Back in Michigan, spring of 1937 saw the creation of the Diocese of Lansing, mostly out of territory from the Diocese of Detroit. In the Diocese of Grand Rapids in the summer of 1937, Bishop Pinten announced 14 priest assignments. In November he publicized four more. Then again before Christmas he made another seven transfers of his priests, 25 assignments in four months. On February 26, 1938, it was announced that Rome had created another new diocese in Michigan, much of its territory this time taken from the northeastern portion of the Diocese of Grand Rapids. In retrospect, after the revelation that the Saginaw Diocese had been formed, this wide-scale shifting of priest personnel seemed to many to be Bishop Pinten's way of sending into the new jurisdiction those priests whose service he would no longer want and securing for the Diocese of Grand Rapids those he chose to keep. In any case, his health continued to deteriorate thereafter, and he lived in ever greater seclusion. His resignation was announced on November 1, 1940, the 50th anniversary of his ordination as a priest. After 14 years of service to the diocese, he retired to his home in Marquette, living in seclusion, and dying there on November 6, 1945, at the age of 78.

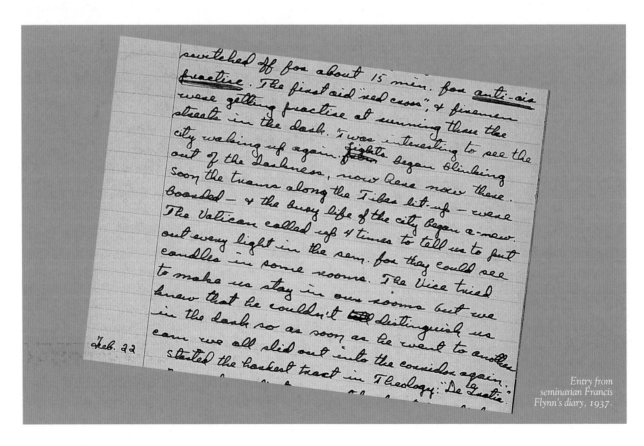

Entry from seminarian Francis Flynn's diary, 1937.

During his administration two parishes were established, five churches and one chapel were built, as were one convent and one school. Eleven rectories were also built or purchased. The diocese was debt-free.

Map of Grand Rapids Diocese with redrawn boundaries in 1938.

Sanctuary of St. Mary's Church, Muskegon, 1937

VALLEY OF DARKNESS

1940 - 1953

THE DARKNESS THAT WOULD SOON ENGULF THE EARTH was already cloaking Europe and Asia as the 1940s began. In the Grand Rapids Diocese as in the rest of the country, people seemed to have all they could do to cope with the continuing anxieties of the economic depression. Out of necessity, if not out of spiritual motivation, they had developed a simple and frugal lifestyle. Enjoyments and recreation were often what people created for themselves. A strong sense of community and a reliance on one another helped to steer a path through the unpromising days of little or no work and little or no income. Wars and rumors of war only cast further gloom and fear.

Into this troubled atmosphere came a ray of sunshine and hope, Joseph Casimir Plagens, as the successor to Bishop Pinten and fifth bishop of the Grand Rapids Diocese. He breathed a peaceable

gospel spirit. Born in Poland in 1880, he migrated with his parents to Detroit when he was four years old. He was only 23 when he was ordained a priest and only 26 when he began serving his first pastorate in Port Austin. He loved music, both singing in choir and playing organ, piano, and violin. Bishop Gallagher consecrated him auxiliary bishop of Detroit in 1924 and came to appreciate and rely on his tact and ability to mediate disputes and factional differences, especially in ethnic parishes.

He was named bishop of Marquette in 1935. In his five years of ministry there he built a lovely new cathedral after the previous one had been destroyed by fire. Parishes throughout the huge expanse of territory in the upper peninsula became familiar with his kindly presence through his pastoral visits. When one of his parishes in Detroit where he had been pastor, Sweetest Heart of Mary, published a glowing

1941	1942	1943	1943	1945	1947	1950	1952	1953
Pearl Harbor bombed	Fermi splits atom	Copland composes *Appalachian Spring*	Movie *Casablanca*	V-E Day	Robinson integrates baseball	U.N. forces in South Korea	Hydrogen bomb first exploded	Queen Elizabeth crowned

tribute in his honor on the occasion of his 10th anniversary as bishop, most felt the remarks were not exaggerated: "… he pacified storms… he preached and lived charity… he commanded dignity."

When he arrived in Grand Rapids on February 17, 1941 for his installation at the cathedral the next day, his first words were "Peace to this city and to all the people who dwell therein." The people in his new diocese to whom he brought this pacific spirit were hunkering down for war. With the sacrifices of the depression era still a normal part of their lives, they seemed to take in stride the additional restrictions that bracing for world war would bring. Rationing of food, clothing, and fuel became the order of the day, with books of stamps required for purchase. Some items like coffee and butter became rare. People were encouraged to grow and raise as much of their own food as possible, so "victory gardens" became popular even in urban settings. As the nation pulled together every possible resource, scrap drives were conducted to collect iron, tin, copper, rubber, and nylon from homes and schools.

Loved ones were continually leaving for the battlefront from 1941 onward. Prayers for the soldiers and the war dead became frequent and public. Soon after the declaration of war on December 8, 1941, Bishop Plagens issued a pastoral letter to be read at all Masses the Sunday before Christmas. In it he urged all "our beloved people to acts of penance, daily attendance at Mass, frequent, even daily, Holy Communion, and constant prayers for our president and our soldiers…." At the end of 1942 Bishop Plagens encouraged a day of prayer for victory and peace before the sacrament of the Eucharist on December 8. He urged families to pray the rosary together every day and priests to celebrate Mass "once each week for the men in the services, both living and dead."

As a practical post-script, he also wrote: "We suggest that in the spirit of sacrifice the faithful refrain from all pleasure driving and thus conserve gasoline for attendance at church services."

This spirit of sacrifice was widespread. In early 1942, Catholics throughout the diocese were approached to contribute to a special collection for the American Red Cross. The Grand Rapids Catholic Daughters of America held a drive at the same time for making altar linens to be used for religious services in battlefields and war camps. Later that year the Women's Guild of St. Stephen Parish in East Grand Rapids faced what many another parish society confronted: the shortage of coffee, sugar, and meats which would therefore require the cancellation of such events as annual parish suppers. Such shortages, however, did not prevent children from Sacred Heart School in Grand Rapids from preparing gift packages for children in war-stricken countries before Christmas of 1942 or from sending boxes of candy to the soldiers at Fort Custer in Battle Creek that same Christmas. Neither, amazingly, did wartime constraints halt the groundbreaking for a new St. Michael's Church in Muskegon in February 1942, under the leadership of Father Andrew Sikorski.

More than in previous conflicts involving this country, World War II drew a patriotic and pastoral response from clergy wishing to serve as chaplains. The first to enlist from the Grand Rapids Diocese was Father Charles E. Steves. He left for the army in late 1941 from his post as assistant at Sacred Heart parish in Mt. Pleasant. He was eventually followed in the army by eight other diocesan priests: Fathers John W. Collins, Gerard F. Guzikowski, Ralph J. Kelly, Herman S. Kolenda, William E.

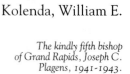

The kindly fifth bishop of Grand Rapids, Joseph C. Plagens, 1941-1943.

Powers, Linus M. Schrems, Speer Strahan, and James P. Yager. Serving as chaplains in the navy were Fathers Anthony C. Bourdow, Raymond B. Drinan, Charles W. Popell, and Joseph I. Sruba. Within a year of the war's declaration the Redemptorists from St. Alphonsus parish in Grand Rapids would have seven of their priests serving as chaplains, beginning with Father Mark VanGorp, Father August J. Peters, Father Edward J. Comer, and Father Francis Tobin.

From his chaplaincy service in Italy with General Mark Clark's Fifth Army, Father Tobin wrote to his parents in late 1943: "I don't have to urge them to come to church… the church was filled…. There's no such thing as a Eucharistic fast over here. I give the men general absolution and tell them to go to confession afterwards. And they certainly make use of the privilege…. There's something contagious about the faith of the Catholic boys, which kindles a kindred flame in their non-Catholic comrades…." Father Tobin came from a family of three sisters who became nuns and two brothers who were ordained to the priesthood.

I n another part of the world with another part of the war, a diocesan priest-chaplain, Father Speer Strahan, wrote of his experiences at Pearl Harbor just after December 7, 1941, in a national Catholic publication, *Commonweal*. He described how on the day following the Japanese attack, he heard confessions "ceaselessly" on the very fields leading to the Pacific where the dead had been stretched out in countless numbers. After the long hours of confession, many of the soldiers assembled, kneeling in wide circles before him for Holy Communion. Two impressions stayed with him: their deep religious fervor and, especially in those circumstances, the power of the Communion prayer he was required to say in Latin as each one received: May the Body of our Lord Jesus Christ guard your soul into everlasting life.

In an amazing coincidence, there was a second priest-chaplain from the diocese at Pearl Harbor on that "day of infamy." Father Raymond B. Drinan had just finished celebrating Mass aboard a hospital ship when the Japanese attack began. Later he served in the battles of the Coral Sea and Midway and was with

the armed forces that stormed the Solomon Islands. On a visit in the spring of 1943 to see his mother in Muskegon and his brother, Father David Drinan at Mount Mercy in Grand Rapids, he addressed the student body at the Mount, remarking: "To me there is a vivid contrast between the impact of the war on the boys fighting it and on the folk still at home. In the action zone men have become startling reverent and have turned to prayer. Here at home people are talking too commonly about how much money they are making."

H e may have met some people back home who were flushed with enthusiasm over the growing employment opportunities that supported the war effort after the bleak days of the worst of the depression. Still, most lived far from the lap of luxury. When Lent of 1943 approached, Bishop Plagens acknowledged the rigors which the war brought so close to home as he published the usual Lenten regulations for Catholics. "In a spirit of mortification we exhort all the faithful to refrain from public amusements and social entertainments and pray God to grant to the world an early and just peace." He went on to say: "In consideration of the difficulties in obtaining food in this time of war, for this year only we dispense the faithful of the diocese from the obligation of fast and abstinence on all the days of Lent with the exception of Ash Wednesday and Good Friday…. Fridays are to be kept as days of abstinence only." However, he urged priests and people to hold special Lenten devotions "in every church and chapel in the diocese at least twice a week in the evening, the Way of the Cross with benediction and prayer for peace on one evening and a special Lenten sermon with benediction [of the Blessed Sacrament] on another evening."

A nother adjustment to new conditions the war brought was the novelty of an afternoon and evening Mass, never before allowed in the diocese, on the feast of the Ascension, 1943. Presumably, there was no general communion for those attending, as the communion fast from the previous midnight still prevailed. For nearly a year, beginning in late 1942, there had been a U.S. Army

Air Force Weather School located in downtown Grand Rapids. Its purpose was to train hundreds of weather forecasters for duty in all theaters of war. To accommodate the Catholic personnel whose class times prevented them from attending morning Masses, arrangements were made for the later Masses "to be offered in the post chapel in the Pantlind Hotel." Father Thomas J. Bolger and Father Thomas O. Martin were assigned as chaplains to the weather training school.

Another feature of the weather training school was a program of hospitality on the part of Catholics in the Grand Rapids area. With an estimate of at least 25% of the trainees listed as Catholic, a cooperative effort was made between the weather school and representatives of diocesan lay organizations to open up Catholic homes for hospitality to the military.

Meanwhile clergy from the diocese continued to enlist for service as chaplains. One pastor from the diocese had an unusual swearing-in ceremony. Father John W. Collins was pastor of St. Mary's parish in Charlevoix. In May of 1943 he took the oath of an army officer at the weather training school in Grand Rapids. It was administered by John A. Collins, his father and the mayor of East Grand Rapids.

While school children showed that they, too, could be counted on to contribute to the war effort through their scrap drives and gift packages to the troops and to fellow children in the war zones, they also had to prepare for the dangers of the war. Air raid drills became a regular feature of school discipline, with children practicing to respond by hiding under their desks at school or marching in orderly fashion down the streets to their homes. Adults also learned the seriousness of city-wide air raid drills when sirens wailed and blackouts were ordered. Civil defense wardens were trained to patrol neighborhood blocks to enforce the blackout. Fines were stiff for any violation, running to $100, 90 days in jail, or both. Even though the threat of enemy attack on the towns and villages of a diocese in the heartland of a vast country was made to seem a real possibility, people often took the occasion of the nighttime blackouts to gather with family and

neighbors on their porches and enjoy popcorn and lemonade in the summer twilight and darkness until the all-clear sirens sounded.

Two young brothers and their friend who lived in the triangle of parishes in Byron Center, North Dorr, and New Salem had a much closer contact with the forces of Japan than an air raid might simulate. At about 4:00 p.m. on February 23, 1945, Kenneth Fein, age 10, and his brother Robert, age 12, along with their friend Larry Bailey, were playing outdoors in the rolling countryside when they spotted a strange object in the sky moving rapidly from west to east. At first they thought it was a gull, then maybe a kite. As they chased after it, they could see that it was a balloon that was fast losing altitude. To their delight it landed on the farm of Chris Stein near the intersection of 146th Avenue and 21st Street in northern Allegan County. The intensely curious boys grabbed what they could of the 19 ropes of 49 foot length attached to the balloon and attempted to drag the balloon home. It was 33 feet in diameter. Their neighbor, Joseph Wolf, saw them struggling with their find and helped load the harness of the balloon in his pickup and drove to the Fein homestead.

Kenneth Fein of north Allegan County, who as a boy helped snare the mystery balloon.

Genevieve Fein, the boys' mother, had their pastor called. "In those days," she said, "when anything happened you always called the priest." Father Ernest J. Walters was the pastor at St. Sebastian Church in Byron Center. When he saw the entire contraption, he advised that they should immediately call the Kent County sheriff. Two deputies quickly came and thought the discovery was a weather balloon but were informed by the weather bureau that it was not. Then the Federal Bureau of Investigation took over. Two FBI agents came the next day to question the family. They removed all the evidence from the house, and nobody heard another word about what it might have been. For national security reasons there had been a news blackout, and the information remained classified.

Only in 1986, 41 years later, did it become known that the Japanese government had launched over 10,000 such balloons in early 1944. The goal was to reach the northwest coast of the United States and Canada with incendiary bombs to cause firestorms in the forests and panic in the general population. If the balloons succeeded, the Japanese government planned a germ warfare attack against livestock and crops. Only two such bombs reached as far as Michigan. One of them ended up in the Fein basement.

Mysterious wartime balloon.

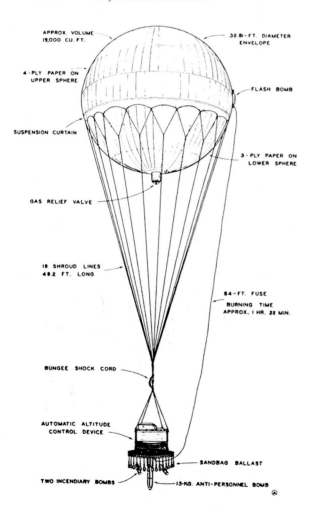

As the war took its toll on the battlefields where it was being waged, it also took its sad toll in homes across America and in all the combatant countries. Eventually it even engulfed civilians in direct assaults and bombardments, with segments of the population or entire cities obliterated in Europe and Asia. The moral distinction between civilian and combatant was treated as too hard to separate and honor, or even non-existent, especially as munitions factories and assembly lines for planes, tanks, and other war-related equipment were located in the midst of cities or population centers, not only abroad but also at home. If Detroit was the "arsenal of democracy," Muskegon and Grand Rapids were also doing their fair share of manufacturing war materiel right within their city limits.

Prisoners of war, taken on all sides and presumed to be protected under international law by the Geneva Convention of 1929, were brought to Michigan, as to other parts of the country, by the U.S. government. The army set up tent camps or barracks to utilize the prisoners for farming, as many who had been farming were either serving in the military themselves or were recruited for the war effort in factories and industry. In Michigan there were as many as 25 prisoner-of-war facilities, five of them in the territory of the Grand Rapids diocese: Fremont, Grant, Hart, Lake Odessa, and Mt. Pleasant.

The prisoners were German, and in places like Hart and nearby Shelby, where 600 of the POWs had been sent, their work was in the orchards to harvest the cherry crop. In Fremont 500 POWs had been sent by August of 1944 for agricultural and canning operations connected with the Gerber Products Company. In Lake Odessa the POWs received weekly visits from the German-speaking Monsignor J. Bernard Hansknecht, pastor of St. Mary's Church, Grand Rapids. Monsignor's nephew was a sergeant in the U.S. Army at the time, and Monsignor's aunt, Mother Liboria Hansknecht, ran a hostel for refugees in Rome. Mother Liboria was known by the young relatives as "reverend aunt" and Monsignor as "reverend uncle."

Funeral Mass for Bishop Plagens at St. Andrew's Cathedral, April 6, 1943.

The patriotic spirit at home showed itself not only through cooperation with scrap drives, rationing, and victory gardens, but through increased attendance at churches for novenas and prayers for peace. Anxiety for the safety of family members serving in the war zones was close to everybody's heart. Religious and patriotic fervor often worked hand-in-hand, as the national flag was honored by being brought into the church, often paired with the papal flag. In addition, special flags were created, with blue stars representing each parishioner serving in the war and gold stars those who had died or been killed in military action. When service flags with the blue and gold stars were first unfurled in a parish or religious institution, official ceremonies usually accompanied the event, with the mayor or civic officials on hand, along with the bishop or his representative. Prayers, dedication speeches, blessings, and the national anthem were the order of these ceremonies, as the "colors" were formally escorted and raised by military detachments and parish societies.

There was not much public notice when Bishop Plagens had a representative take his place at these or other such ceremonial events. He had maintained a constant round of pastoral visits in the diocese. What most did not know was that Bishop Plagens had suffered a heart attack only four months after his arrival in the diocese. He suffered several other mild attacks after that but continued to push himself to fulfill his commitments. On March 19, 1943, Bishop Plagens ordained five deacons to the priesthood: Joseph E. Murphy, John W. McGee, Gerard F. Guzikowski, Thaddeus R. Sniegowski, and Albert R. Bernott. Over a half-century later one of the ordained distinctly remembered how the bishop took some medication during the ceremony, but only after Communion, in order to respect the fast before receiving. Immediately after the ordination he was confined to bed, first at his home and the next day at St. Mary's Hospital in Grand Rapids, where he lingered until his death on March 31 at age 64. The bells of the city's Catholic churches tolled the sad news, while the ordination class of 1943 would ruefully quip that it must have been they who did him in.

The tenure of Bishop Plagens in the Diocese of Grand Rapids was just two years, from his installation in February 1941 to his death. During that short time he had endeared himself to many through his gracious spirit. The morale of the clergy in particular had been raised considerably. In the cruel and uncertain climate of world war, it was reassuring to have generous-hearted spiritual leadership from their bishop. With his passing so quickly, they could only pray that this quality of ministry would somehow be sustained.

The answer to those hopes and prayers was a surprising choice as bishop of Grand Rapids. In October of 1943, the Vatican announced that the pope had selected Monsignor Francis J. Haas as the sixth bishop of the diocese. He was an academic and an activist, a Midwesterner from Wisconsin and an east coast professor and dean at the Catholic University of America in Washington, D.C. Serving the church as a priest was his life's work, while at the same time he served his country as a mediator in labor disputes. Social justice to him was the heart of the gospel. Those who knew and admired him said that was what gave him such a great heart.

Monsignor Haas had been an instructor and rector at St. Francis Seminary in Milwaukee. As an academic his field of interest was social institutions and the unequal distribution of wealth in the world. He became passionate about the rights of workers to a living wage and the government's share of responsibility toward the poor. His mentor was Monsignor John A. Ryan of the Catholic University and director of the Social Action Department of the National Catholic Welfare Conference. The charter documents which formed his commitment were the gospels and the encyclical letters of Pope Leo XIII (*Rerum Novarum*, 1891) and of Pope Pius XI (*Quadragesimo Anno*-"On the Reconstruction of the Social Order," 1931). In these letters the popes defended the right to private ownership while at the same time arguing for a living wage for workers and for reasonable working hours and working conditions. These, they wrote, could best be accomplished through workers' associations or unions. They advocated for cooperation among representatives of labor, industry, and the public in order to bring justice and charity into society.

Bishop Haas serving meals to residents of the Little Sisters of the Poor. He was the sixth bishop of Grand Rapids, 1943-1953.

These ideals and teachings have formed the foundation of Catholic social teaching in the modern era. They were Monsignor Haas' mission. In the course of applying them to the American scene, he taught, wrote textbooks for college as well as elementary levels, advised church and government officials, and above all served as mediator in over 1,800 labor-management disputes. He was appointed by President Franklin D. Roosevelt in May of 1943 as chairman of the Fair Employment Practices Committee. In fact, it has been said that no other priest in the history of the country has served the government through membership on so many boards and committees.

Why he was chosen to be the spiritual leader of the Grand Rapids Diocese may have much to do with the respect that the archbishop of Detroit had for Monsignor Haas. In the course of the many strikes and labor unrest in Detroit, Archbishop Edward Mooney consulted frequently with Monsignor Haas and came to trust his advice and value his friendship. So, too, did other leaders of the hierarchy, such as Archbishop Samuel Stritch of Chicago and the apostolic delegate in Washington, D.C., Archbishop Amleto Cicognani. It was the apostolic delegate who led the consecration ceremonies of the new bishop at St. Andrew's Cathedral on November 18, 1943, along with Archbishop Mooney and Archbishop Moses E. Kiley of Milwaukee. Over the next decade Bishop Haas would deepen his collaboration and friendship with Archbishop Mooney.

It was not difficult to like the new bishop. Personable and friendly, he enjoyed the company of others. Six feet tall with a lumbering walk, he had a ready smile and a warm personality. If some never forgot the high-pitched, screechy voice and diminutive appearance of Bishop Pinten, others would always fondly recall the foghorn of a voice and engaging demeanor of Bishop Haas. With his concern for ordinary people, he could be seen on his walks, stopping at shops along the streets or visiting the circus when it came to the outskirts of town and set up its tents. He would always ask employees about their wages and working conditions. As he seemed to consider no one strange or alien, he would strike up a conversation easily. However, a good driver he was not, as, lost in thought, he would drive up to his office at the chancery when it was located next to the cathedral,

Bishop Haas and Archbishop Mooney at the consecration of Bishop Thomas Noa (left to right), March 19, 1946.

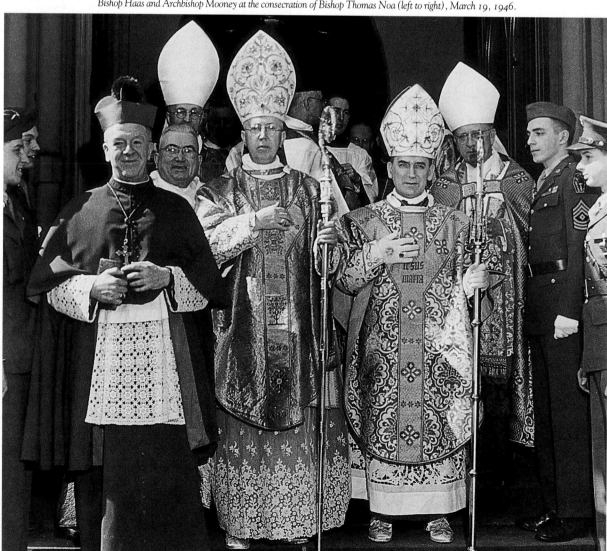

stop in the middle of the street, leave his car, and hand the keys to the first person he met in the office. With a mixture of impatience and embarrassment, he would groan, "Park the car!"

As the tragedy of the world at war would continue until 1945, the Catholics in the Grand Rapids diocese nevertheless found in their new leader an energy and vision not seen since the days of Bishop Kelly 20 years before. They responded in creative ways to channel his priorities of social justice and charity into new organizations and institutions for the service of others. In some cases they were able to build on initiatives that had small but important beginnings years earlier.

In the death registry of St. Andrew Parish there is an entry under the date of January 29, 1884, regarding the death of Wade Hampton, "Colored man," age 60, who died of consumption and was buried in the St. Andrew Cemetery. This may be the first reference to a black Catholic in the history of the diocese. Blacks, however, did not come to the area in significant numbers until just before and especially after the second world war. In 1938 Father Arthur F. Bukowski, the new and first president of Catholic Junior (later Aquinas) College, began a "Center for Negro Instruction" on Grandville Avenue in Grand Rapids with the blessing of Bishop Pinten. Later it came to be known as the Martin de Porres Center. The driving force behind the project and the one who encouraged Father Bukowski's involvement was Edward J. Farrell. Father of two priests, Fathers M. Donald and Edmund J. Farrell, he was manager of the St. Vincent de Paul store which housed the new center. Programs on the life of Christ and Catholic instruction were offered, initially to 27 blacks and two Indians. With help from college student volunteers the programs were expanded to include hospitality, entertainment, and a vacation school for children. In May of 1942 a second center was opened on Logan Street and was called Augustine House.

When he gave his first press conference in Grand Rapids in late 1943 and was questioned pointedly for his views on an array of public issues, Bishop Haas responded just as pointedly on the issue of racial discrimination. He "expressed hope for the attainment of social and economic justice for the Negro... 'not gradually, one brick at a time... one brick every hundred years.'" To demonstrate his commitment, Bishop Haas decided to travel to St. Ann's church in Baldwin when a class of 18 blacks and 7 whites had been prepared for reception into the Catholic Church in 1946. He baptized the candidates himself.

Sharing the bishop's spirit of urgency was a young couple, new to Grand Rapids in 1947, Lewis and Dorothy Clingman. Both were grounded in work for social justice and integration as Catholics in Chicago. They became the resident directors of Augustine House. "We set up camp on the second floor," Dorothy would recall over 50 years later, and "we would have classes downstairs. We had to have a piano there, and they could play the piano.... The

Dorothy and Lewis Clingman beginning a lifetime together and of service to education and social justice within the diocese.

kids could come in from the neighborhood, and we'd have little crafts there, you know, like making doll clothes… [and] the girls from Mercy School of Nursing came over… and they would bring little gifts to the youngsters…."

In the aftermath of a war which destroyed homes, cities, countrysides, and the social fabric of nations, and turned the wealth and talent of millions toward death and devastation, a time for building up again swept the world. In Europe and Asia the renewal of ordinary life often had to start from nothing. In the Grand Rapids Diocese, as in the United States generally, projects and improvements had been delayed or restricted by the constraints of the war. Bishop Haas seized the opportunities of peacetime to create apostolates and ministries that would have long-reaching and powerful effects on the faith-life of the Catholic community throughout the diocese. His first concerns were to serve the most neglected.

In 1950 seminarians Leo S. Rosloniec and Edwin A. Thome were the first to be sent from the Grand Rapids Diocese to study theology and complete their preparations for ordination to the priesthood at Assumption Seminary in San Antonio, Texas. This was not just an additional venue for priestly training but part of a plan to familiarize future priests with the language and culture of Spanish-speaking seasonal workers in the orchards and farms of west Michigan. Eventually nearly all seminarians at the college level were recruited for summer assistance to the migrant workers by teaching catechism to the youngsters, driving the visiting priests from Mexico to the fields and camps where the migrants worked and lived, and communicating with local pastors and parishioners about developments of the apostolate. Father Aloysius Ulanowicz of St. Bartholomew parish, Newaygo, was assigned as the director of the new apostolate.

Among his parishioners at St. Bartholomew's was an immigrant from the Netherlands, John Dekkers, who with his wife, Arlene, son John Jr., and close friend Adrian VanLoon, adopted the apostolate to the migrants as their own. Donating several acres of land for a church for the Spanish-speaking, Mr.

Dekkers set out to secure the materials for the building at a time when they were hard to come by and he himself helped with the construction. When he faced opposition, he prayed for the help and guidance of Our Lady of Guadalupe. By 1948 the Chapel of Our Lady of Guadalupe, constructed from material of St. John's at Ensley, was dedicated in Grant, with Bishop Haas coming to confirm 140 of the migrant workers. Two years later a similar chapel was inaugurated in the basement of the cathedral for services in Spanish.

Silverio Cerda and Yolanda Ramirez reenact the miracle of Our Lady of Guadalupe, Cathedral of St. Andrew, 1998.

The church, and for that matter the civic community, had much work to do in serving the needs of the elderly. The Carmelite Sisters of the Divine Heart of Jesus were well known to Bishop Haas, as their mother house was in Milwaukee. He urged them to come to Grand Rapids to staff a new "home for the aged" that he contemplated setting up in a remodeled structure on the corner of Wealthy Street and Madison Avenue. Though the project began in 1944, wartime restrictions on construction materials prevented the opening until 1952, when it was dedicated as St. Ann's Home.

Equally urgent in the bishop's mind and equally neglected were the children of the poor. As he wished to serve their immediate needs for food, clothing, safety, and shelter as well as their long-range needs for education and a healthy family environment, he proposed the establishment of a professionally trained staff and organization called the Catholic Service Bureau, later the Catholic Social Services. With offices in Muskegon and Grand Rapids, the Bureau was headed by Father Joseph Walen. Fresh from graduate studies in social work, which the bishop insisted on, Father Walen began a ministry which would include Catholic Charities, St. John's Home, and the new Bureau. With the approval of Bishop Haas, the Bureau sought assistance beyond church sources for a ministry that served many who were not members of the church. In 1948 the Catholic Service Bureaus in both Muskegon and Grand Rapids began to receive funding from the local Community Chest campaigns for their care of neglected children. Another trademark of Bishop Haas's approach to church ministries which had a social or civic impact

was to invite the participation of qualified and knowledgeable laymen and laywomen. Both as staff and as members of advisory boards, their presence and expertise began to change the face of traditionally based outreach or apostolic work.

Nowhere was this more evident or dramatic than in the Tri-State and Diocesan Congresses which Bishop Haas held annually from 1947. Envisioned as a "vast project for adult education," the congresses brought together noted speakers, lay and clergy, from around the country to address topics of concern to people of faith in such broad areas as industry, rural life, education, health care, and charities. He selected Monsignor Edmund F. Falicki as executive director of the congresses. Known as the sternest of disciplinarians in his post as rector of St. Joseph Seminary, Monsignor Falicki also demonstrated strength of focus and organizational abilities which served the bishop and the congresses effectively. In succeeding years lay people served as co-

Bishop Haas initiated "congresses" on a tri-state and diocesan level in 1947 as a "vast project for adult education," held in the Civic Auditorium of Grand Rapids.

Parish delegates to the diocesan congress.

chairs, with Dr. Monroe B. Sullivan and Mrs. Charles S. Dominski being the first. No one was to be excluded from the proceedings. "All the meetings will be open to the public," the bishop announced. "In fact, the public is warmly invited to attend."

Attend they did, in such large numbers as to fill the main hall of the Civic Auditorium in downtown Grand Rapids, spilling over into smaller meeting rooms for panel discussions and a remarkably informal sharing of ideas among the noted experts, visiting hierarchy, lay men and lay women, youth delegates, and clergy. When the first congress, the Tri-State (Michigan, Indiana, and Ohio), was so successful with 6,000 attending the opening Mass and up to 4,000 participating in the work sessions, Bishop Haas decided to sponsor future congresses solely for the Grand Rapids Diocese. They proved equally successful. Topics in succeeding congresses were "Religion and Citizenship," "The Catholic Woman in the Community," "Problems of Unemployment," "A Living Wage for Decent Family Living," "Helps for Family Life on the Farm," and "Recreation in Family Life."

Customarily, Bishop Haas presided at the opening Mass and sometimes invited a guest preacher, such as

Auxiliary Bishop Allen J. Babcock of Detroit in 1948. At the conclusion of the three or four days, he would close the congress by presiding at a solemn Benediction of the Blessed Sacrament and offering his personal words of appreciation. The congresses reflected the bishop's own well-known interests and commitments as a teacher and pastor of the church. They also created enthusiasm while they advanced knowledge and understanding of the Catholic faith and its real-life applications personally and in the family, as well as at work and in public life. They also provided a forum, rare and perhaps unequalled in the country, in which such a cross section of the Catholic people could interact so freely with one another on matters of their faith.

While Bishop Haas coped, somewhat reluctantly, with the usual requirements of administration, his real love was as teacher and pastor. He had plenty of challenges to be both in a geographically large expanse of diocesan territory at a time when the whole country was energized by the end of the war and the return of the military to civilian life. In the midst of these challenges, he was obligated to report to Rome on the state of the diocese in 1949. These visits to the pope and his offices every five years by the world's bishops are called "*ad limina,*" that is, to the thresholds of the tombs of Saints Peter and Paul. While in Europe, he also took the opportunity to visit Germany, the home of his paternal grandfather, and Ireland, home of his mother's parents.

In Germany, his father's relatives had been in communication with him after the war. He had assisted them with packages of shoes and clothes. On this trip he also wished to visit camps where people displaced by the upheaval of the war were housed temporarily as reconstruction slowly took place throughout Europe. In the American zone of West Germany the camps were the former barracks of the German army. Bishop Haas wrote back to the Catholics of his diocese: "The persons in these camps are suffering far less than they did in the homes which they were forced to leave… they have enough to eat and wear, although their living quarters are far from adequate. In many cases, two or more families are crowded into a single room…. They are, for the most part, without any hope for the future…." Their

Refugees from Lithuania with Msgr. Joseph A. Lipkus at SS. Peter and Paul School, Grand Rapids.

plight left a deep impression on the visitor who himself lived on hope for the future and who always brimmed over with practical plans for sharing both his faith and his hope with as many as he could.

The United States Senate passed the Displaced Persons Act on June 18, 1948, and it was signed into law by President Truman shortly after, thus allowing refugees to come to the United States. In Germany alone there were some 60,000 Lithuanian and 100,000 Latvian war refugees, among others. Through Bishop Haas' visit and invitation, many found their way to West Michigan. Included in their number were 21 priests, almost all Lithuanian. In addition, one priest came to the diocese from Czechoslovakia (Father Walter Marek) and one from Latvia (Father Stanislaus Matiss). There was even a bishop among the refugees who found a welcome to Grand Rapids, Bishop Joseph Rancans.

Bishop Rancans was a colorful figure. Tall and courtly, he was more at home speaking elegant Latin than he ever became able to handle English. He was 65 when he arrived in Grand Rapids in 1951, after living as a displaced person and political refugee in Germany for six years from 1944. He had served the church in Latvia as seminary professor and rector, pastor, historian, and author of devotional books. He served his country as representative of Latvia to the Holy See, as member and vice-president of parliament, and as a leader of the political underground resistance against Nazi Germany. From his unlikely base in Grand Rapids, living and working as chaplain at St. Ann's Home, he assisted in administering the sacrament of confirmation within the diocese and visited Latvian Catholics, who revered him, throughout the United States and Canada. Never losing hope for an independent Latvia after the ravages of Nazi and Soviet occupation, he died and was buried in Grand Rapids in 1969. Twenty-six years later his remains were exhumed from Resurrection Cemetery in the city of Wyoming for reburial in the Basilica at Aglona in the free and independent Latvia he had worked so valiantly to bring about.

Father Walter Marek's route to the diocese came by way of Czechoslovakia, through the camps for the displaced in Germany, where he spent two years after fleeing communist oppression for his work in the resistance movement back home. After his "chance encounter" with Bishop Haas in Frankfurt, he, too, received an invitation to come to the diocese. By 1951 he was serving as second assistant priest at Sacred Heart Church in Muskegon Heights. With his expertise in violin, piano, and organ, he met others in the arts, including Fritz Stansell, who was beginning an enterprise called the Blue Lake Fine

Father Walter Marek came from Czechoslovakia to serve in Muskegon Heights and at the Blue Lake Fine Arts Camp.

Bishop Joseph Rancans of Riga, Latvia (left) with Bishop Haas, Bishop Albers of Lansing, and Bishop Woznicki of Saginaw.

Arts Camp north of Muskegon. Father Marek also had his bank-owner father's business acumen, and so the priest-musician found himself on the camp's board of directors and its treasurer for 30 years. An impressive hall in the rustic beauty of the camp was named after him. Father Marek then fulfilled a dream of founding a similar camp in his hometown of Horni Jeleni, the Czech Music Camp for Youth. "My life unexpectedly turned so beautiful," he reflected, as he reestablished ties over 40 years later with a homeland that had thrown off the shackles of communism in the "Velvet Revolution."

When it came to children and youth, Bishop Haas expended not only much personal time and energy to hand on the faith to another generation, but he also motivated and inspired many others in the same cause. Kay Kirby had been continuing her work with the religious education of children who were not in Catholic schools. She and a growing number of interested and like-minded women had formed the Catholic Instruction League and had expanded their work from St. Alphonsus parish in Grand Rapids into neighboring parishes and then into Allegan, Marne, and Muskegon as more and more catechists received training. At the beginning of the war classes had to be dropped because of gas rationing. Later, as they resumed, a public school librarian, Eugenia Schmitz, joined the cause, lending her gift for organization to the recruiting and training of new catechists. They met every month as catechists, usually some 60 strong,

to compare notes and conduct business. They also sought out help for bettering themselves for their mission, enlisting Sister Leonard Lynch from Marywood and Monsignor Edmund F. Falicki from St. Joseph Seminary. Sister Lynch would spend an hour of their monthly meetings guiding them through the methods of teaching, and Monsignor Falicki, in turn, provided an hour of instruction in Catholic doctrine.

These gatherings formed the first certification program for catechists in the diocese. Within the diocesan structure the Catholic Instruction League was a committee of the Diocesan Council of Catholic Women. Bishop Haas, however, decided it was time for the League to operate under its own charter, and so in 1946 he incorporated it into the Confraternity of Christian Doctrine (CCD) with Monsignor Falicki as diocesan director.

Still, Bishop Haas felt that there were thousands of children beyond the reach of the growing corps of lay catechists or of Catholic schools. He was especially concerned about the children in the outlying and rural expanses of the diocese. Having heard of a program which taught children the Catholic faith through correspondence, he asked the Marywood Dominicans in 1947 to develop something like it for the diocese. Sister M. Rosella Powler directed the Religion Correspondence Course, and Sisters Mary Liguori DeHaus and Marie Dominica Viesnoraitis wrote a textbook for it, illustrated by Sister M. Rosalia Genovese. Pastors were involved in the program by submitting names of students in their area. Students

Sister Marie Rosella Powler, OP, and Sister M. Rosalia Genovese, OP, review student letters from the Religion Correspondence Course.

Sister Marie Dominica Viesnoraitis, OP, with textbooks she authored for the Religion Correspondence Course.

received their letter of invitation to join from the Dominican Sisters, who also sent lessons in the mail for the students to complete and return. The Sisters corrected, graded, and returned the lessons, sending back gold stars and holy cards for work well done. Entire families often found themselves drawn into the studies. The program was free of charge for the students, with the Sisters volunteering their services and the remaining costs underwritten by the diocese. At its peak development in 1960 students from grades 4 through 12 in the program numbered 2,220. As the budget for the program was $13,000, the cost was slightly more than $5.00 per pupil per year.

Back in his Washington days, Professor Haas had become familiar with an American-bred group of priests whose mission was the home country itself. The Missionary Priests of the Congregation of St. Paul (the Paulists) had a seminary just down the street from the Catholic University of America, where Monsignor Haas was dean of the School of Social Science. Since they usually located their mission in the center of large urban areas or college campuses, Bishop Haas liked their method (so much like his own) of bringing the gospel and the teachings of the church to people directly. Besides, their apostolate was primarily directed towards those who were not members of the Catholic Church but who had an interest in learning about it and possibly joining as members. They specialized in offering courses for adults that Catholics also could participate in and thus learn anew what they had studied only as children or youngsters. They accepted the invitation of Bishop Haas in 1947 to come to Grand Rapids, even though the city was considerably smaller than the sites of their other centers across the country. First housed in a three-story building at 329 Monroe Avenue in 1948, the flourishing ministry moved to even larger quarters on Ionia Avenue downtown in 1964.

With the same impulse to teach and pastor as widely as human ingenuity might devise, Bishop Haas launched a newspaper for the diocese in September 1948, *The Western Michigan Catholic* with Father Joseph Walen as editor. Since 1883 *The Michigan Catholic* of Detroit had served the Catholics of the entire state. With the editor-owner, William Hughes, hailing from a Grand

Rapids family, *The Michigan Catholic* first began publishing a Grand Rapids edition in 1887 until 1919, when *The Catholic Vigil* became the Grand Rapids diocesan weekly. When the *Vigil* ceased publication in 1929, *The Michigan Catholic* took up the slack again with a weekly section for the Diocese of Grand Rapids. Now with a paper designed to serve the Catholics of the western side of the state, the bishop wrote in the inaugural issue: "It will … enable our many families in rural areas without Catholic schools to obtain doctrinal information to supplement the catechetical work of the pastors. The paper will serve to strengthen Catholic life in all of our parishes by assisting the efforts of the priests in having a well-informed laity."

"Well-informed, educated, and motivated Catholics" was a continual refrain with Bishop Haas. In that spirit he welcomed Serra International to establish a club in the diocese in March of 1948. Founded by laymen for laymen in the state of Washington just 14 years earlier, the aims of Serra (named after the 18th century California Franciscan missionary priest, Junipero Serra) seek to encourage and support the calling to priesthood and the religious life, as well as to deepen the understanding and practice of the faith among its lay members. The

Mr. Ralph Hauenstein of St. Stephen's Church in East Grand Rapids was military chief of intelligence for Europe during World War II and later president of Serra International.

Ordination to the priesthood at St. Andrew's Cathedral, June 3, 1950.

first president of the Grand Rapids club was J. Bernard Haviland and the first chaplain, Father Joseph Ciesluk. The next year a chapter was begun in Muskegon with Dr. Andrew J. Donnelly as president and Father Francis Flynn as chaplain. The Grand Rapids club would have the distinction of seeing two of its leaders named as president of the worldwide membership, J. Bernard Haviland and Ralph Hauenstein, and one member on the international board of trustees, Dennis Leiber.

Mr. Hauenstein, former city editor of *The Grand Rapids Herald*, was well informed and motivated on more than matters Catholic. In World War II he had been a U.S. Army colonel and chief of intelligence for the European theater of operations. In that capacity he received the most confidential information in the conduct of the war, including what has been called the war's biggest secret. Beyond "top secret" and "most secret" was "Ultra." This was the secret that the allies had broken the Nazi military code early in the war and were able to decode enemy messages. As Mr. Hauenstein would reveal only after a half century had

passed since the war, "There were some instances where Hitler would give an order to one of his commanding generals, and we would have that message before the general got it." Historian Stephen Ambrose remarked about the Ultra code: "It won the war sooner. It saved countless lives.... We don't know what would have happened if we had fought the war without Ultra." Among the many honors that would later come to Mr. Hauenstein was that of being appointed a lay auditor for the final session of Vatican Council II.

If lay Catholics and their ongoing education and formation in the faith were a high priority with Bishop Haas, so were his seminarians and their training for the priesthood. Besides attending to their spiritual needs, he kept their physical well-being at heart. At the diocesan preparatory seminary in Grand Rapids he noticed on one of his visits that milk was missing on many tables but available on others. Upon inquiry, he learned that milk was an extra personal cost to the seminarians, which many could not afford. He immediately ordered it as a staple for everyone. In 1949 Bishop Haas joined Cardinal Mooney of Detroit and his other fellow bishops in Michigan in establishing St. John's Provincial Seminary. Located some 25 miles west of Detroit in what had been secluded countryside near Plymouth, St. John's was planned as the educational and spiritual formation center for seminarians from the dioceses of Michigan in their final years of preparation for ordination to the priesthood. In its nearly 40 years of service as a seminary, it would provide the state of Michigan with well over a thousand priests and the Diocese of Grand Rapids with several hundred. Many laymen and laywomen also received training in theology and spiritual formation there in its later years.

Shortly after Bishop Haas was consecrated for his ministry in the diocese, he had quickly rallied many helpers to expand the care and service of the church for meeting the wide variety of needs facing the diocesan community. Even though World War II was still going on, there was an optimism and determination that it would soon end in victory. People seemed to anticipate that prosperity would also follow. When the bishop, therefore, announced ambitious plans in 1944 to expand the Catholic high schools of Muskegon, Grand Rapids, and later Cheboygan, thousands of lay people contributed not only money but time and labor as well. In Grand Rapids alone, 2,500 workers made door-to-door canvassing of all known parishioners to ask for their financial donation and pledge. They responded to their spiritual leader's description of the drive as "a vast city-wide religious crusade" because it enabled the church to carry out Christ's command to teach all nations. Each drive was more successful than the last, setting records as the largest financial undertakings in the history of the diocese up until that time. People of other religious affiliations also joined the effort with generosity, and Bishop Haas publicly acknowledged their help, saying that "they recognized… something of far-reaching benefit to all."

The lay leaders of these drives, along with their bishop, were emboldened by their experience and success, prompting Bishop Haas to formalize the

Grand Rapids Catholic Central High School students with Bishop Haas during 1944 fund drive.

campaigns into yearly events called "The Fund for the Faith." They featured the same door-to-door solicitation of every Catholic household with the goal, as the bishop explained it, of providing funds "for the orderly and vigorous extension of the faith throughout the diocese." In announcing the reasons for making these drives an annual occurrence, Bishop Haas described the diocese of 1950 in these terms: "It may come as a surprise to many of our people to learn that the Diocese of Grand Rapids with its nearly 17,000 square miles and its population of more than a million is, when all is said and done, only a missionary diocese. Actually, the ratio of our Catholic population to the total is much less than 10 per cent. Less than one out of every 10 persons is Catholic. The true figure is perhaps one out of every 12 or 13. Indeed, there is a missionary job to be done. And this job is not merely for 1950, but for many years to come."

He himself would not be given many more years for this mission. As he found himself grieving the loss of friends and mentors in the work for social justice nationally and frequently invited to deliver their final farewells, he also experienced the loss of two great churchmen at home.

Monsignor Joseph Stanislaus Pietrasik, pastor for nearly 40 years at St. Isidore Church in Grand Rapids, died of cancer April 20, 1952, at the age of 77. Born in Poland, raised in Manistee, and ordained in Milwaukee after seminary studies there, he had been the founding pastor of St. Stanislaus Church in Ludington in 1901. Never owning a car, he walked everywhere and was well-known for his availability to his parishioners. He was an official consultor to three bishops in succession, Bishops Pinten, Plagens, and Haas. Above everything else, he was revered for the encouragement and support he gave to young men and women to enter the priesthood and religious life. During his tenure at St. Isidore, 31 men were ordained to the priesthood and some 60 women entered the religious life as School Sisters of Notre Dame, Sisters of Mercy, and Dominican Sisters.

The revered pastor with some of his protégés, April 1935. Standing: Fathers Frank Kupinski, Louis Wodecki, Casimir Walkowiak, John Boguslawski, Anthony Arszulowicz, Stanislaus Fron. Seated: Fathers Adalbert Radawski, John Maksymowski, Msgr. Thomas Noa, Msgr. Joseph Pietrasik, Fathers Stanislaus Sikorski, Joseph Karas, Andrew Sikorski.

The Fund for the Faith aimed for "the vigorous extension of the faith throughout the diocese" and involved all ages.

A year after preaching the funeral sermon for the patriarch of St. Isidore Church, Bishop Haas preached at the funeral of Monsignor Salvatore Cianci on April 22, 1953. Founding pastor of Our Lady of Sorrows Parish in Grand Rapids and spiritual father of the city's Italian community for 45 years, Monsignor Cianci had also been the first and longest serving chaplain at St. Mary's Hospital in Grand Rapids from 1908 to 1921. He had been continually sought out by many beyond his parish as a spiritual advisor and confessor. Though some may have kept a reverential distance from his blunt and outspoken opinions, many others came to know his warmth, his deep loyalty to Christ, and the

fierce and protective pride he had in his people. In the last months of his life he developed heart problems. As get-well wishes poured in from his many admirers, including Vatican prelates who were his old schoolmates, nothing could help him recover his strength, not even the loving attentiveness of his three faithful dogs. Years earlier the mayor of the city had said of Father Cianci, "There is no man I am prouder to know." Within a month filled with many similar eulogies, Bishop Haas himself was hospitalized.

From the end of May to the middle of July and then again from the end of July to the beginning of August,

106

Msgr. Salvatore Cianci was a strong influence on his Our Lady of Sorrows parishioners and on the civic and religious community of Grand Rapids.

he was treated for two successive heart attacks. Feeling recovered enough and energized, he hosted the participants of the National Liturgical Conference at their convention in the Grand Rapids Civic Auditorium, attending three sessions from August 17 to 20. At the end of the conference he delivered gracious concluding remarks, apologizing for speaking from the steps of the stage, as he could not yet climb to the platform. Eight days later he suffered a final heart attack, dying in the early morning of August 29, 1953. He was 64 years old, the same age as his predecessor at his death.

By most standards, the 10 years of Bishop Haas'

stewardship of the diocese had been most productive and creative. He had authorized the founding of 11 new parishes from Muskegon to Indian River to Lake Odessa to Grand Rapids. Many of these would become some of the largest communities of Catholics in the diocese. In addition, he raised 10 former missions to the full status of parish. He is also credited with establishing 20 mission churches and 19 elementary schools. More remarkable than even the numbers and the structures, however, was the welcoming spirit which Bishop Haas engendered. He helped create a climate that allowed an ever-increasing number of lay people to participate in the life of the church and its mission. His funeral was

The cathedral choir on Easter Sunday, 1950. Joseph Sullivan, far right, was organist and choirmaster 1948-1984.

probably the largest interfaith and interracial diocesan event until that time, not to mention the largest representation of government, business, and labor representatives the cathedral had ever witnessed.

As the recipient of many awards in his lifetime, perhaps one of his most treasured was given the year before he died. The Order of B'nai B'rith Interfaith Award was given in recognition of his "lifetime of activity in the field of bettering human relations, which has added to the well-being of all persons who have come within the influence of his work. His life

work has been bound up with the ideals of peace, of culture, of conciliation, of fair employment practices, assistance to the aged, and the preaching of tolerance." The citation went on to call Bishop Haas a blessing to himself and to humanity, because he had fulfilled the injunction of God to Abraham, "Be thou a blessing."

What Bishop Haas left for future generations of Catholics to accomplish was the application of his cherished ideals of Christian social justice to life within the church itself.

PEACE AND QUIET

1 9 5 3 - 1 9 6 9

WHEN THE DOCUMENTS OF SURRENDER WERE SIGNED aboard the battleship *Missouri* on a table desk manufactured by the Metal Office Furniture Company of Grand Rapids (now Steelcase), the end of World War II in 1945 signaled the beginning of a long-desired peace and quiet. At least, that is what many people dreamed would happen: a return to a normal life of work, family, education, church, some measure of security, and the joys and challenges of ordinary life. Who could suspect that the next half-century would rank among the most turbulent and blood-soaked in human history, next to the recent war itself?

For a few years it seemed that the promises of peace would come true. Work in cities and on farms was generally available for veterans eager to pick up their lives where they had left off. Many projects had been long delayed by the war. There were homes and schools to be built, roads to be repaired, factories to be constructed, and, as Bishop Haas had demonstrated, churches to be established and new ministries to be created in order to bring the gospel directly to people of every age and condition of life.

But some changes brought about by the war would not disappear. Because so many men had gone off to battle, women had been desperately needed in the work force on the home front. When the men came back from war, many women did leave offices and factories to go back to their work at home full-time. But not all of them chose to do so. Women's experience of working outside the home, with its additional income and increased independence, began a change in the workplace and in American society that would only grow in succeeding years.

1954	1954	1954	1962	1963	1964	1965	1966	1967
Separate but equal education unconstitutional	Mc Carthy hearings	School children inoculated against polio	Cuban Missile Crisis	J.F. Kennedy assassinated. M.L. King *I Have a Dream*	The Beatles tour U.S.	U.S. combat troops in Vietnam	Chavez organizes United Farm Workers	Six-Day War between Israel and Arab nations

Signing of surrender agreement ending World War II.

For their part, the returning military found that the GI Bill of Rights or Servicemen's Readjustment Act signed by President Roosevelt in 1944 provided opportunities for their education and housing that were too generous to pass up. So many took advantage of college scholarships that by 1952 about half of all veterans, or 7,600,000, received some form of education or training through its provisions. Enrollments in Catholic colleges across the nation swelled, including at Aquinas College in Grand Rapids, which expanded its campus in anticipation by purchasing the Lowe estate in 1945. With their advanced education and increasing professionalism, Catholics graduating from college would never be the same. As a result, neither would their church. They became increasingly able and willing to assume leadership in their parishes and in the diocese. Bishop Haas welcomed this advance and sought ways to enable their further development in the understanding and practice of their faith. His successor would do even more.

Additional changes brought about by the war production effort that would continue and grow in the years following the war were the expansion of the population into rural areas surrounding cities and

Pope Pius XII.

the movement north of the country's black and Hispanic populations. Internationally, what seemed only to keep increasing was the distressing missionary zeal of communism. In the years after World War II the Soviet Union swallowed up neighboring countries, forcing them to be satellites. Along with China, it brutally suppressed any opposition, persecuting and eliminating by force religious as well as political dissenters.

In Europe, as reconstruction of demolished cities went forward with generous American financial assistance, people reassessed their thinking about the world, about God, and about human life in the wake of the savagery they had just witnessed. For those of religious faith, a new spirit of ecumenism emerged, as they revealed how they had discovered a common bond in facing hardship and persecution together. In the immediate post-war years Pope Pius XII was widely hailed by Jews and Christians alike for his spiritual and moral leadership during the upheaval of the war. However, after his death a great controversy developed over whether he had done enough to save Jews from the holocaust and condemn Nazism. Whatever other world leaders did on their behalf, which was little or nothing, the pope's efforts to rescue Jews had taken place through quiet diplomacy, rather than openly and publicly, as later critics thought the catastrophe demanded.

Within the church itself, Pope Pius undertook several initiatives during the war years and immediately after which would have lasting impact on Catholics. In 1943 he issued an encyclical letter, *Divino Afflante Spiritu*, which endorsed many of the scholarly methods in archaeology and language studies which had brought fresh insight into the understanding of the bible. This letter encouraged Catholic scholars to make new translations of the bible from the original languages in which the sacred scriptures had been written. It also gave Catholic scholars the freedom to explore ancient methods of composing literature, with a view toward discovering the forms through which the human writers of the bible, under the inspiration of the Holy Spirit, had expressed God's word. The pope's document opened up seminaries, colleges, and universities within the church to the study of the scriptures. Equally influential were two other letters by the pope, *Mystici Corporis* in 1943 and *Mediator Dei* in 1947. The first letter laid the foundations for understanding the church from a biblical point of view rather than from only an institutional or legal aspect. The second led to an awareness of liturgy in the life of the church, of praying and worshipping publicly as a community in ways that would draw forth active involvement from the participants.

In 1953 the pope approved an easing of the 400-year-old church law requiring a fast from food and liquids before receiving holy communion. No longer would a total fast from the previous midnight be required. The revised law eventually required a fast from liquids and food only an hour before communion. Water could be taken anytime, and the sick could take medications and liquids, other than alcohol, anytime before communion. While the new regulations were hedged in with various precautions and restrictions, an era of eucharistic discipline and practice was thus ended.

The philosophical musings of postwar European thinkers on the meaning of existence would not preoccupy the ordinary American Catholic, or for that matter, the ordinary pastor or bishop. Neither, at the time, would the intellectual exertions of the pope on such admittedly important matters as the nature of the church, its worship, and the bible. The changes in fasting before communion, however, did receive wide attention, as they affected practicing church members directly. Other changes by Pope Pius in reviving ancient rituals to celebrate the Holy Week liturgies also gained some notice. More forcefully and widely communicated, however, was

Praying the rosary as a family became a popular devotion among Catholics in the 1950s.

the strong, consistent, and public anti-communist stand of Catholic leaders worldwide, beginning with the pope. In the United States anti-communism was at the forefront of politics as well. The 1950s saw Senator Joseph McCarthy escalate his investigations into espionage among government employees at the same time as the nation went to war again when communists in North Korea invaded the south of that country in 1950. The longed-for peace was proving short-lived.

In the realm of spiritual devotion Pope Pius had accentuated Catholic reverence for the Virgin Mary, first by solemnly proclaiming the dogma of the Assumption of Mary in 1950, then by declaring a year of pilgrimage in honor of Mary in 1954, and by encouraging devotion to Our Lady of Fatima. The Fatima devotions reinforced a strong anti-communist stance among Catholics with a call to repentance and continual prayer for the conversion of Russia. The message of Fatima included predictions of wars and persecutions if the prophecies delivered in 1917 to the three young children in Portugal by the Mother of Jesus were not heeded. Catholics were alert to this message at home and on the new battlefront in Asia. The practice of praying the rosary with family members, in church or with neighbors, grew in the 1950s. Among the fighting units in Korea the pilgrim statue of Our Lady of Fatima was brought for crusades of prayer for peace, just as in neighborhoods at home. Typical of the devotion and its message was an address given to a gathering of 150 members of the Muskegon deanery of the Diocesan Council of Catholic Women, meeting at St. James Parish in Montague in October of 1952. They heard encouragement for the "Block Rosary," a practice of gathering neighbors living within the same block to pray the rosary together in one of their homes as a way of expressing their shared faith and solidarity.

Bishop Allen James Babcock, seventh bishop of Grand Rapids, 1954-1969.

It was on the last day of March in the "Marian Year" of 1954, seven months after the death of Bishop Haas, that Bishop Allen James Babcock was named by the pope as the seventh bishop of the Grand Rapids Diocese. He had been auxiliary bishop to Cardinal Edward Mooney in Detroit and pastor of Blessed Sacrament Cathedral there. Born in Bad Axe in the thumb area of Michigan in 1898, he completed his seminary studies at Assumption College in Sandwich, Ontario, and at the North American College in Rome. As a young priest he served as assistant pastor to the college students at the University of Michigan in Ann Arbor and then as vice-rector of the North American College. His term of service at his alma mater in Rome began in 1936 and was cut short in 1940 by the outbreak of hostilities in Europe, leading to the Second World War. The North American College was closed and the seminarians, along with the faculty, were sent back to the States to complete their studies.

When he first arrived as bishop in Grand Rapids on the day before his formal installation of May 20, 1954, he paid a visit to the Cathedral of St. Andrew and then greeted more than 2,000 high school and elementary school students, seminarians, and faculty gathered outside the church doors to welcome him. He graciously thanked everyone for the traditional "spiritual bouquet" of prayers presented to him by Catholic Central principal, Monsignor William J. Murphy, remarking that the numbers of prayers and works of mercy offered on his behalf were "astronomical." Cardinal Mooney preached the sermon at the Installation Mass, and Bishop Babcock delivered a brief but moving address. "We are all charged with the work of being witnesses of Christ," he remarked. "Please join with me... in the dedication of our lives...." As he developed this inaugural theme, an eloquence in preaching that would become familiar over the next 15 years was revealed for the first time to his people.

Catholic grade school and high school students welcome Bishop Babcock to the diocese, May 19, 1954.

These seemed boom years of Catholicism in America once more, reminiscent of the explosion of growth after the Great Depression, with seemingly ever greater numbers of priests, religious, churches, and schools. From 21 million members belonging to the Catholic Church in the United States in 1940, the number had doubled to 42 million in 1960. In the course of his tenure, Bishop Babcock approved the construction or expansion of over 50 churches. Some were small missions or chapels, like St. Ambrose in Delton or Our Lady of Guadalupe next to the cathedral. Others were nationally acclaimed for the design of the church structure, like St. Jude in Grand Rapids under the pastorate of Monsignor Charles D. Brophy and St. Francis de Sales in Muskegon during the pastorate of Father Louis B. LaPres. One extraordinary construction project was the world's largest crucifix as part of a parish and shrine in the northern woods of the Lower Peninsula at Indian River. Built over soil that the young pastor, Father Charles D. Brophy, brought from Kateri Tekakwitha's grave at La Prairie near Montreal, the majestic crucifix and shrine were to become a major destination for pilgrims throughout the state and country. Moreover, with the approval and encouragement of Bishop Babcock, some eight schools were expanded and 26 were established and built, among the latter being Muskegon Catholic Central, West Catholic High School in Grand Rapids, and Manistee Catholic Central High School.

As much as he did to foster the growth of Catholic schools in the diocese, Bishop Babcock also embarked on a vast development of religious education for children not enrolled in the parochial schools. He himself was not a student in a Catholic school until he was a freshman in high school. From his own experience he was eager to extend opportunities for religious education to as many children and youth as possible. "If you treat them like second class citizens, they will behave like second class citizens," was his frequent comment.

To help him create a first class program, he appointed Father Victor Gallagher in 1957 as the director of the Confraternity of Christian Doctrine (CCD), who, in turn, recruited Father James C. Cusack to assist in the venture. They set out with determination and vigor, first to inform themselves of the needs of the diocese as well as of the thinking and advances in the field of catechetics (from a Greek word meaning to teach and question by word of mouth). They tapped into the astonishing ferment in scripture studies, liturgy, and religious education that had been developing in Europe, especially since the end of the Second World War and was now reaching at least academic Catholic circles in the United States. From their parish in Reed City (St. Philip Neri), they organized workshops for laity, sisters, and clergy, to share with them the exhilarating and challenging developments in religious education studies that they themselves had been discovering. In 1958 Bishop Babcock invited the Victory Noll Sisters from Huntington, Indiana, to join the venture. Officially known as the Congregation of Our Lady of Victory Missionary Sisters, they were specialists in religious education. Beginning their work in the northern areas of the diocese at Mancelona and Kalkaska, Sisters Josephine

Cross in the Woods Catholic Shrine, Indian River.

Konrad, Martha Wordemann, and Joan Arnold methodically took up in each place a parish census and began what became a massive teacher-training program.

One special feature of the program was the offering of the training courses in various regions: Muskegon, Mount Pleasant, Mancelona, Kalkaska, and Grand Rapids. For eight weeks every fall and eight weeks every spring classes met for two hours a week over the course of two years. Sisters from other congregations assisted in the training, as did clergy from the diocese. Over the next eight years nearly 1,000 catechists were awarded certification. Eventually two Notre Dame Sisters joined the diocesan staff, Alberta Thelen and Ruth Kuntz.

On October 9, 1958, Pope Pius XII died after nearly 20 years in office. Among the attendants at his lying-in-state were seminarians from the North American College, including Charles R. Dautremont of Grand Rapids. When the cardinals hastened to Rome for his funeral and the election of his successor, no one seemed prepared for the candidate they chose. Nearly 77 years old, short, rotund, and by his own complaint to God, not photogenic enough to be pope, Angelo Roncalli seemed the very opposite of the lean, ascetic, mystical, aristocratic Pius XII. Born in a peasant family of 13 children, the new pope took John XXIII as his name, even though an anti-pope had used it before. As chatty as Pius had been reserved, he soon gave a pay raise to the carriers of the papal ceremonial chair who by tradition had to hoist him aloft in the *sedia gestatoria* for people to see as they carried him in procession. He figured they earned it because of his extra weight.

Because of his age and geniality, many observers within the church, perhaps even the cardinal electors, thought of John XXIII and his budding papacy as a pleasant but short breathing spell for the church to absorb the voluminous teachings and decisions of Pius'

Fr. Victor P. Gallagher (seated) and Fr. James C. Cusack at signing of contract with Victory Noll Sisters Mary Whitfield (left) and Mother Cecilia Schmitt, OLVM in 1958.

lengthy and eventful years in office before moving on to another serious period of governance. That would prove to be a condescending and quite mistaken judgment. For within three months of his election, while at the Basilica of Saint Paul-Outside-the Walls, Pope John announced to his startled cardinals that he had decided to convene a worldwide council of the church. His decision seemed to come as a bolt out of the blue. So few knew of Angelo Roncalli's life-long private study of the councils of the church and of his research into the life of St. Charles Borromeo, cardinal of Milan and one of the great Fathers of the Council of Trent (1545-1563). These formed the inner landscape of Pope John's mind and spirit. He was even crowned pope on St. Charles' feast day, bluntly remarking in his sermon: "The life of the church has its moments of stagnation and renewal." Even as preparations for the council slowly were organized, the pope on his own initiative struck the one word "perfidious" from a Good Friday prayer that

Catholics had been saying for centuries. It had described Jews. In that small but highly symbolic decision, the pope signaled what kind of council he had in mind and that if you believe what you pray and pray what you believe, as an old Latin saying implied, then Catholics had some important revising to do.

Since Bishop Babcock had been serving as chairman of the department of lay organizations for the United States bishops, he was appointed by Pope John XXIII to serve on the preparatory commission of the lay apostolate for the proposed council. This required him to travel to Rome six times before the council convened in order to develop the working drafts on the topic of the role of laity in the church, from which the 2,500 Fathers of the Council would deliberate. In his own diocese Bishop Babcock had initiated the Diocesan Council of Catholic Men in 1954 to complement the active involvement which the Diocesan Council of Catholic Women had in the work of the diocese since 1939. From this diocesan council had come a

Grand Rapids seminarian Charles R. Dautremont with Pope (now Blessed) John XXIII at North American College, Rome, 1958.

Senator John F. Kennedy campaigning for the presidency in Grand Rapids, October 1960. Building in center housed The Western Michigan Catholic.

president of the National Council of Catholic Women, Mrs. Gerald B. Bennett of St. Francis Xavier Parish, Grand Rapids.

In the meantime, Catholics in the United States experienced a change in their own self-identity, as they participated in record numbers in the national presidential election of 1960. When the Catholic candidate, John F. Kennedy, was elected, an enormous barrier was suddenly broken, no matter how narrow and disputed the margin of victory. Boosted by the new president's considerable charm and gift for motivating others, Catholics seemed to gain a new self-confidence and entered more fully than before into the mainstream at all levels of American life. The young president's call to assist the poor in developing countries through the Peace Corps sparked the idealism, generosity, and spirit of adventure among many young Catholics, as among young people generally around the country. At the same time Pope John was issuing a plea to Catholics of North America to assist their fellow Catholics among the poor of Latin America. Bishops were encouraged to share their priests for missionary work in areas of Latin America where priests were scarce.

Bishop Babcock responded by establishing a mission in Santiago, Chile, under the sponsorship of the diocese and in cooperation with the Holy Cross Fathers of the Indiana Province. As envisioned when it was first announced in January of 1965, the diocese planned to provide lay workers, seminarians, priests, and religious education material for the mission in a slum area of 12,000 inhabitants. Director of the project was a Holy Cross priest who was a native of Manistee, Father Joseph F. Pawlicki. The mission was named *Cristo Nuestro Redentor* (Christ Our Redeemer).

As in so many Latin countries at the time, huge numbers of farmers and country dwellers were migrating to cities to earn more money and improve their lives. Unskilled and untrained for industry and with no place to live, they built shacks out of cardboard and tin, with no electricity, water, or sanitary facilities. With the degradation and despair that would overcome them, they were prime targets for disease and hunger, as well as for opportunistic communist agitators. Father Pawlicki and his helpers envisioned in their plight a community of Christians whose love for Christ and for one another would grow strong enough to lead them to organize and change their environment. As Father Pawlicki wrote in a report in September of 1965: "Drinking water is the prime need of the whole arid area. It is hard to imagine such a need, not to be able to turn on a faucet for at least cold water."

Bishop Babcock made a personal visit to the mission in December of 1966, accompanied by Monsignor Charles D. Brophy and Father Joseph C. Dunphy. Yet the diocesan partnership would come to an end when Father Pawlicki had to resign because of ill health in October of 1971. By then the Grand Rapids Diocese also found itself in a changed situation, with fewer resources of personnel and finances. With reluctance it withdrew from the Santiago venture on June 31, 1972.

The Grand Rapids Dominican Sisters had heard the same plea for help in Latin America given by papal representatives to the National Congress for Religious held at Notre Dame in August 1961. There the request was specific: each congregation of religious was asked to send 10 per cent of its personnel over a 10-year period. Mother Victor Flannery consented, reporting to her sisters: "All exhorted us to give personnel – not merely what could be spared but to sacrifice the best…. With this in mind I am asking for volunteers for this new mission work…. God's blessing will be with us if we try – in spite of our very grave needs at home – to serve in a small way the exploding population of Latin America." The Dominican Sisters had chosen Chimbote, Peru, for their mission, 250 miles north of Lima where the Dominican Fathers had jurisdiction over that territory called a "prelature." With characteristic thoroughness, the volunteers who were chosen, Sisters Marie Dominica Viesnoraitis and Herman Marie Maez were first sent for an intense four-month language and inculturation course in Cuernavaca, Mexico, under the direction of Monsignor Ivan D. Illich. Before they went to their mission, Mother Victor, the prioress, and Sister Aline Needham, one of her council members, went to Peru themselves to lay the groundwork for their sisters.

I n 1953 and 1954, missionaries came from overseas to serve the Grand Rapids Diocese, when first the Consolata Fathers and then the Consolata Sisters arrived from Italy to take up their

Bishop Babcock (center), Father Joseph C. Dunphy, and Msgr. Charles D. Brophy (from left) leave to visit the diocesan mission in Santiago, Chile, December 1966. Miss Gertrude Horgan of Aquinas College and Father Max Frego see them off.

assignments at Our Lady of Sorrows parish in Grand Rapids. The sisters pursued studies at Aquinas College while teaching in the parochial school, but eventually (in 1962) they established a mother house in Belmont for the training and formation of new candidates for their institute of sisters. In 1969 Sister Celsa Silvestri, who had led the first group of sisters to Grand Rapids, became the superior general of the entire institute of missionary sisters, headquartered in Turin, Italy.

It was with a like-minded missionary spirit that Bishop Babcock began a much-expanded pastoral ministry to college students. Like Bishop Kelly, he had as a young priest served the students and faculty at the University of Michigan in Ann Arbor. Now in his own diocese he decided to establish parishes close to the campuses of Ferris Institute (later Ferris State University) in Big Rapids and Central Michigan University in Mount Pleasant. Catholics had long been discouraged from attending public or secular schools and colleges as a danger to their faith. Those who did attend were expected to nourish their faith in the nearest parish. With a specific outreach to college communities, Bishop Babcock acknowledged the reality of increasing numbers of Catholics both on staff and as students in the public college sector, as well as the special problems and opportunities for Catholics in public higher education. St. Mary's Parish began at Central in October 1960 with Father John N. McDuffee as its first pastor. St. Paul's Campus Parish at Ferris started in 1958 under the leadership of Father Francis A. Hackett for a brief time and then Father John A. Najdowski. Under Bishop Babcock's direction the campus ministry was expanded to include the newly-founded (1967) Grand Valley State College (now University) in Allendale and the community colleges in Muskegon and Grand Rapids.

No less mission-minded was another pioneering outreach during Bishop Babcock's administration. The first bishop of Grand Rapids to utilize the medium of radio on a somewhat regular, if infrequent, basis was Bishop Haas. However, in 1947 Bishop Haas ordained as priest a young man from SS. Peter and Paul Parish, Ionia, who had apprenticed at WOOD radio in Grand Rapids when he had taken a sick leave from his studies at St. Mary's Seminary in Baltimore. With his deep, rich, and melodious baritone voice, Hugh Michael Beahan turned his brief sabbatical interest into a lifelong passion and powerfully effective ministry. As perfectly suited for the medium as his voice was, even more was Father Beahan's gift for communicating. Beginning his radio mission out of a former coal bin in the basement of St. James Church in Grand Rapids, where he was an assistant, he went on to establish with his brother Fred the Aquinas Broadcasting Society, with Bishop Babcock as chairman. In the tower of the administration building on the campus of Aquinas College Father Mike, as he was known, located WXTO FM radio station. It was licensed by the Federal Communications Commission and built practically from scratch by radio engineering enthusiast Father Charles P. Ausberger, assistant at nearby St. Thomas Parish. Its call letters were an abbreviation for the Greek word for Christ. There from 1962 to 1970 the first radio station in West Michigan to broadcast classical music also aired news, the "saint for the day," as well as lectures and discussions of religious interest. Internships were available for students of speech and drama. One of the interns, now the Honorable Dennis B. Leiber of Grand Rapids, years later recalled the easy and patient manner of Father Mike, as he "persistently coaxed fragile equipment and nurtured meager student talent."

In the early days of local television Father Beahan began a program on WOOD TV in Grand Rapids called "Fifteen with Father." From 1953 to 1976 the program aired every week, featuring Father Mike analyzing and discussing matters of current religious or moral interest to the general public. Nationally Bishop Fulton J. Sheen was attracting attention from 1951 to 1957 for his dramatic and even spell-binding televised lectures during prime-time. While others could not make a successful transition from faceless radio to the unforgiving cameras of television, audiences in West Michigan saw in Father Mike, as in Bishop Sheen, a gifted and compelling messenger of the gospel. For each of his programs, moreover, Father Mike was required by cautious church

Father Hugh Michael Beahan at the start of his 27-year ministry on television, 1953.

authorities to submit his written text beforehand for approval of doctrinal and moral content consistent with the official teachings of the church. This practice, therefore, also meant that he had to commit each program's text to memory.

As television stations were required to provide a percentage of their air-time to public service programming, Father Mike arranged with WOOD TV to begin televising the Mass on Sundays from their studios in Grand Rapids in 1955. Father Mike became producer, director, and narrator of the Mass, explaining to viewers quietly and authoritatively (while he himself was unseen) the unfolding ritual. A guest priest was the celebrant and the congregation came from parishes or groups usually from neighboring parishes in Grand Rapids. By 1966, through the encouragement of Monsignor Charles Popell, rector of the Cathedral of St. Andrew, a large donation by Mrs. Catherine Rose equipped the cathedral with its own TV studio and cameras, and the Mass began to air from the cathedral,

among the first in the nation to be able to do so, live and every Sunday. Father Mike arranged the transition and helped the cathedral in training volunteers from the parish to operate the cameras. So successful was the televising of the Mass that the Grand Rapids station arranged hookups with other affiliated stations within the broadcast network, which carried the Mass to a far-flung congregation in Cadillac, Traverse City, and Alpena. With the signals traveling across the waters of the Great Lakes, people often had clear reception in Wisconsin, the Upper Peninsula, and Canada, as well as points in northern Indiana and Ohio. A preview of this phenomenon had been the installation ceremonies of Bishop Babcock in 1954, when for the first time in the diocese such ceremonies were televised and broadcast through a similar hookup.

In all such arrangements Father Beahan lent his indispensable expertise. With his high public profile and extraordinary gifts, he was much in demand as a speaker for civic, religious (many of them ecumenical)

Sisters preparing for television appearance in 1950s.

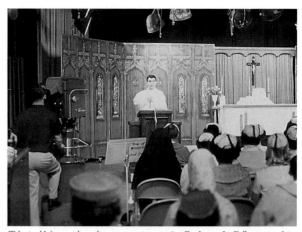

Televised Mass with studio congregation, 1960. Fr. James L. Fellows at pulpit.

and business events. All the while, he fulfilled his parish assignments, initiating and guiding such groups as Catholic Young Adults, which provided spiritual and social activities for hundreds of post-high school singles from the mid-1950s to the early 1960s. No priest since Father "Mac"(Patrick McManus) of St. Andrew days in the 1870s had been as widely known and revered as Father Mike. He had been given awards of recognition by groups as varied as the Shriners, the Christian Reformed Laymen's League, the Catholic Broadcasters Association, and the United Fund of Kent County. He died of cancer at the age of 60 in 1980 while rector of the cathedral, witnessing bravely to his faith during his sufferings through his weekly column in *The Western Michigan Catholic*.

While the expanse of territory comprising the diocese was still large, the efficient and convenient railroad network of Bishop Richter's time had fallen into disuse or disappeared entirely. The automobile was the bishop's mode of transportation to all points of the diocese. The demands of administering such a diocese as well as participating in preparations for the Vatican Council were heavy,

prompting Bishop Babcock to seek from the pope an auxiliary bishop. In 1962 Charles A. Salatka, son of Lithuanian parents, vice-chancellor and pastor of St. Michael's Parish in Coopersville was appointed auxiliary bishop. He was the first to be named to that position, as Bishop Schrembs and then Bishop Gallagher had been named as coadjutor with right of succession to Bishop Richter.

In the late 1950s and early 1960s two renewal movements came to the diocese, the Christian Family Movement (CFM) and the Cursillo movement. CFM originated in the work of a Belgian priest, Father Joseph Cardijn, who sought to engage young people in nothing less than a reform of society itself through the application of their faith with a method of "observe, judge, act." In the United States, groups of lay people involved in Catholic Action, as the approved lay apostolate was called, elected a Chicago couple, Pat and Patty Crowley, to lead them in the spiritual development of families for

Auxiliary Bishop Charles A. Salatka, 1962. Later, bishop of Marquette and archbishop of Oklahoma City.

the purpose of renewing the social order. The movement thus combined the features of an emerging lay leadership with personal renewal for the sake of community renewal beyond the church, reaching into matters of social justice. Meeting in small groups in one another's homes, CFM energized a new generation of lay Catholics before the Vatican Council gave its own mandate along similar lines.

Around the same time, the Cursillo movement arrived from Spain via Texas and the Southwest. The Cursillo was designed as a short but highly intensive course in the fundamental teachings of Christianity. The compact days of the short course include prayer, teachings, interaction, and a commitment to renewal beyond the retreat experience. Separate Cursillos were arranged for women and for men, for Spanish-speaking and English. The first Cursillo in the diocese was held in the basement of St. Andrew's Cathedral April

4-7, 1963, with some 40 participants singing, praying, learning, eating, and sleeping on cots there. The reactions of participants then and thereafter were usually highly enthusiastic. As with each succeeding new development in the quickly changing church, Bishop Babcock's approach to the Cursillo movement favored slow, cautious, orderly, and careful testing. As events would proceed in and out of the church in the 1960s, his method itself would be sorely tested.

The list of the tumbling and crashing cascade of events in the '60s and '70s would tell why all segments of church and society, too, found themselves tested. The pronouncements and decrees of Vatican II from 1962 to 1965 changed everything in the church, from the language in liturgies to the physical arrangement of space and furniture within church buildings. Changed, too, was the relationship of laity to clergy, of bishop to priest, of pope to bishop,

Bishop Babcock with Pope Paul VI
during Vatican Council II,
October 22, 1964.

of church to other churches and faiths, of church to the world, of church to the bible, even of church to Christ, as the Savior became widely understood as brother in our shared humanity, in addition to being Lord. Even though the writings of Pope Pius XII on the nature of the church, of the liturgy, and of the bible laid the groundwork for much that the council built upon, church members around the world found their development quite a surprise. While most Catholics welcomed or at least accepted the changes, especially in worship, others felt confused or betrayed. Pope John died on June 3, 1963, after issuing a landmark letter, *Pacem in Terris* (Peace on Earth), which won him the Balzan Peace prize. He left unfinished, though set on its course, the work of the council, to the leadership of Pope Paul VI.

American society was assaulted by a series of assassinations, of President Kennedy in 1963, of Rev. Martin Luther King, Jr. and Senator Robert Kennedy in 1968. The Vietnam War was spinning out of control, becoming the longest and most ineffective in American history, with exorbitant loss of life, limb, and spirit, and crippling loss of trust in the government and military. For young men eligible for the war, draft resistance, escapes to Canada or Europe, and conscientious objection became new realities. The civil rights movement, while gaining national momentum, was brought vividly by television to American homes, just as the Asian war was, with scenes of rioting, brutality, and protest in their own city streets. The student free speech movement on the campus of Berkley, California, sparked sit-ins and takeovers on campuses across the country, as education moved from the European model of an acknowledged authority-centered process to a student-centered one.

With the hippie movement and free-love style culminating in the Woodstock music-and-live-in of 1969, some felt their America had died, while others thought it had never been so alive.

So inflamed were the feelings of the times, that within the church some segments could no longer communicate with one another. Humor seemed suspect or dead and gone. Among the clergy, the clear demarcations of rights and duties previously held between pastors and assistants fell, with many pastors lamenting the ensuing loss of respect or at least the signs and tokens of respect. Lay people, likewise, were of various minds about the informality fostered by young priests or by the semi-circular style of new churches, bringing them into an unfamiliar, and for some, uncomfortable closeness as a community. New associations were formed in the diocese, one by the younger clergy and one by the senior pastors, each lacking confidence in the other and each seeking the attention of the bishop. In keeping with the decrees of the Vatican Council, Bishop Babcock gradually formed consultative groups, such as the Senate of Priests. For the first time, he invited the participation of the junior clergy in advising him on the annual assignments to parishes of assistant priests. Tensions, however, were often high among the clergy, as policies and views of church order continually came into conflict while the changes called for by the council were implemented.

Bishop Joseph C. McKinney was consecrated as auxiliary bishop in September 1968.

Diocesan Development Fund dinner at Grand Rapids Civic Auditorium, 1969.

At St. Lazare's Retreat House, founded in 1952 as a place of tranquillity on the shores of Spring Lake and entrusted to the care of the Vincentian Fathers, the clergy of the diocese customarily made their days of spiritual retreat every fall and spring. During the late '60s and '70s, not even those peaceful haunts could shield the priest-retreatants from the controversies of the times. At one table discussion like many another, Father John W. McGee, a progressive himself and knowing more than most about the turbulent years of other eras in the life of the church, pounded the table for emphasis as his jowls shook and his face reddened, voicing dismay with bearded younger clergy, as well as with the manner and morals of long-haired hippies. All across America this "war between the generations" was playing itself out. For Catholics it was complicated by the reform unfolding within the church, yet with that reform the overall

membership in the diocese, as around the world, had no serious objection. In fact, most welcomed it as long overdue.

In 1968, Pope Paul VI issued his teaching on birth control after a long scientific and moral study begun under Pope John XXIII. It was in 1960 that a Catholic doctor, John Rock, co-developed a fertility control pill, with the statement that it would assist nature in regulating birth. The pope ruled that it was an immoral interference with nature, and dissent broke out across the church, sharpening already existing tensions. As these and the ordinary burdens of ministering to his flock in the 29 counties of the diocese weighed ever more heavily on Bishop Babcock, he obtained from the pope a new auxiliary bishop, since Bishop Salatka had been named bishop of the Marquette diocese in January of 1968. Appointed in July of 1968 when he was only 39 years old, Joseph C. McKinney had grown up in St. Mary's Parish, Grand Rapids, was educated at the parish school, at St. Joseph's Seminary, at the Seminaire de Philosophie in Montreal, and at the Pontifical Urban University in Rome.

With most of the diocese unaware, Bishop Babcock had been diagnosed in 1967 as having throat cancer. He nevertheless continued his normal rounds of ministry, including confirmations in the northern parishes. By 1968, however, his doctors had cautioned him against driving, so he was flown north and back by the diocesan superintendent of schools and pilot, Monsignor Herman H. Zerfas. In the spring of 1969,weakened by his illness and his throat dry from medication, he persisted in leading the annual Diocesan Development Fund (DDF), the much-expanded successor to the Fund for the Faith. He attended and addressed the pre-campaign dinners which had become a special feature of the fund-raising effort during his administration. These took place at sites across the diocese, such as Gaylord, Traverse City, Cadillac, Mount Pleasant, Muskegon, and the last in Grand Rapids. There at the Civic Auditorium dinner would be served to as many as 2,300 people. These would be his last public appearances in the diocese. Though now worn and weary, with the cancer unabating, his eloquence had not diminished. His bearing still had great dignity, and his manner remained unfailingly gracious. He died on June 27, 1969, at age 71.

A SPIRIT
LIKE THE WIND

1969 - 1989

WHEN JOSEPH M. BREITENBECK was announced as the eighth bishop of Grand Rapids on October 15, 1969, many on the west side of the state, especially among the sisters and the clergy, already knew of his reputation as a skilled and dynamic auxiliary bishop in Detroit. Though the consultation process by which the Vatican surfaces names of candidates for the episcopacy is shrouded in secrecy, the new bishop's name was always the most frequently mentioned in pre-announcement speculation. As the personal secretary to Cardinal Mooney for 14 years, he had vast experience and knowledge of the workings of the church throughout Michigan. Because of the cardinal's responsibilities and stature in the church, he also enjoyed innumerable contacts around the country, in Rome, and around the world, not only among church people but also in the professions as well as in diplomatic and government

circles. He became expert at utilizing such a rich and varied network of resources for assisting the mission of the church.

Born and raised in Detroit, he was educated there, including three years of pre-law studies at the University of Detroit, then at Sacred Heart Seminary, at the North American College in Rome, and in Washington, D.C. at the Theological College of the Catholic University of America. When Pope Pius XII died in October of 1958, Monsignor Breitenbeck accompanied Cardinal Mooney to Rome for the conclave which was convened to elect the next pope. Just before the solemn procession to the conclave was due to begin, his attentive secretary knocked at the door of the room where the cardinal was resting from a dizzy spell. Not hearing a response, he entered and rushed to the bedside where the

1969	1972	1973	1973	1979	1980	1981	1986	1989
Armstrong first man on moon	Nixon visits China and Russia	Roe vs. Wade	U.S. troops withdraw from Vietnam	Mother Teresa wins Nobel Prize	Walesa leads Poland's Solidarity Movement	AIDS identified	Chernobyl nuclear disaster	Berlin Wall falls

Students at North American College, Rome in late 1930s. Right of center in first row is vice-rector, Msgr. Allen J. Babcock. In first row, second from left, is seminarian Joseph M. Breitenbeck.

cardinal lay dying. Instead of accompanying him to the Vatican, Monsignor Breitenbeck had the sad and solemn duty of bringing home for burial not only the superior he served but his close friend and beloved mentor.

When John F. Dearden became the next archbishop of Detroit, Monsignor Breitenbeck served as his secretary for a year before he was named pastor of Assumption Grotto Parish. With more than 4,000 families, the parish presented the new pastor with a challenge not only to his administrative skills but especially to any personalized form of

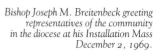

pastoring. With the determination and zest that became his trademark, Monsignor Breitenbeck organized the systematic visitation of every parish household by himself or one of his assistants, insisted on greeting parishioners at the church doors after every Sunday Mass – at the time still something of a novelty for Catholic priests – and placed a high priority on attending to the hospitalized and homebound either personally or by his staff.

What was a pastor's style and method for reaching out to a large parish with dependable and personable

Bishop Joseph M. Breitenbeck greeting representatives of the community in the diocese at his Installation Mass December 2, 1969.

service became a bishop's style and method for ministering to an entire diocese. When he had become an auxiliary bishop in 1965, the responsibilities of Bishop Breitenbeck widened to include ministry to the women religious of the archdiocese as their vicar. He eventually was named chairman of a national liaison committee for women religious superiors. More widening, however, than anything else was his attendance, even as bishop-elect, at the closing sessions of the Second Vatican Council in the fall of 1965. For the rest of his years he would remain firmly and deeply committed to its decrees and goals, becoming the longest serving and sole surviving Council Father in the state of Michigan.

T he installation ceremony of Bishop Breitenbeck at the Cathedral of St. Andrew on December 2, 1969, featured addresses of welcome by Sister Mary Aquinas Weber, prioress of the Grand Rapids Dominican Sisters, Felix C. Suchowolec, president of the Diocesan Council of Catholic Men, Monsignor William J. Murphy on behalf of the clergy, in addition to the greetings of Cardinal Dearden and of Grand Rapids commissioner Joseph Sypniewski. This inaugural representation of clergy, laity, and women religious would become a hallmark of the new bishop's administration, as would the honored presence in the front pews of religious leaders from other communities of faith and of many civic guests. In his brief and graceful words of welcome, however, Monsignor Murphy made reference to news reports about dissent in the church, and specifically among some clergy, over *Humanae Vitae*, the letter of Pope Paul VI reaffirming the church's stand against contraception. "What is true of the universal church is doubtless true of some of the priests of this diocese. But I know that today we are all in joyful unanimity over this action of the Holy Father – your selection to be our bishop and our chief pastor."

To preserve and nourish such a spirit of unanimity, Bishop Breitenbeck pledged to live out the still-fresh decrees of Vatican Council II on the role of the bishop in his relationships to the various segments of the church represented at his installation. Referring to priests as "my closest friends and my most trusted collaborators," he likewise reaffirmed that laity and religious, civic officials and members of other faiths

Bishop Breitenbeck prayed in the St. Ambrose Chapel of the cathedral on his first day in the diocese, November 28, 1969, with Msgr. Charles Popell (left) and Bishop Joseph McKinney.

must all strive together to contribute to the common good. Even before his formal installation, he held a series of separate receptions for the clergy, sisters, and diocesan employees. Following the ceremonies and an open reception at West Catholic High School in Grand Rapids, he soon embarked on a whirlwind tour of the diocese, greeting people who wished to meet him at Mt. Pleasant, Gaylord, Traverse City, Muskegon, Manistee, and once more in Grand Rapids at the cathedral, all within a two-week period before Christmas. As the years of his service to the diocese unfolded, all the themes present at his installation, and a few unheralded ones, would become prominent features of his administration and of Catholic life in West Michigan.

The continuing education and spiritual formation of his priests would become a constant and abiding feature of the Bishop Breitenbeck years. Among the bishops of the country he was a pioneer in both initiating programs for his clergy and in his commitment to providing opportunities for them beyond the diocese. When the graduate house of the North American College in Rome began offering a three-month sabbatical of courses for priests in theology, scripture, and spirituality, he immediately invited two diocesan priests to participate, renewing the invitation for two to attend every spring and every fall. Fathers Leo Rosloniec and David Gemuend were the first priests of the diocese to enroll (in 1972), living at the 17th century Casa Santa Maria on Humility Street in the heart of old Rome near the Trevi Fountain. Bishop Breitenbeck himself signed up in 1974, studying once more at his old alma mater, where he had done post-graduate work in canon law from 1947 to1949. He also initiated an ongoing program within the diocese so that priests could be continually updated in pastoral studies and skills and participate in spiritual retreats or days of prayer. In 1985 he launched an annual conference for all priests in the diocese, to be held each autumn at a center or resort removed from the cares of pastoral assignments. His goal was to renew fellowship and the spirit of unity among clergy and bishops, as well as to strengthen their commitment to Christ and to the service of the church.

Spiritual renewal and the full realization of every Christian's baptismal empowerment was at the heart of Vatican Council II, and it was meant to be the ongoing work of the whole church. When the diocese approached its centennial anniversary in 1982-83, a consensus grew among the clergy that the best way to observe the occasion would be through an experience that would affect the entire Catholic community spiritually. Bishop Breitenbeck seized upon this advice and welcomed into the diocese the national Renew program. Rather than one or two large ceremonial festivities in celebration of 100 years as a diocese, every parish became part of a five-year spiritual deepening of Catholic faith. Leaders from each parish received training in guiding the program in their own community. Parishioners met in one another's homes in groups of eight or more to share the sacred scriptures with an experience refreshingly new for most Catholics. Activities and liturgies within the parishes were coordinated according to the themes of each six-week segment every fall and spring. Without an explicit mandate from Bishop Breitenbeck that every parish was obliged to participate, there was nearly total involvement across the diocese, albeit with varying levels of enthusiasm and commitment. A diocesan Mass of Thanksgiving at the Catholic Central Athletic and Convocation Center in Grand Rapids drew the Renew experience to a formal close on November 18, 1984. Many parishes, however, incorporated the format of small group meetings for scripture, reflection, and prayer as on ongoing feature of parish life. Flowing also from the Renew experience, with its emphasis on Christian charity and justice rising from an awakened spiritual life, the Secretariat for Social Concerns was established in the diocese in 1984.

Bishop Breitenbeck inaugurating Renew in cathedral, September 1982.

The Renew program involved all segments of the church (the sisters, laity, and clergy) and increased the level of participation in parish and diocesan ministries.

Msgr. Charles Brophy (right of center) and Father Charles Hall (second right from Msgr.) with parishioners.

Msgr. Edward Alt (center) at Renew discussion with Deacon Dale Hollern (left) and Father George Fekete (second from right).

The 1970s were traumatic for the nation because of the Vietnam War and the crisis in the presidency (1972-1974) from the Watergate fallout. Before that decade began, there had been a one-day "moratorium" in colleges around the country to protest against the war. Classes were suspended, while students gathered for assemblies, rallies, and speeches. Such protest escalated when four students at Kent State University were killed during a confrontation with the Ohio National Guard in the spring of 1970. The war, however, continued and even widened into Cambodia and Laos. When it finally ended, America would become a refuge for victims fleeing the victorious communist regime. In western Michigan alone some 15,000 Vietnamese would eventually be resettled, enough of them of the Catholic faith to form their own new parish by the end of the millennium, Our Lady of La Vang in Wyoming with Father Peter Hoang-Xuan-Nghiem as pastor. From their numbers as well would come four young men ordained for the diocesan priesthood, Fathers Phillip D. Nguyen, Loc Trinh, Phong Q. Pham, and Peter Vu.

In June of 1971 the Vatican announced the formation of two new dioceses in Michigan, the dioceses of Gaylord and Kalamazoo. The territory of each new jurisdiction was formed from the territories of existing dioceses. Two-thirds of the new Gaylord diocese was formed from the northwestern territory of the lower peninsula that had constituted 14 counties and over 50 parishes and missions of the Grand Rapids Diocese. The Kalamazoo Diocese was formed mostly from the territory of the Lansing Diocese, but Grand Rapids contributed two counties and 15 parishes and missions. Two additional counties with their eight parishes were assigned to the Saginaw Diocese. The secrecy of the procedure provoked dissatisfaction, but not of the scale as when the diocese of Saginaw had been formed in 1938. Nevertheless, several priest-brothers from the old Grand Rapids diocese now found themselves assigned to different dioceses after the division. The resulting redrawing of the lines made of Grand Rapids a compact 11-county diocese with 104 parishes and missions.

At St. Francis de Sales, Holland (top picture), Father Stephen S. Dudek (left) celebrates the wedding of bride My Thi Nguyen Nghi and groom Thomas Pham, with relatives and Father John Au (right), September 24, 1994. The Vietnam War brought an influx of refugees to the diocese. Bishop Breitenbeck (bottom picture, left) welcomes them with Msgr. Herman Zerfas at right.

The present size of the diocese was finalized in 1971, comprising 11 counties out of its original 39.

The '70s and '80s witnessed an explosive growth of ministries in the life of the church, most noticeably during the five-year-long Renew experience. Parishioners were eager to offer themselves for service both within their congregations and beyond. One new ministry was especially close to Bishop Breitenbeck's heart. With Sister Rose Callahan, OP named as director in 1969, he established a ministry to those with special disability needs in September of that year. His own sister had

been born with mental retardation and has remained in special care all her life. With service now from the diocese, parishes were assisted in identifying those in need. Religious education materials were provided, as well as special catechists, for nurturing the faith life of the mentally and physically disabled.

Other developing ministries in the diocese were directly inspired by the Second Vatican Council. A program of training was initiated for the permament diaconate in 1971. Open to married men, the permanent diaconate as part of the ordained priesthood was reinstated by the council, though it had gone into disuse during the early centuries of the church. The first candidates for the Grand Rapids Diocese were ordained by Bishop Breitenbeck in 1974.

Another burgeoning development of Vatican Council II was the revised Rite of Christian Initiation for Adults (RCIA). Instead of the priest alone offering information or a course of classes to adults interested in becoming Catholic and then privately baptizing the prospective converts, the RCIA revived an ancient practice of the church by involving the entire parish community in the sharing of faith with those who wished to join the church. With such ongoing parish involvement, the RCIA became a built-in spiritual renewal dynamic for the entire community. The process, by design, gradually assimilates prospective members into the church and into a specific community through teaching, friendship, prayer, and sharing in the mission of the church. As parish after parish adopted the rite in the 1970s and 1980s, the numbers of candidates (those who had been previously baptized) and catechumens (those not baptized) grew to such an extent that Bishop Breitenbeck began holding two services of welcome and of "election" at the cathedral. At these services he formally selected those presented to him to proceed to full initiation into the faith. At the Easter Vigil in their home parishes the catechumens would then be fully initiated through baptism, confirmation, and Holy Eucharist. The baptism of candidates from other Christian communities would be honored and not repeated. Instead for them there would be a profession of faith and the celebration of their confirmation and first Eucharist. By the end of the millennium several hundred adults in the diocese each year would become members of the church in this way, with thousands of parishioners assisting as sponsors, teachers, and companions in prayer along the journey.

Sister Rose Callahan, OP, directed the ministry to the disabled which Bishop Breitenbeck initiated in 1969.

In these two decades there was sometimes cause for joy and satisfaction in the life of the church side-by-side with cause for sorrow or anguish. While Villa Elizabeth in Grand Rapids had opened (1967) in the last years of Bishop Babcock's administration as a beautifully equipped nursing home for the elderly, the Little Sisters of the Poor had to close their venerable institution for the elderly poor in 1970 in spite of heroic efforts to keep them in the diocese with their valuable ministry. Bishop Breitenbeck even journeyed to their headquarters in La Tour, France, to plead the case for their remaining in Grand Rapids, but their shortage of sisters determined the closure. Also, Bishop Babcock in the mid-1960s had contemplated further expanding the facilities at St. Joseph Seminary on Burton Street in anticipation of greater numbers of young men seeking a vocation to the priesthood. He had already approved the building of a new gymnasium for the seminarians in 1956 and a college residence and classroom building (St. Henry's Hall, named in honor of Bishop Richter) in 1957.

In the late 1960s, however, the seminary was emerging from disputes on how to implement the council decrees as well as changes in education

Candidates for the permanent diaconate and their wives, with Bishop Rose at the cathedral, March 11, 2001. The first permanent deacons were ordained by Bishop Breitenbeck in 1974.

and discipline in the life of the students. It was decided to separate off the junior college program from the Burton Street complex. Bishop Babcock secured the Thomas estate in proximity to Aquinas College, and there the Christopher House was established in 1969, named in honor of the seminary's longtime and beloved nurse and infirmarian, Sister Christopher Steinforth, OP. Seminarians could attend classes at the college while living in a community devoted to their

Marge Haarman assists one of the Little Sisters of the Poor whose service in the diocese ended in 1970.

spiritual formation as future priests. Father Robert J. Rose became the first dean. Yet after 72 years of service the high school program was ended in 1981; the anticipated numbers of applicants did not increase but instead plunged precipitously, as happened all across the country. From those 72 years had come a long line of dedicated priests who served the diocese and even more laymen whose faith enriched their marriages, homes, work and parishes. In addition, from the old seminary came several distinguished leaders in the hierarchy who pastored dioceses and shared in the governance of the universal church: Cardinal James Hickey, Cardinal Edmund Szoka, Archbishop Charles Salatka, Bishops Paul Donovan, Joseph Green, Joseph McKinney, Thomas Noa, Kenneth Povish, Robert J. Rose, and Charles White.

the Grand Rapids Diocese Jane Muldoon, wife of surgeon James, devoted 25 years to the struggle against abortion. She became the Michigan Right to Life president in 1974 and its executive director in 1980. Bishop Breitenbeck, for his part, became involved in one of the greatest controversies of his administration over the abortion issue. In 1974 Aquinas College decided to award U.S. Representative Shirley Chisholm an honorary degree for her work on behalf of women, other minorities, and the poor. The representative, however, was also a public proponent of abortion rights. As the offer of an honorary degree was not withdrawn by the college, Bishop Breitenbeck announced that he felt compelled to resign as honorary chairman of the Aquinas Board of Directors. The episode was painful for the college, and the bishop's decision gained national attention. A dozen years later, he himself would be given an honorary degree by the college, along with his friends, Father Theodore Hesburgh of Notre Dame and Catholic industrialist, Mr. Raymond Knape.

A bitter event of the '70s was the Roe vs. Wade decision by the United States Supreme Court. In 1973 it legalized abortion and brought in its wake one of the most contested and divisive elements in American life. The Catholic Church joined with others seeking to create a climate of respect for life that would be protected by law. In

A nother sorrow in the post-Vatican II years was the alarming exodus of priests and nuns from their vocation in the life of the church. In the Grand Rapids diocese some 47 priests left the active ministry in the two decades following the council. The Grand Rapids Dominicans counted 167 who left the sisterhood. While the reasons for leaving may have been as varied as the individuals, the church's requirement of celibacy was often a commonly voiced one. Bishop Breitenbeck continued to

Father John W. Collins, left, with his father, John Collins, longtime mayor of East Grand Rapids, and Bishop Breitenbeck on August 3, 1978.

stay in contact, especially with the priests who left the active ministry. He would invite them periodically to come together for dinner and conversation, even into his retirement years.

A movement that began in the late '60s and would continue to grow throughout the country and in the diocese for the next two decades was the charismatic movement. Open to the active presence of the Holy Spirit, charismatics were marked by a New Testament style of enthusiastic prayer, music, and worship, and in some cases by a communal form of Christian living. The movement came to Grand Rapids from the University of Notre Dame. In 1967 Monsignor Arthur F. Bukowski, president of Aquinas College, hosted a prayer meeting in his home with Sister Mary Amata Fabbro, OP, newly returned from doctoral studies in scripture, Dr. Bert Ghezzi and his wife Mary Lou, all formerly associated with Notre Dame. Also attending were Father Charles R. Antekeier and students from Aquinas College. Other prayer meetings followed at the college, with the numbers growing so large that Father Antekeier offered the parish hall at St. Mary's in Grand Rapids, where he was the associate priest. When that space could no longer accommodate the numbers, the meetings moved to West Catholic High School, where 400 to 600 regularly gathered. Auxiliary Bishop McKinney was devoted to the movement and eventually became the national liaison to the charismatic renewal on behalf of the United States bishops. Several other priests joined the

movement but Father Antekeier remained chiefly identified with its work and activity in the diocese.

Other movements also entered Catholic life in the diocese at this time, such as the Marriage and Engaged Encounter, which challenged and strengthened efforts to deepen the faith commitment of couples about to marry or already in marriage. With origins in Spain like the Cursillo movement, Marriage and Engaged Encounter offered an experience in personal dynamics in a retreat-style environment, deepening the faith level of the participants while assisting them in developing their communication skills with one another.

A mong the slow but sure developments in the diocese has been its incorporation of blacks within the life of the church. In a European-based church transplanted to America, European immigrants themselves did not find it easy to meld into the mainstream of church life, not to mention American life. In the aftermath of the assassination of Dr. Martin Luther King, Jr., interracial relations were intensely strained throughout the country. Yet at the same time, following upon Dr. King's civil rights mobilization, there was an unprecedented cooperation among whites and blacks and people of all faiths in the common effort to achieve true equality in America.

A t Ferris State College in Big Rapids, the few hundred black students in the student body, mostly from the Detroit area, were in shock

St. Joseph Seminary students and faculty, spring, 1962. Faculty (from left) Fathers Leo S. Rosloniec, John J. Thome, John P. Weisengoff, Msgr. Joseph E. Shaw, Msgr. James P. Moran (rector), Auxiliary Bishop Charles A. Salatka, Fathers Joseph J. Zaskowski, Joseph C. Mc Kinney, Msgr. Thomas O. Martin, Fathers Gerard F. Guzikowski and Robert J. Rose.

and anger after the killing of Dr. King in April of 1968. They gathered in the student center in a stormy meeting to decide what to do. They were offered the use of the St. Paul's Campus Chapel as a place to have a tribute for Dr. King. The offer was quickly accepted, and a solemn march began down the hill to Damascus Road and the chapel by the Muskegon River. The pastor, Father John A. Najdowski, had been hastily advised of developments by a phone call. By the time the marchers arrived at St. Paul's, the pastor was vested for the service and standing at the front door to welcome the mourners. It marked the beginning of an often disputed use of St. Paul's as a center for black students to meet and socialize.

The events of 1968 also galvanized many of the junior clergy and lay leaders to lend their support to a ministry in the diocese that would address the needs of minorities. Bishop Babcock began a study in 1968, enlisting the help of a young activist in the work of racial justice in Chicago. Dr. Monroe B. Sullivan had been chairman of the civic reception welcoming Bishop Babcock when he first arrived in the diocese in 1954. Fourteen years later his son and namesake conducted several meetings on the issue of race relations in the diocese and recommended the establishing of a human relations department. The Catholic Human Development Office was formed in that year, with Mr. Calvin Jeter as its first director.

In 1971, when the parochial school of Our Lady of Sorrows in Grand Rapids was closed, Consolata Sister Sebastiana Ghidelli led efforts to turn the building into a private non-

Bishop Babcock established the Catholic Human Development Office in 1968, with Mr. Calvin Jeter as its first director.

denominational neighborhood school with very low tuition fees. She became its first principal. Most of the students were from low-income families and were African-American. The neighborhood families so appreciated the new Southeast Education Center and the quality of education it was providing that the Grand Rapids Board of Education was willing to take over and expand the school as an alternative education program in 1974. Similar creative outreach efforts had been taking place within Catholic schools, as at St. Andrew's School in Grand Rapids under the direction of Sister Marie Michael Jacobs, OP. In Muskegon Heights the Catholic Community Center had opened in 1963 and served low-income minorities with religious education as well as assistance with food and clothing.

Consolata Sister Sebastiana Ghidelli, right, with co-worker Valerie Wesley of the Southeast Education Center in Grand Rapids.

The ministry of the church among blacks, however, received its biggest boost when Father Bernard Hall of Washington, D.C. was ordained a priest of the diocese in 1977. Still the only African-American priest of the diocese and now suffering gravely from multiple sclerosis, Father Hall brought passion and pride to black Catholics. One of them, Fran Dalton, in recalling her life in the church, wrote wistfully: "It is surprising how comforting a black authority presence can be." She had made these remarks about having a black teacher, Mr. Jacob Robinson, at Catholic Central High School. With Father Hall on the scene, an organization was formed in 1980, the Afro-American

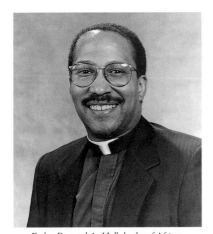

Father Bernard A. Hall, leader of African American Catholics in the diocese.

Marie Mylan was active in church and civic life and the first woman to head the Diocesan Development Fund.

Judge Noel P. Fox sought to end discrimination through his work on the bench.

Lay Catholic Caucus, later known as the Black Catholic Caucus. Its goal was not to separate from the mainstream of the church but to help create a sense of identity and solidarity among black Catholics within the church, since they were a minority within both church and country. In addition, blacks would be encouraged to know their own gifts and to bring their culture to the life and worship of the church. Jean Robinson remembered how "quiet and still" Catholic worship seemed after her non-denominational Protestant church services, where they were "always making a joyful noise unto the Lord." In Catholic churches she noticed the quiet was broken only "when the priest began to speak in a strange language," which she later discovered was Latin. More difficult than the language or the style of praying was the persistent racism oftentimes unsuspectingly yet sometimes blatantly displayed by members and institutions within the church.

Among the friends and collaborators of Bishop Breitenbeck in the excitement and tumult of the '70s and '80s were Marie Mylan and Noel P. Fox. Miss Mylan had been active as a member of St. Andrew's Cathedral, assisting Monsignor Popell in raising funds for the renovations and additions to the cathedral in the early 1960s. Bishop Breitenbeck named her as the first woman to head the Diocesan Development Fund drive in 1974. She had a gift for organizing and motivating, which she put not only at the services of the church, but for underprivileged children, for women, and for the arts. With her pilot's license she flew her own plane around the country and world. She helped form the Women's Resource Center in Grand Rapids, organized the first ecumenical week of prayer for Christian unity in Grand Rapids in 1971, and served on the Michigan Women's Commission at the appointment of Governor William G. Milliken. Described as "a stately lady who meets people with a direct and searching gaze," she had been thanked by Norman Cousins of *The Saturday Review* for her "heroism, thoughtfulness, and good humor." She died at the age of 88 in February of 1985.

U.S. District Judge Noel P. Fox was very much in the public arena, and he brought the convictions of his Catholic faith with him. Born in Kalamazoo and raised in Muskegon, he graduated at the top of his class from Marquette University in Milwaukee. He was an expert in labor law and was appointed to the federal bench by President Kennedy in 1962. Among his controversial decisions was his ruling in 1979 that the treaties between the United States and the Indian tribes of northern Michigan of the 1800s had to be honored: Indians were entitled to fish commercially in parts of Lakes Huron and Michigan. Before making his decisions, he would listen to arguments on site, if the issues seemed to call for a visit. He heard arguments for land acquisition regarding the Sleeping Bear Dunes National Lakeshore at a Lake Michigan beach there. For a case involving questions of separation of church and state in a Traverse City school, he visited the classrooms of the school. When he died in June of 1987, Bishop Breitenbeck said, "I knew Judge Fox as a brother," and remarked that being in his presence was "an honor and a pleasure" any time. One of his fellow judges called him "a pioneer in attempting to eradicate discrimination in race, religion, color, sex, and age."

As some institutions and long-time features of Catholic life met their demise in this era of transformation, others were renewed or came into being with a new birth. On a farm of 230 acres near Lowell, the Franciscan Sisters of the Eucharist established The Franciscan Life Process Center in 1972. Several sisters with advanced degrees, along with a professional staff, developed a comprehensive program of therapy, counseling, education, and prayer at the rural center, as well as offering service in the center of Grand Rapids. In Muskegon Heights the followers of the former Russian baroness, Catherine de Hueck Doherty, came from Combermere, Ontario, to set up Madonna House, a "house of listening, a house of prayer." The first resident lay missionary, Theresa Marsey, began the apostolate in 1979, providing a place to talk about God and to God, as well as the opportunity for sharing the burdens of the heart with a willing listener.

In the same era as these developments, Catholic marriages were suffering from divorce at nearly the same 50 per cent rate as marriages generally. The church instituted in 1970 a revised process for judging the nullity of marriage called the American Procedural Norms. Approved by the Vatican, this process sought to examine causes prior to marriage that might render the consent of one or both individuals null and void for various reasons of deficiency. The pastoral goal was to restore church members to full communion and to heal the wounds of relationships that had not endured. The procedures were not always so benignly understood or accepted. Yet by the late 1970s the Grand Rapids diocesan tribunal under Father John F. Porter was completing as many as 250 cases annually.

Dr. Norbert J. Hruby was the first layman named as president of Aquinas College, 1969.

The papacy itself experienced dramatic changes. When Pope John Paul was elected in 1978 following the death of Pope Paul VI, the world seemed entranced by the warmth of his smile and the informality of his public audiences. Within 33 days he was gone, dying suddenly of a heart attack. The choice of his successor electrified the world, as the first non-Italian pope in over 400 years strode onto the world stage as Pope John Paul II. A vigorous 58 years old, the Polish pope was a tried and tested warrior against totalitarianism, fearless and shrewd. As an actively involved Father of Vatican Council II, he would spend all the years of his papacy making the council the centerpiece of his teaching and administration, while assertively confronting leaders of governments on behalf of justice, equality, and freedom for their citizens. Yet, with the attempt on his life in broad daylight by a would-be assassin in St. Peter's Square, within only a year of his election, it was doubtful whether he would be able to continue in his ministry for long.

Twenty years later, doubts were still being expressed as he toiled on. His papacy has been marked by unprecedented world-wide travels in public witness to the Catholic Christian faith, huge gatherings of the faithful, young and old in attendance, an often rigorous and restrictive application of the council decrees in his administration and in his expectations for Catholic living, and a continual ecumenical and interfaith outreach. At the same time he provocatively reasserted the prerogatives for Catholic identity.

As chief shepherd in the diocese, Bishop Breitenbeck was scrupulously loyal to the pope and to the union of the world-wide college of bishops with the pope. At the same time he remained open to further developments in the church with regard to the status and role of women and of married priests who had left the active ministry. He believed in breaking down barriers, as in his appointment in 1988 of the first woman to be named chancellor of the diocese, Sister Patrice Konwinski, OP, or in his sending five sisters and two priests to postgraduate studies in theology at the Catholic University of Louvain in Belgium in 1971. When he traveled around the diocese to celebrate the sacrament of

Pope John Paul I.

Pope John Paul II ordains Grand Rapids deacon Edward A. Hankiewicz to priesthood at St. Peter's in Rome, June 1994.

A gathering in Rome, late May 1978. Left to right: Bishops Dabrowski and Breitenbeck, Cardinals Woytyla, Dearden, Wyszynski, and Carberry.

confirmation, he delighted in handing his crozier or pastoral staff to a young female confirmand as a token of the future and in posing for a picture together.

Of course, the mundane details of administration were also part of his responsibility, and he liked to streamline and reorganize whenever a new approach or structure seemed to offer hope of effective service. Like his predecessors, he continued to develop the method of fund-raising for the mission of the diocese. The Catholic Services Appeal (CSA) became the successor to the Diocesan Development Fund, with the new features of assigned financial goals for parishes and the return to the parishes of funds raised over and above the assigned target. He also consolidated, after some resistance, all parish and diocesan monies into the Diocesan Deposit and Loan, so that parishes in need could borrow at a modest rate of interest from the pooled assets of all other parishes and the diocese.

Sister Patrice Konwinski, OP, first woman named chancellor of the diocese, 1988.

I n his own personal lifestyle, he chose to live modestly, abandoning as soon as he could the graceful but mansion-like residence he had inherited as bishop at 2006 Lake Drive in Grand Rapids, and withdrawing to a smaller house he had built in the country near Parnell. Controversy did not seem to disturb him, though it could create pickets, confrontations, and even the occasional threatening letter. He relished bringing the witness of his faith to the public arena, authoring a pastoral letter on peace (March 25, 1982: "the huge… expenditures for the designing and furthering of nuclear arsenals are… stealing bread from the mouths of the hungry…."), and serving on a statewide committee to make the courts of justice more accessible and fair for ordinary citizens.

His administrative style had been marked by the same meticulous attention to detail required of him as the effective secretary and assistant to two cardinals. There were frequent memos evaluating diocesan functions, prompt thank you notes, and the occasional expression of impatience or frustration, for which an apology was sure to follow. There probably had never been more meetings, more committees, and more task forces in the history of the diocese than under his administration. As he turned 75 in 1989, Bishop Breitenbeck seemed glad to be able to retire from them all. With increasing back pain, he was relieved to hand on the crozier and mitre, openly voicing his hopes that his successor would consolidate and confirm what he had done. Next to the founding bishop's 33 years of service, Bishop Breitenbeck's 20 years in office have been the longest.

A FLOWERING

1989 - 2001

FRESH FLOWERS WERE PLANTED all around the outside of the cathedral in anticipation of Bishop Robert J. Rose's installation on August 30, 1989. Inside there had to be, of course, some roses. On that warm and sunlit day, the first bishop of Grand Rapids to be born and raised in the city itself was led to his chair of authority, the cathedra, by Cardinal Edmund Szoka of Detroit. As a native son, he was known for his deliberative and reflective personality, for his sharp and bright mind, and for the warmth of his personal encounters. These gifts showed when he spoke at his inaugural Mass. "I have not come home to Grand Rapids," he said modestly and candidly, "with a blueprint or a readymade diocesan plan in my suitcase."

He had already been a bishop for eight years in the Diocese of Gaylord. There he traveled from the Lake Michigan coast to the Lake Huron shores, from the straits to farmlands to forests, listening intently to his people's needs at all his pastoral visitations. Listening, he always felt, was essential for his teaching as well as for his planning and administrating. It was a thorough, methodical, and slow process – too slow for some, who would be impatient for quicker decisions and a more dramatic style of leadership. "We need to do our homework thoroughly," was his inaugural resolve, "in faith, before the Lord, under the guidance of his Spirit." The "we" of his statement was as important as the rest of the components, for he would remain committed to a collaborative style of leadership. Besides being a style suited to the widespread participation of all segments of the post-Vatican II church, it was simply his nature and his gift.

Educated at St. Francis Xavier school in Grand Rapids and at St. Joseph Seminary a few blocks away, he then studied (1950-1952) at the Seminaire de Philosophie in Montreal, where Chief Blackbird had

1989	1990	1991	1995	1997	1998	2000
Tiananmen Square protests	First gene therapy on humans	Soviet Union dissolves	Oklahoma City Federal Building bombed	Scottish scientists clone sheep	Impeachment of President Clinton	Pope John Paul II opens Jubilee Year

also been educated by the Sulpician Fathers a hundred and fifty years before. He was sent in 1952 for his theological studies to the Pontifical Urban Seminary in Rome, where Chief Blackbird's son, William Macatebinessi, and Augustine Hamelin had been seminarians in 1832. There he was ordained a priest a few days before Christmas in 1955. Most of his work as a priest would be devoted to teaching and administration in seminaries, first at his alma mater in Grand Rapids, then at the newly established Christopher House near Aquinas College, and finally as rector for St. John's Provincial Seminary in

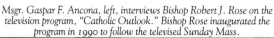

Bishop Robert J. Rose at his inaugural Mass in Grand Rapids, August 30, 1989 as ninth bishop of the diocese.

Plymouth, Michigan from 1971 to 1977. Before being named bishop, he had served as pastor at Sacred Heart Church, Muskegon Heights from 1977 to 1981. From his student days on, he always enjoyed playing the piano and organ, as well as the study of languages both classical and modern even as a form of recreation. With his own ancestry of Dutch, French, and Norwegian, he delighted in the mixture of races and nationalities, especially Asian and African, that constituted the student body of his seminary years in Rome.

The diocese he came to shepherd was, by his own happy evaluation, a thriving one after the 20 years of Vatican II reforms and renewal under Bishop Breitenbeck. It was also sound financially. So Bishop Rose began his methodical visitation of parishes, beginning with the cathedral where he had taken up temporary residence, and continuing with several parishes each year. These were not casual or purely ceremonial visits, but usually an extended weekend of celebrating the liturgies, preaching, general receptions, meetings with parish leaders, educators, and pastoral staff, visiting children in schoolrooms or religious

Msgr. Gaspar F. Ancona, left, interviews Bishop Robert J. Rose on the television program, "Catholic Outlook." Bishop Rose inaugurated the program in 1990 to follow the televised Sunday Mass.

education centers, and finally sitting down for a personal review with the pastor. These, in turn, led to a diocesan assembly in 1995 which met at the Grand Rapids Catholic Central Athletic and Convocation Center to deliberate priorities for the diocese. From the recommendations of those several hundred predominantly lay delegates, Bishop Rose prepared a pastoral vision statement to guide the work of his administration as well as of the parishes, with the focus on family, vocation, and justice.

What intruded shockingly on these thoughtfully laid deliberations was the national and local crisis of sexual abuse of children charged in highly publicized cases to members of the clergy. The greatest sadness and outrage was for the victims and how to bring them justice and healing. The church was challenged to develop fair and sensitive procedures that would do justice to the rights of victims as well as perpetrators, and at the same time to safeguard the reputation of the innocent, whether victims or the accused. The church also had to re-evaluate what forms of therapy or rehabilitation could be effective and what further assignments, if any, were proper for clergy found to be offenders. While the publicity was universal and relentless and the shame in the church deep and pervasive, the crisis did propel the church across the country and in the diocese to pioneer procedures and policies for its personnel, schools, and institutions. Bishop Rose went personally to the homes and the side of victims and their families for exhaustive listening sessions. He did the same for church congregations afflicted by the revelations. He enlisted his staff in a prolonged and intensive pastoral effort to bring justice and healing, especially the chancellor, Sister Patrice Konwinski, OP; his vicar general, Monsignor Terrence L. Stewart; and Monsignor John A. Najdowski, vicar

A 1951 photo of a young Father John W. McGee inspecting the beams charred by the 1901 cathedral fire.

The cathedral renovation of 1998-2000 included the exterior from the 12-foot-high cross to the foundations and the interior from ceiling to basement.

for priests. While the crisis abated by the end of the '90s, the wounds would be long in healing.

There were other wounds of an institutional nature that also needed healing, primarily the attitudes and actions associated with prejudice and racism. Bishop Rose sought to immerse his diocesan offices and their staffs in an ongoing confrontation with the reality of racism. He joined forces with other religious and civic organizations in an Institute for the Healing of Racism, so that the church could give authentic witness to the good news of Christ both within its membership and to the world. In the Hispanic community he encouraged the development of a new pastoral plan for the diocese. It was issued in 1997 under the leadership of Mr. Luis Beteta, Director of Hispanic Ministry, and Father Stephen Dudek, Associate Director, and called for a *"Pastoral de Conjunto,"* a collaborative ministry that would permeate all levels of church life in the diocese.

The plan documented how the presence of Hispanics had grown beyond the days of seasonal migrant workers into a resident population in the diocese approaching nearly 20 percent of the total Catholic population.

One sphere of leadership in which Bishop Rose was surprised to find himself playing the central part was the largest capital campaign in the history of the diocese. To raise funds for the restoration of the Cathedral of St. Andrew, an endowment for Catholic education, and a new diocesan spirituality and ministry center at St. Henry's Hall, along with one year's assessment for the annual Catholic Services Appeal, a total goal of $18 million was set for a campaign in 1998. Called "In the Name of the Lord" after his own motto as a bishop, the fund-raising effort set some heads shaking in disbelief at so high a target. When the campaign was completed, the pledge returns totaled $24 million. While church members proved generous and pastors indispensably brought the appeal to every parishioner, Bishop Rose himself addressed many a group and uncharacteristically and effectively attended many a social function.

Flanked by masters of ceremonies Fathers Thomas G. Simons, William H. Duncan, and deacon Michael Wood with Book of the Gospels, Bishop Rose blesses the baptismal font near the entrance of the restored cathedral, Chrism Mass, April 18, 2000.

President Juan Olivarez, center, at his installation as head of Grand Rapids Community College, October 22, 1999. Other dignitaries shown include Lt. Governor Dick Posthumus (far left), Grand Rapids Community College Student President Kimberley Van Solkema, and at far right, Dr. Arend Lubbers, Grand Valley State University President.

This financial generosity of ordinary Catholics was echoed in the last years of the century and the dawning of the new millennium in a flowering of philanthropy on the part of several Catholic businessmen, industrialists, and laywomen. Not only did they contribute to the civic community, but they generously endowed schools, hospitals, and churches within the diocese. An even more striking feature of Catholic life at the dawn of the new millennium is how pervasively Catholics occupied positions of leadership and service throughout the public sector, from the courts to corporate boardrooms, from police and fire departments to the classrooms, from the media to government agencies. It was, therefore, an especially significant and festive day when Dr. Juan Olivarez, himself a migrant worker as a boy in Oceana County, became president of Grand Rapids Community College in October of 1999.

Interior of restored cathedral. Stars in blue ceiling form constellation in night sky at date of first bishop's consecration, Henry J. Richter, April 22, 1883.

145

The journey of faith
has often seemed long and arduous.
It has been going on since
Abraham first heard God calling him,
and he with his wife Sarah
left home.

It took a dramatic new turn when
those adventuresome Magi
crossed unfamiliar territory
and bravely followed their star.
Where they halted they
brought their gifts and fell down in worship.
Their story of finding Christ
has become our own.

Having ourselves discovered
where the star came to rest, we have also
learned that Christ Risen was
already accompanying the great pilgrimage
and sharing the dangers
and triumphs of the journey.

May the telling of that story
cause his day to dawn.

Gaspar F. Ancona

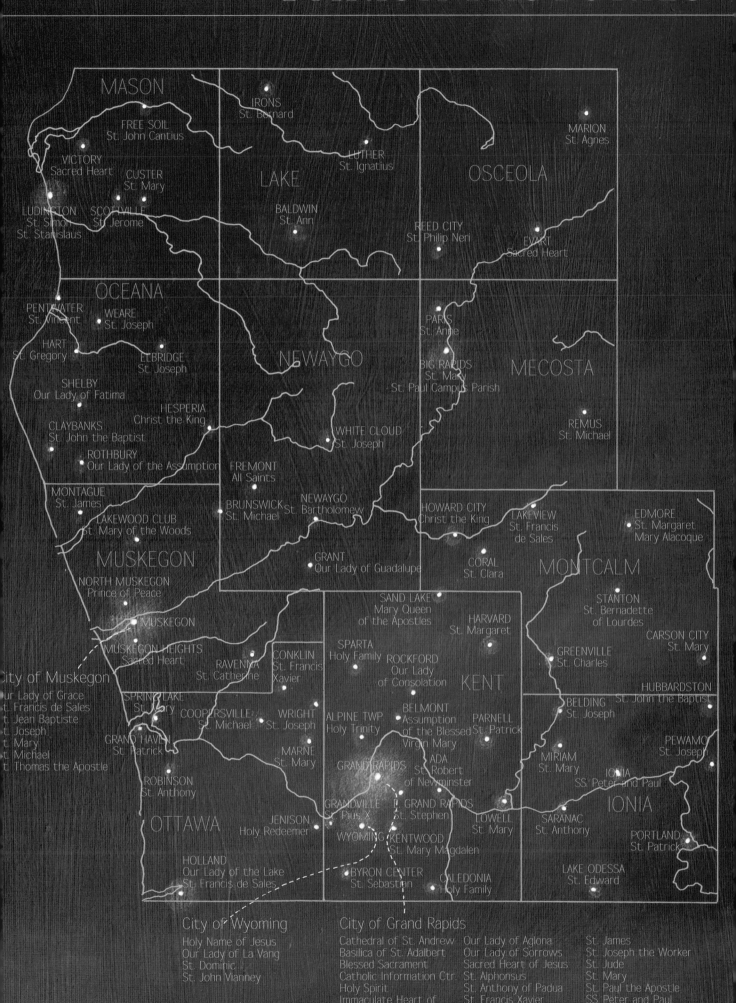

MASON

FREE SOIL
St. John Cantius

VICTORY
Sacred Heart

CUSTER
St. Mary

LUDINGTON
St. Simon
St. Stanislaus

SCOTTVILLE
St. Jerome

IRONS
St. Bernard

LUTHER
St. Ignatius

LAKE

BALDWIN
St. Ann

OSCEOLA

MARION
St. Agnes

REED CITY
St. Philip Neri

EVART
Sacred Heart

OCEANA

PENTWATER
St. Vincent

WEARE
St. Joseph

HART
St. Gregory

ELBRIDGE
St. Joseph

SHELBY
Our Lady of Fatima

HESPERIA
Christ the King

CLAYBANKS
St. John the Baptist

ROTHBURY
Our Lady of the Assumption

NEWAYGO

WHITE CLOUD
St. Joseph

FREMONT
All Saints

PARIS
St. Anne

BIG RAPIDS
St. Mary
St. Paul Campus Parish

MECOSTA

REMUS
St. Michael

MONTAGUE
St. James

LAKEWOOD CLUB
St. Mary of the Woods

MUSKEGON

NORTH MUSKEGON
Prince of Peace

MUSKEGON

MUSKEGON HEIGHTS
Sacred Heart

City of Muskegon

Our Lady of Grace
St. Francis de Sales
St. Jean Baptiste
St. Joseph
St. Mary
St. Michael
St. Thomas the Apostle

BRUNSWICK
St. Michael

NEWAYGO
St. Bartholomew

GRANT
Our Lady of Guadalupe

HOWARD CITY
Christ the King

LAKEVIEW
St. Francis
de Sales

CORAL
St. Clara

EDMORE
St. Margaret
Mary Alacoque

MONTCALM

STANTON
St. Bernadette
of Lourdes

CARSON CITY
St. Mary

SAND LAKE
Mary Queen
of the Apostles

HARVARD
St. Margaret

SPARTA
Holy Family

ROCKFORD
Our Lady
of Consolation

KENT

GREENVILLE
St. Charles

HUBBARDSTON
St. John the Baptist

BELDING
St. Joseph

RAVENNA
St. Catherine

CONKLIN
St. Francis
Xavier

SPRING LAKE
St. Mary

COOPERSVILLE
St. Michael

WRIGHT
St. Joseph

ALPINE TWP.
Holy Trinity

BELMONT
Assumption
of the Blessed
Virgin Mary

PARNELL
St. Patrick

GRAND HAVEN
St. Patrick

MARNE
St. Mary

GRAND RAPIDS

ADA
St. Robert
of Newminster

MIRIAM
St. Mary

PEWAMO
St. Joseph

IONIA
SS. Peter and Paul

ROBINSON
St. Anthony

OTTAWA

JENISON
Holy Redeemer

GRANDVILLE
St. Pius X

E. GRAND RAPIDS
St. Stephen

WYOMING

KENTWOOD
St. Mary Magdalen

LOWELL
St. Mary

SARANAC
St. Anthony

IONIA

PORTLAND
St. Patrick

HOLLAND
Our Lady of the Lake
St. Francis de Sales

BYRON CENTER
St. Sebastian

CALEDONIA
Holy Family

LAKE ODESSA
St. Edward

City of Wyoming

Holy Name of Jesus
Our Lady of La Vang
St. Dominic
St. John Vianney

City of Grand Rapids

Cathedral of St. Andrew
Basilica of St. Adalbert
Blessed Sacrament
Catholic Information Ctr.
Holy Spirit
Immaculate Heart of
Mary

Our Lady of Aglona
Our Lady of Sorrows
Sacred Heart of Jesus
St. Alphonsus
St. Anthony of Padua
St. Francis Xavier
St. Isidore

St. James
St. Joseph the Worker
St. Jude
St. Mary
St. Paul the Apostle
SS. Peter and Paul
St. Thomas the Apostle

St. Robert of Newminster

Ada

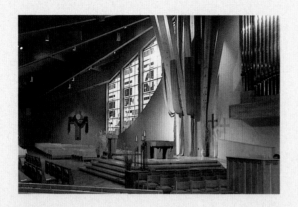

and the parish census swelled to about 400 families. With an eye toward the future, a new church was constructed in 1976; it seated about 700 people. Later in that decade a parish center, Newminster Hall, was added. It accommodates the many social and educational functions of the parish family. This facility also included several smaller rooms for meetings and educational purposes. In 1995 a wing of eight classrooms was added.

"Newminster" today marks the ruins of a Cistercian abbey in the north of England. However, in a scenic sweep of Western Michigan, it also serves to name a vibrant, growing, beautifully sited parish complex at the eastern border of Grand Rapids. The parish territory embraces Ada, Cascade, and parts of the surrounding communities.

St. Robert of Newminster Parish was established by Bishop Francis J. Haas on November 14, 1951. Father Frederick Voss was named as pastor. The next day, he led 84 parishioners in the first service at the Kennedy Restaurant on M-21 in the village of Ada. The first church, built in 1952, was a colonial style building of red brick that seated 320 people.

In the 1960s the Ada-Cascade area experienced rapid growth

The dynamic of growth continued during the next two decades, leading to the construction of the current church. Designed in a contemporary style, it seats 1,300 people, with an overflow area that can accommodate another 400 worshippers. The church reflects a community dedicated to meaningful and lively worship.

Today, with Father R. Louis Stasker as pastor, St. Robert of Newminster is a dynamic community of almost 2,000 families. The parish boasts a large and comprehensive religious education program, with over 1,300 children and young people enrolled. The youth ministry program reaches out to a large population of middle and high school students. The music ministry consists of several choirs comprised of both children and adults. A variety of musical styles complements liturgical celebrations. Numerous outreach ministries reflect the parish's commitment to service and social justice.

Holy Trinity
Alpine Township

I N 1848, with the encouragement of Father Andreas Viszoczky, German Catholic families in and around Alpine Township in Kent County began construction of a mission chapel at the corner of Baumhoff and Five Mile Road. On September 12, 1852, Father Julian Maciejewski was appointed first priest in charge of the mission. Detroit Bishop Peter Paul Lefevere blessed the church in 1853. In 1875 the congregation moved to a new church on a larger site on Alpine Church Road.

In 1901, over 50 years after the construction of the first church, the rectory was finished and Father Francis Berhorst became the first resident pastor. A new school and convent were built and Dominican Sisters arrived to administer and teach.

The last German-speaking pastor, Father Charles Bolte, was installed on July 1, 1923, and remained until his retirement in 1964. His 40 years saw considerable building and growth in the parish and the surrounding area, including various land additions, electrification in 1925, a new school in 1934, and the third church in 1957.

On Palm Sunday 1965, a tornado hit Alpine Township. Parish buildings were all either severely damaged or destroyed. The school, rectory, old convent, and the above-ground portion of the church were demolished. Only the church basement and the new convent were saved. The new and current church with the attached rectory was blessed on May 5, 1968.

Today, with Father Daniel DePew as pastor, the parish is blessed to have as associate pastor Father Thomas McKinney, who shares his wisdom and spirituality with parishioners—though he could easily have retired after a crippling accident. The church has an active LifeTeen program, Sunday evening Masses, and a Welcoming Home program for inactive Catholics. The community is currently developing a new master plan for the future.

St. Ann
Baldwin

AS EARLY AS 1912, records show St. Ann's Parish in Baldwin as a mission of St. Philip Neri's Parish in Reed City. The church building, dedicated on August 15, 1924, was enlarged in 1943 and again in 1965. The Baldwin mission was transferred to St. Joseph's Parish, White Cloud, in 1948.

In 1972 St. Ann's was elevated to the status of parish. The pastor of St. Joseph's, Father David Hawley, was transferred to St. Ann's to become its first pastor; he was also pastor of St. Bernard's Parish, Irons. A rectory was completed in January 1973. Later that year, St. Bernard's, Irons, was separated from St. Ann's, and St. Ignatius, Luther, became a mission of St. Ann's.

A parish hall was constructed in 1979 for parish functions and the meals program sponsored by the parish. St. Ann's parishioners and its pastors, Fathers Hawley, Raymond Bruck, and Joseph Fix, have been very dedicated to programs of social justice and Christian service. Among other activities, the parish has played a major role in Habitat for Humanity projects. The present pastor is Father Rock Badgerow.

St. Joseph
Belding

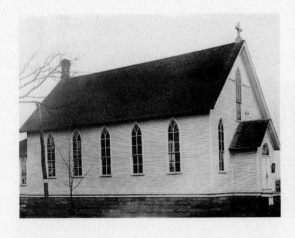

of the need for a larger church and, in the summer of 1921, Catholic farmers and other able-bodied men dug the basement. On October 12, 1923, the new church was dedicated, the pastor being Father Joseph A. Maier. In 1937 St. Joseph's became a part of the Diocese of Grand Rapids.

St. Joseph has been blessed with many religious vocations: Father Joseph E. Meade, C.Ss.R., Brother G. Martin Brown, O.S.B., Sisters Diane M. Dehn, O.P., Mary Frances Doyle, S.S.J., Marie Teresa Honson, O.P., and Deacon Howard A. Scheid, who was one of the first permanent deacons ordained in the Diocese of Grand Rapids.

In 1998 Father Troy A. Nevins received his first pastoral assignment – the parishes of St. Joseph and St. Mary.

An important part of the parish is St. Joseph's School, which opened in September 1957 under the guidance of Father Charles E. Steves, pastor from 1946 to 1974. The religious education program is supervised by Linda Brondige and the Rite of Christian Initiation of Adults (RCIA) is directed by Jill Nelson.

The present membership is 958 (343 families) and there are many active organizations within the parish.

ST. JOSEPH'S was established in 1891 in the village of Belding, Ionia County, Michigan, as a Catholic mission of St. Mary's Parish, Miriam. At that time it was part of the Diocese of Detroit. The original church building was built in 1894 on the corner of Bridge Street and M-44.

In 1913 St. Joseph's was given full parish status and Father John Zindler was named pastor. Belding grew to become the "Silk City of America" and parish membership greatly increased. Property was purchased in anticipation

Assumption of the Blessed Virgin Mary

Belmont

IN THE EARLY 1900S, Grand Rapids Bishop Henry Joseph Richter saw the need for a parish in the area north of Grand Rapids. On July 13, 1913, Father Casimir Skory met with a group of Catholic families from the Belmont area. At that meeting, it was decided by a majority vote to purchase the church structure of St. Adalbert's Parish, dismantle it, move it from Grand Rapids to Belmont, and reassemble it. Assumption of the Blessed Virgin Mary Parish was born and formally dedicated on May 31, 1914.

The parish was served by priests from St. Adalbert's until 1925, when Bishop Edward D. Kelly appointed Father Casimir Szyper as first pastor. The ensuing years brought several priests to guide the parish community and, as it grew, so did the desire and focus on a parish school.

To acquire the funds needed to make the school a reality, the parish held festivals, raffles, and dinners for several years. The building boom for the parish really started when Msgr. Joseph Podhajski was pastor (1953-1970).

In 1958, a campaign was launched to raise the remaining funds needed to start construction of not only four classrooms and a multi-purpose room but also an attached convent which would house the Consolata Missionary Sisters from Italy.

The 1980s brought more parish growth and the need for a larger church and more school classrooms. With Father John Porter as pastor, a fund drive was initiated and groundbreaking for the new church took place on November 27, 1986. When the wrecking ball demolished the old church structure, a tumbling steeple marked the end of an era.

A new era began as the new church was dedicated on February 2, 1988, by Bishop Joseph M. Breitenbeck. With Father James Bozung as pastor, the parish has members from 790 households.

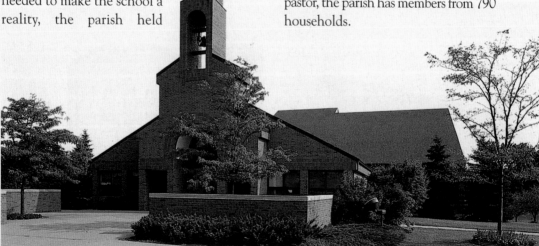

St. Mary
Big Rapids

THE CATHOLICS OF BIG RAPIDS were visited by priests from St. Mary's Parish in Grand Rapids as early as 1857. The community continued as a mission of Grand Rapids and later of St. Mary's, Muskegon, until it received its first pastor, Father H. M. Schaeken, in 1873. The parish had built its first church in 1869.

Father Andrew Herbstrit became pastor in 1874. That same year, the church was enlarged to serve the growing congregation. The first school was opened in 1878 with a lay teacher. The Sisters of Mercy took over the school the following year and also opened Mercy Hospital in 1879 to serve the needs of local lumbermen. Big Rapids served as the mother house of the Sisters of Mercy until 1914.

St. Mary's Parish served as the mother parish to many new parishes and missions in the surrounding areas of Remus, White Cloud, Reed City, Newaygo, and elsewhere.

On January 1, 1901, St. Mary's Church burned down. A new brick church was built and dedicated on December 21, 1902. This church was replaced in 1962 with a modern structure, which was dedicated on December 8, 1963.

Father Emmeran Quaderer, pastor from 1957 to 1967, recognized the need for a better ministry to the students of Ferris State Institute (now Ferris State University). He worked with the bishop to build a Catholic chapel at the school. This chapel became St. Paul's Campus Parish.

St. Mary's Parish celebrated its centennial in 1973 and its 125th anniversary in 1998. A parish center was completed in 1996. Many new ministries and service projects have been taken on by the parish in recent years, during the pastorate of Father Michael McKenna.

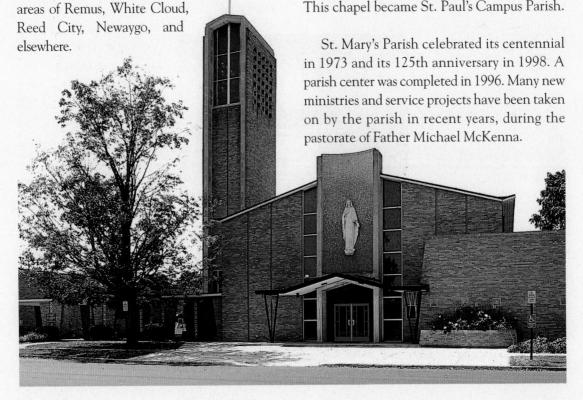

St. Paul Campus
Big Rapids

I N THE DECADE following World War II, the burgeoning college student population put a severe strain on traditional diocesan parishes to serve the Catholic students pouring into colleges and universities throughout the state. At Ferris State University (then Ferris Institute), over 700 Catholic students swamped St. Mary's, the local parish, and plans took shape to build a Catholic chapel to serve this growing population. Thus, on November 1, 1959, St. Paul's Chapel was blessed and dedicated by Bishop Allen J. Babcock of the Diocese of Grand Rapids, who named Father Francis L.Hackett the first pastor.

Over the past 41 years, St. Paul's, led by Father Hackett and his six successors, has served the Ferris State community by providing many services for the student body and Ferris community. These initiatives have included drug and substance abuse counseling, the Rite of Christian Initiation of Adults (RCIA), Habitat for Humanity support, religious education, and pre-Cana assistance.

Perhaps one of the campus parish's most significant programs was the 1993 union with its new sister parish, San Andreas, in rural Guatemala. Working closely with students and faculty, St. Paul's built and financed a free dental clinic for the Indian residents of the San Andreas area. Ferris professional staff, along with students and religious members of the parish, have visited the Guatemalan parish several times. The entire congregation has supported ongoing fundraising efforts to keep the dental program thriving and also financed the purchase of a new sports utility vehicle for the San Andreas religious staff for use in the rugged mountain terrain.

Serving thousands of young college students in addition to its mission initiative in Guatemala, St. Paul's has been a vibrant religious and social force despite its relatively short history. The student chapel has striven to implement its mission statement, "…to dedicate ourselves to living the Gospel of Jesus Christ…and to build a community of faith at Ferris State University and in the broader parish community." Father Wayne B. Wheeler, Jr. is the current pastor.

St. Michael
Brunswick

THE FAITH COMMUNITY of St. Michael's, Brunswick, began in 1885 as a mission of St. Mary's, Big Rapids. The first church building, a wooden structure, was completed and dedicated in 1887. The parish continued as a mission, first of St. Jean Baptiste, Muskegon, and later of St. James, Montague. A cemetery was added to the property in 1903. A rectory was built, but it was not used by a priest until 1922. In 1925 St. Michael's Parish was assigned its own mission, All Saints, Fremont. In 1948 the northern sector of the parish was established as another new mission, Christ the King, Hesperia.

A parish hall, begun in September of 1951, served as a temporary church from June 1, 1952, until June 5, 1953. The present church of brick and stone, constructed mostly through volunteer labor, was blessed and occupied for its first Mass on June 6, 1953. On March 12, 1954, lightning caused a fire in the hall, but the church suffered only minor damage.

A convent was begun in 1955. In 1956 the parish hall was converted into classrooms for a parish school, the first and only Catholic school in Newaygo County. The parish added a classroom and bathrooms in 1961, a new parish hall in 1972, and a kindergarten and library in 1989, although kindergarten classes had begun four years earlier in the parish hall.

St. Michael's School, pre-school through eighth grade, is dedicated to educating the whole child. The school offers a strong academic curriculum, a pleasant learning environment, up-to-date technology, supportive parents, and a strong network of volunteers under the guidance of a dedicated faculty. The library, equipped with over 3000 volumes, offers an inviting atmosphere for study.

Pastoral and Finance Councils, elementary religious education, and the Rite of Christian Initiation of Adults (RCIA) play an important role in the life of the parish. Father Donn P. Tufts is pastor.

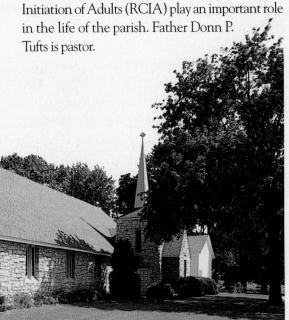

St. Sebastian
Byron Center

Ministering the Eucharist on Good Friday: Mary Ancona and her son, flanked by servers Leah Brummel and Adam Wolf.

Procession with Bishop Rose and Warren Reynolds

St. Sebastian Church on the wedding day of Ronald and Adrianne Wolf, Oct. 28, 2000

ESTABLISHED IN 1852, St. Sebastian's Parish began as a community of immigrant German farmers. John Jacob Wolf donated the property on which a log building was constructed for the first church. Priests from Grand Rapids and Wright, 18 and 25 miles north, served the pioneer community.

From 1890 to 1901, St. Sebastian's united with St. Mary's Parish in North Dorr. Under the leadership of Father Anthony Eickelmann, the present church was built in 1901. Riding by horse to Jamestown and by interurban to Holland after his Sunday services in Byron, Father Eickelmann also pastored the Catholics of the lakeshore area. Father Ernest J. Walters served longest as pastor, from 1921 to 1968.

The North Dorr Hotel, moved in 1909 to the church property, became school, convent, and hall. It burned down in 1976. A parish activities hall was built in 1975 and expanded in 1993 with six classrooms. The 1897 rectory was refurbished in 1994. The church was made barrier-free and a gathering deck was constructed in 1997-98. In 1999 St. Sebastian's more than doubled its land holdings with the purchase of 14 acres. The parish is thus poised to grow with the surrounding developments in Byron Township. Msgr. Gaspar F. Ancona is the current pastor.

Holy Family
Caledonia

HOLY FAMILY PARISH in Caledonia was formed in 1969 with the merger of St. Mary's, Cascade, and St. Joseph's, Leighton. St. Patrick's, Bowne, was incorporated into the parish in 1981.

St. Mary's Church in Cascade was built in 1856 by Irish immigrants. The church was served by priests from St. Patrick's in Parnell and St. Andrew's in Grand Rapids until 1891, when Father James Byrne became the first resident pastor. A new church had been built in 1888, and it served the parish until Holy Family's church was constructed in 1970.

St. Joseph's Church in Leighton Township, Allegan County, was built in 1872 or 1873. It was a mission of Hastings, New Salem, North Dorr, Cascade, and Gun Lake before becoming part of Holy Family Parish.

St. Patrick's Church in Bowne was founded as an outgrowth of St. Patrick's, Parnell, about 1866. A small church was built in 1868 and a larger one in 1887. Priests came from Parnell, Hastings, and Grand Rapids until the mission was attached to Cascade in 1891. After 1969, St. Patrick's was a mission of Holy Family, Caledonia. When St. Patrick's Church burned down in 1981, the members joined Holy Family Parish.

In 1965 the three church communities of Cascade, Leighton, and Bowne established a combined religious education program. With their old churches becoming increasingly inadequate, the Cascade and Leighton congregations chose to consolidate into Holy Family Parish in Caledonia. The merger was completed in 1969. The people of St. Patrick's, Bowne, chose to retain their separate status as a mission of Holy Family until their church was destroyed in 1981. Holy Family Church was constructed in 1970. The growing parish community currently numbers 1,000 families and is under the leadership of Father David E. Le Blanc.

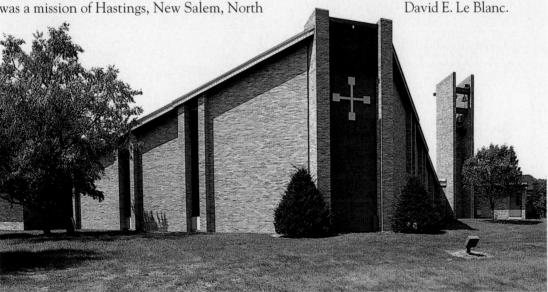

St. Mary
Carson City

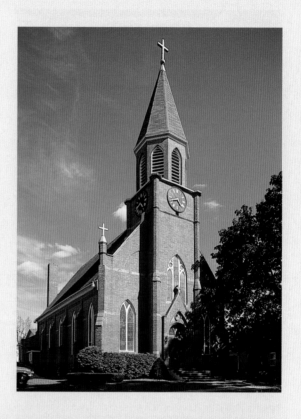

THE CATHOLIC COMMUNITY at Carson City originally worshipped with the parishioners of St. John the Baptist Parish in Hubbardston, Michigan. In 1896, however, Father Kyran Whalen became the first pastor of the newly established parish of St. Mary's.

In those early years, Father Whalen served the missions of Harvard, Greenville, and Maple Valley, as well as the people of St. Mary's. The Mass was celebrated in various local halls while the church in Carson City was built. The first Mass in the new building was celebrated on Christmas Day 1896. A rectory was built in 1898 and a parish school, St. Mary's Academy, was opened in 1906.

St. Mary's Parish now shares a pastor, Father William J. Reitz, with St. John the Baptist in Hubbardston.

St. John the Baptist
Claybanks Township

THE MISSION of St. John the Baptist traces its heritage to 1857, when the first Mass was celebrated in Oceana County's Claybanks Township at the home of Mr. and Mrs. Owen Farrell. Father Steinhauser walked through the trackless wilderness forest from Muskegon to celebrate the Eucharist with six Catholic pioneer families who lived in the area. In the years following, various other priests trekked from Muskegon, Ludington, Big Rapids, and Spring Lake to minister to the tiny flock.

The congregation acquired its first home when it purchased a small school in 1870 on the farm of A. S. Anderson on the shores of Lake Michigan. Mass was celebrated there about four times a year.

In 1882 the community was linked to St. James Parish in Montague, a relationship that continues to this day. In 1884 Father Edward LeFevre was appointed pastor for the area. He spurred the construction of a new church at its present location atop a scenic ridge on 50th Avenue, a four-acre plot donated by John Miller. The first Mass was celebrated in the structure on March 6, 1886.

In the years that followed, many pastors served the congregation at Claybanks. Liturgies were held once a month for many years, until Father Russell Passeno was assigned to Montague in 1931 and began celebrating Mass every Sunday at St. John's.

Today the parish counts about 30 families as full-time members. But each year countless tourists and seasonal residents find their way up the gravel road to celebrate Mass with St. John's family. Although many improvements have been made over the years, the 114-year-old church looks much as it did when it was built, and in many ways the present community remains as tightly knit as that of the first pioneers.

St. Francis Xavier
Conklin

WITH THE PERMISSION of Bishop Henry Joseph Richter, St. Francis Xavier Church in Chester Township was built in 1892 under the direction of Father Ege, pastor of St. Joseph's Church, Wright. The building cost $4,000, as most of the materials were donated by the 19 founding families.

As a mission, St. Francis Xavier was originally served by various priests. It became a parish on October 1, 1945, with the appointment of Father Betka as pastor.

Since 1952, through special arrangement, the children of the parish have attended St. Catherine's School, Ravenna. A festival dinner helped to pay bus and tuition expenses.

Improvements to the church in 1959 included an addition with a vestibule and lavatories, redecoration of the church, new classrooms in the basement, a new organ, and a parish library.

Before his appointment as auxiliary bishop in 1968, Father Joseph McKinney, the pastor, directed the building of the Shrine of the Resurrection in

the parish cemetery, commemorating the 75th anniversary of the building of the parish. Its dedication included an outdoor Mass.

St. Francis Xavier takes pride in its parishioners who have entered religious life: Father Leonard Gross, Brother Vincent Gross, and Sisters Ann Joel Van Oeffelen, Mary Dorothy Yegge, and Mary Lucinda Lehmkehl.

Events marked by the parish in recent times include Father Max Ostrowski's golden anniversary of ordination on April 30, 1989, and the celebration of the parish's 100th anniversary in November 1992. This latter occasion was marked by many festivities, including the celebration of Mass by former pastors.

St. Francis Xavier Parish now numbers 150 families and shares its pastor, Father John F. Porter, with St. Catherine's Parish, Ravenna. It continues to grow as a family, worshipping together. The parish is especially proud of its quaint and beautiful statues and altar.

St. Michael
Coopersville

ST. MICHAEL'S CHURCH is located about four miles northwest of Coopersville, Michigan. This rural farming area was once part of Dennison, an early settlement that developed mainly because of logging activity beginning in the 1850s. Only traces of Dennison remain today.

Early families of St. Michael's were primarily Irish, along with some Germans and people of other nationalities. These families were served by occasional visits by mission priests who traveled, at first, on horseback. Services were held in the homes of families until the first structure, a wood frame church building, came into use. It was constructed in 1882 on land that had been donated in 1879. The church was formally dedicated in 1888. It was named for the patron saint of the mission priest then overseeing the congregation, Father Michael Dalton.

St. Michael's was first a mission of the church in Grand Haven and then, in 1924, of St. Mary's in Marne. The mission obtained the status of parish in 1950.

In 1962 St. Michael's completed an expansive building project consisting of a new convent and a school with a large all-purpose addition that functioned during the following years as a church. This construction was accomplished under the parish's first pastor, who served until 1962. That same year he was ordained bishop and was shortly thereafter appointed to the Marquette Diocese. In 1977 he became Archbishop Charles A. Salatka of the Oklahoma City Archdiocese.

In 1988 a large new church structure was completed under the pastorship of Father William Langlois. Later, additional space was added to the school and the all-purpose area became a family center. The convent, built to house the Sisters of St. Francis who were the first to staff the school, has been converted into an administration building.

St. Michael's Parish is involved in Grand Valley State University's Campus Ministry. Father John F. Vallier is pastor.

St. Clara
Coral

S t. Clara's Mission had its origin over 100 years ago when a tract of land was donated by James Coady. The first church building was a small log structure located on Amble Road. Previous to the building of the church, services were held in the homes of local residents. The priest rode on horseback from Grattan to minister to the people.

In the early 1870s the church was moved to Maple Valley and a neighboring house was obtained for a rectory. The Fathers Seybold and Goossens were priests who served the parish in that era. Later the parish was serviced from Carson City.

The parish became a mission of Greenville in the early 1900s. In 1937 it was attached to St. Mary's Parish in Sand Lake. Time ravaged the old church structure and a new one was constructed in 1945, with all useable materials transported to Coral, where the new church was erected.

St. Mary
Custer

S T. MARY'S CHURCH in Custer had its beginnings in 1865 with about 14 families as the original members. They were of Irish, English, French, and Scottish descent, most of them coming from Canada. Father Paquin celebrated Mass in the homes of John Howard, Edward Stocks, William Connelly, and Mathew Hoey once a month. The priest came from St. Simon's Parish in Ludington, generally by train, although he came by livery for sick calls. Other priests in those early years were Fathers Theis and Hayden.

Members met in 1884 and decided to build a church. All worked together, Catholics and members of other religious communities, to construct the building in which to honor God.

Father Paquin directed the project and John Howard was the carpenter. Some 20 families contributed funds, materials, and labor.

In the early 1890s the ladies of St. Mary's met to organize an Altar Society and named it in honor of St. Rose of Lima. In 1895 the Holy Name Society was organized under the guidance of Father Joseph Pietrasik. St. Anthony's Society was organized in 1917. Mrs. Z. Biabek (now Donnora) organized the Rosary Society in 1926 and was its first president.

During these years St. Mary's was a mission of St. Jerome's in Scottville. Priests during this time were Fathers Brogger, Karas, Dark, and Tomaszewski. In 1932 Father W. Viesnoraitis was named pastor and under his guidance construction on a rectory was started. The parish celebrated its golden jubilee in 1937.

Father J. Alksnis was named pastor in 1944. He was succeeded by Father Benedict Marciulionis, with Father George Riauba as assistant, in 1948.

In 1955 a parish school was constructed. The Sisters of St. Casimir were its teachers. The school closed in 1967 when the sisters left to teach in the inner city in Chicago. It is now rented to the Mason County Eastern Schools and is used for first- and second-grade classrooms. Father Isidro Gargantiel is pastor.

St. Stephen
East Grand Rapids

IN 1924 Bishop Edward D. Kelly purchased land on the corner of Rosewood Avenue and Franklin Street in East Grand Rapids for a new parish. At the time, two small houses, a barn, four shacks used by transients, and a large pond were on the site. A roller coaster a few blocks away at Ramona Park made an impressive sight.

Construction of a church-school building was completed in 1925, and the new St. Stephen's Parish was now a reality. The first Mass was celebrated May 11, 1925, by St. Stephen's first pastor, Father Leo Farquharson. The school's first nine students graduated in June 1926.

For some years afterwards, an old farmhouse on the property served as a convent. At first Father Farquharson roomed with the Burns family; then he moved into a small office in the school which contained a bed, a hot plate, and an icebox.

As the parish grew, a Women's Guild and a Holy Name Society were formed, and they initiated numerous fund-raisers to help retire the $88,000 debt. In 1941 the present rectory was built at a cost of $40,000. In 1943 a memorial shrine was erected on the lawn of the rectory to honor the men and women from the parish who served in the armed forces during World War II.

After the war it became apparent that the parish was outgrowing its facilities. In 1951 a capital campaign to raise $400,000 began. This program added five classrooms, a gym, a new convent, an extension to the church, new pews, and new equipment for the school. In 1959 and 1960 a second expansion of the school added eight more classrooms.

As the church absorbed changes brought about by Vatican II, Msgr. Edward Alt, the fifth pastor of St. Stephen's, was confronted with another renovation to the church. During this period the parish made a special effort to offer the opportunities of its grade school to the total community.

During the 1970s and 1980s St. Stephen's Parish continued to grow and change. As more women joined the workforce, the Women's Guild faded, but other parish activities were born, including adult education lectures, receptions, and the Rite of Christian Initiation of Adults (RCIA). Father Mark C. Przybysz serves as pastor.

St. Margaret Mary
Edmore

IN 1961 Father Edwin Thome was assigned as a resident priest to serve the missions of Sheridan, Stanton, Six Lakes, Edmore, and Vestaburg. The territory was divided into two mission centers, Stanton and Edmore. St. James Mission House in Edmore was purchased to serve as a rectory, education center, and chapel.

Plans were begun at the time for a new church in Edmore. St. Margaret Mary Church was dedicated on June 9, 1963. The mission of Edmore was changed to the status of parish in 1965 with Father Thome as pastor and St. Bernadette's in Stanton and St. Francis de Sales in Lakeview as missions.

Father Thome was transferred in 1969. He was succeeded by Fathers James Bozung, Eugene Alvesteffer, William Zink, Fredrick Brucker, Louis Baudone, Donn Tufts, Isidro Gargantiel, and Vincent Bryce, O.P.

St. Bernadette was elevated to parish status in 1974, but the Edmore and Stanton parishes have always shared a pastor. A new rectory in Edmore was built by the two parishes in 1975, and the mission house was sold.

St. Joseph
Elbridge

BEGINNING IN 1867, Catholic directories list an Indian settlement in Oceana County as a mission of St. Mary's in Muskegon. This mission was the forerunner of St. Joseph's Parish, Elbridge. It was later transferred to St. Mary's, Big Rapids, and then to St. James, Montague, before a priest was assigned to Elbridge in 1884.

Father Philip Seraphin Zorn, a former Franciscan missionary from Harbor Springs, was appointed by Bishop Henry Joseph Richter to be Elbridge's first resident pastor. The Pay-Maw-Me School was used as the original church.

In 1891, because of Father Zorn's poor health, Elbridge again became a mission of Montague. In 1894 St. Joseph's was comprised of 32 families: three English-speaking (Irish), four German, and 25 Native American. From 1894 to 1919 the community was served by Franciscan missionaries from Harbor Springs and Petoskey. The current church was built and dedicated in 1915.

In 1919 St. Joseph's again became a mission of Montague. Over the next 17 years, the church was attended (often irregularly) by priests from Montague, Muskegon (St. Michael's), Petoskey, and Brunswick. St. Joseph's became a mission of St. Gregory's, Hart, in 1936. It has been connected to Hart ever since, with the exception of the years 1952 to 1972 when it was a mission of Our Lady of Fatima in Shelby.

In the summer of 2000, St. Joseph's was transformed into an evangelization outreach and gathering center for the area Native American community under the direction of the diocesan Native American Ministry. St. Joseph's is now known as the Kateri Tekakwitha Center and St. Joseph's Chapel.

RECORDS indicate that Sacred Heart Mission was founded in Evart in 1874 as a mission of St. Mary's Church in Big Rapids. Mission services were held one day every second week and on Sundays four times a year. Sacred Heart became a mission of St. Philip Neri's in Reed City in 1903.

The first Catholic church in Evart was built on the north side of Cherry and Railroad Streets at a cost of about $3,000. It was dedicated by Bishop Caspar Henry Borgess of Detroit on August 26, 1875. Father Andrew Herbstrit of Big Rapids was the first pastor of Sacred Heart Mission.

The steeple of the first church was struck by lightning and the church burned on July 5, 1922. The damage was so great that it was decided to build a new church on the corner of South Main and Ninth Streets. The church was dedicated by Father Zugelder on June 26, 1923. Father Zugelder served the mission for 29 years.

The second church was ample for the mission's 20 or so families until about 1955. However, the influx of summer residents on the lakes and on the Muskegon River more than filled the building. Many summer visitors sat outside on the lawn listening to the Mass on loudspeakers. In 1960 Msgr. Victor Gallagher and Father James Cusack, priests of St. Philip Neri Parish and Sacred Heart Mission, led the construction of a new church on U.S. Highway 10 west of Evart. The first Mass was celebrated in the building on Easter Sunday, April 2, 1961.

Bishop Joseph M. Breitenbeck established Sacred Heart as a parish on October 11, 1972. The parish at that time comprised about 70 families. The first pastor was Father Melvin Fox. Succeeding pastors have been Fathers Delvin Tilmann, James Chelich, and Rock Badgerow. In 1984 the parish numbered approximately 190 families. The present pastor is Father Joseph Fix.

St. John Cantius
Free Soil

IN 1901 an organizational meeting was held at the Free Soil Town Hall for the purpose of planning the construction of a Catholic church in the Free Soil area of Mason County. With the donation of two acres of land and the purchase of an additional six acres for $100, the church was built, largely with donated labor, from 1904 to 1906.

In 1906 St. John Cantius Parish was established as a mission of St. Joseph's Parish, Manistee. It remained a mission until 1922, when Father Constantine Skrowronski was appointed the first permanent pastor. In the early years, St. Bernard's, Irons ,was a mission of St. John Cantius. Now St. John Cantius and St. Bernard's share the same pastor.

In 1938 a major renovation took place with the addition of a new sanctuary and sacristy, increased seating, and the redecoration of the church interior. In the 1970s and early 1980s, the church windows were replaced, new pews and lighting were installed, a new front entrance which included restrooms and inside basement access was constructed, and other renovations to the kitchen and church interior took place. In the 1990s a new pavilion with a kitchen was constructed, the rectory was partially renovated, and a new section was added on the north end of the cemetery.

St. John Cantius Parish, located in the northernmost part of the Grand Rapids Diocese, consists today of approximately 126 families with Father Thomas Niedzwiecki as pastor. Annually, on the first Sunday of August, the parish serves 700 to 800 dinners at its chicken barbecue.

CATHOLICS in the Fremont area were first noted in the National Catholic Directory in 1873. During the ensuing decades, the Fremont community was served by clergy traveling from Big Rapids, Grand Rapids, and Muskegon, but little is known about how many families attended worship services. At the turn of the century, Mass was conducted in a flat; later, the Masonic Hall above John Pikaart's store was rented.

In 1901 enough money was raised to construct a church. Records show excavation started in 1905 on a lot on South Stewart Street. That November, when the walls were only partially completed, a gale struck and the building collapsed into the basement. Despite this setback, the church was completed in 1906. It was given the name All Saints in 1908.

In 1915 the church community again moved forward and started having Masses twice a month on the second and fourth Sundays, instead of once a month. In 1923 All Saints became a mission church of Brunswick and received its own pastor, Father Leo A. Whalen. It remained a mission church until it was declared an independent parish in 1950, when Father Herman S. Kolenda, living in a furnished apartment near the church, became its resident pastor.

During the 1950s and 1960s, buildings were purchased or rented to house religious education and the rectory. In 1947 the community purchased land to build a church. That church was not built until 1970 and included a modest rectory. This same building still services the congregation, which continues to grow. Under the leadership of Father Richard J. Van Lente, the parish is currently undergoing a fund drive to build an addition that is scheduled to begin in 2001.

St. Patrick
Grand Haven

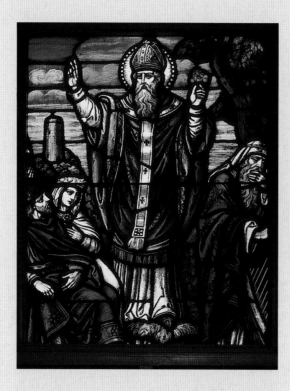

IN 1867 about 40 Grand Haven families were organized into St. Patrick's Parish. A priest would come from Muskegon to say Mass. The majority of the original parishioners were Irish. In 1872 the first church was built and the parish also obtained the services of its first priest. Father Timothy J. Murphy came directly from Ireland.

One of the early supporters of the church was Captain Thomas W. Kirby. He established several companies in Grand Haven and employed hundreds of Grand Haven men. He also contributed greatly to the growth of the Catholic Church in Grand Haven. He served as mayor of Grand Haven for four years in the late 1880s.

In 1911 Father Daniel J. Hyland arrived in Grand Haven and served as pastor until 1948. He was a progressive and public-spirited individual and served for many years as chairman of the Grand Haven Hospital Board. Father Hyland built the first Catholic school; it opened in 1919. Four Sisters of Mercy staffed it. Father Hyland led the parish through a period of industrialization and heavy immigration, a

depression, and two world wars. He distinguished himself as a builder and problem-solver and helped the parish meet the demands of the first part of the 20th century. He died in 1948.

The construction of a boulevard through Grand Haven ran right through the church so that a new one had to be constructed in the mid-'50s. The majority of this task fell to Father Francis Branigan, who served this parish for 13 years. He did so decisively and wisely. He also established the first lay board of advisors in the parish and supervised the building of a parish religious education and family center.

Situated in the heart of town, St. Patrick's has met the needs of its people over a long time span. St. Patrick's has always been a religious community within the context of the larger public community of Grand Haven. As a consequence, its history is a reflection of the history of Grand Haven. Father William A. Langlois is the present pastor.

Cathedral of St. Andrew
Grand Rapids

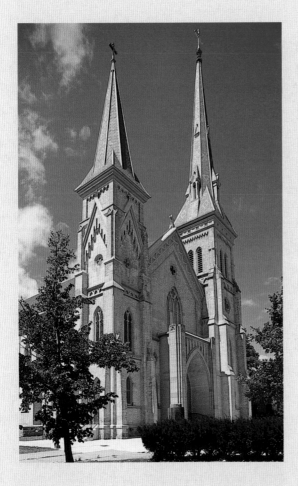

F ATHER FREDERIC BARAGA established the beginnings of St. Andrew's when he built the first church, St. Mary's Mission, in 1833 amid Indian cornfields on the west bank of the Grand River.

Two years later, when Father Andreas Viszoczky became the pastor, he found a small church, rectory, and school building that Father Baraga had built. After the Indian population dispersed, Father Viszoczky built a new church on Monroe Avenue, naming the parish for St. Andrew, his patron saint. This church was soon too small for its growing population and, in 1875, a new church was built at its present location on Sheldon Avenue. The Grand Rapids Diocese was formed seven years later, and the first bishop, Henry Joseph Richter, chose St. Andrew's as his new cathedral. In its long history since, the church building has seen damage from

a major fire and has undergone four subsequent renovations. The last renovation, under Bishop Robert J. Rose, was completed for the celebration of Easter 2000.

During its nearly 200-year history, the face of the parish community has changed. Whereas the first sermons were in English, French, German, Odawa, and Ojibway, today's sermons are in English and Spanish, preached to a diverse congregation. The cathedral counts among its parishioners the largest community of Latinos and African-Americans in the diocese. St. Andrew's School is also known for its multicultural population. With its emphasis on a diverse student body, academic excellence, and parental involvement, the school thrives as a model for other Catholic schools.

Today St. Andrew's Cathedral proudly stands in the central city as a place of acceptance and hospitality to its neighbors and to the community at large. Its principal mission has not changed over the last two centuries: to make Jesus Christ present to His people in word, sacrament, and deed. Father M. Thomas Bolster is rector.

Father Bolster with First Communicants

Basilica of St. Adalbert
Grand Rapids

THE SEEDS of St. Adalbert Parish were planted in 1872 on Grand Rapids' northwest side. The congregation was initially made up of new immigrants from Poland, primarily with German roots but also from areas of Poland with Russian and Lithuanian backgrounds. Its members hailed from throughout West Michigan, from as far away as Muskegon. Over the years, St. Adalbert's Parish became known as the "mother parish" of five others in the West Michigan area.

Dave Raczkowski

The cornerstone of the original church building was laid in 1881. The church was enlarged in 1887 and again in 1907, when construction of the current church began. When the new church was completed six years later, the original church was dismantled and sent upriver to the town of Belmont, where it was faithfully reconstructed. The interior of the present church underwent a major renovation in the 1950s, with installation of marble altars and statuary, marble wainscoting, new floors, and the magnificent marble baldachino that dominates the sanctuary today.

The current church was elevated to the rank of Minor Basilica by declaration of Pope John Paul II in December 1979 and rededicated in February 1980. The 1981 centennial celebration brought the installation of the 72-rank Wicks Centennial Memorial Organ, recently upgraded and rededicated as the Joseph A. Westdorp Centennial Memorial Organ in honor of the parish music director's 40 years of dedicated service to the community. St. Adalbert

Basilica Parish sponsors many choral concerts and solo performances each year and is recognized as having one of the finest musical programs and performance spaces in the area.

The parish school opened in 1884 with 250 pupils taught by the Felician Sisters. The school grew throughout the first quarter of the last century to a peak enrollment of 1573 pupils in 1925. By 1920 the teaching mission had been assumed by the School Sisters of Notre Dame. In 1921 a new building designed to house 1500 students was constructed. As elementary enrollment declined over the years, this space was shared, beginning in 1944, by a high school program which eventually became West Catholic Central High School. The high school moved to a new campus in 1962. Changing demographics and the economics of running a parochial school for a parish student body of just 44 led to the closing of the school at the end of 1999. To all those affiliated with the school throughout its long history, the words can be said: "Well done, good and faithful servant."

The former convent now houses Steepletown Ministries, a joint effort with nearby St. Mary and St. James Parishes. This new center provides programs in bilingual education, a tri-parish youth group, counseling services, a mentoring program, and many other neighborhood outreach services. Under the leadership of Father Thomas J. De Young, the parish's 828 families look forward to the challenges of the new millennium in bringing Christ's love to the people of their community.

Blessed Sacrament
Grand Rapids

Parish women with Pastor Father John Collins at the first meeting of the Blessesd Sacrament Ladies Guild in May 1946. The Ladies Guild is in its 55th year of active service to our parish family.

BLESSED SACRAMENT PARISH was founded to meet the needs of the "baby boom" families after World War II. In 1946 the Grand Rapids Diocese recognized the need for a new parish in the expanding northeast sector of Grand Rapids. Bishop Francis J. Haas established the parish of Blessed Sacrament in March of that year and appointed Father John Collins as the first pastor for 256 Catholic families. Masses were celebrated in various locations, first at the Veterans' Facility, then in the Roxy Theatre. In 1952 a gymnasium-auditorium was added to the school building on Diamond Avenue as a temporary church. Finally, in 1989, a long-awaited church was built and dedicated.

The parish family's primary focus has always been the education of its children. In the early years, students attended other parish schools. In September 1950, 250 students began the school year in their own building, with a staff of six Dominican Sisters from Grand Rapids. The Dominican presence ended in 1982, but the Christian values they taught have lived on; some of yesterday's students became the parents of children attending the school today. At its peak the school enrolled more than 500 pupils; today, approximately 300 students are registered in preschool through eighth grade.

The Blessed Sacrament Ladies Guild, founded by Father Collins in 1946, continues its service to the parish family. The faces, tasks, and projects have changed over the years, but the Guild remains a tradition for parish women.

Pastors have included Father John Collins, Msgr. Anthony Arszulowicz, Fathers Eugene Golas, Louis LaSarge, Henry Dondzila, Robert Hart, and, currently, John Wisneski.

In the new millennium, the Blessed Sacrament Parish Community remains united in the Eucharist, committed to being the Body of Christ while building the Body of Christ by prayer and service.

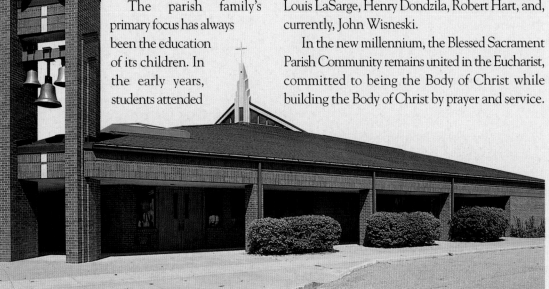

Catholic Information Center
Grand Rapids

IN 1947 Bishop Francis J. Haas invited the Paulist Fathers to begin a ministry in downtown Grand Rapids where people inquiring about the Catholic faith could simply walk into a building where classes and literature would be available. Two Paulist Fathers arrived and, along with the diocese, purchased Jack's Cut Rate Clothing Store on Monroe Avenue where the Hall of Justice now stands. They converted the building into a small chapel, classrooms, and offices, and opened the Catholic Information Center in 1948.

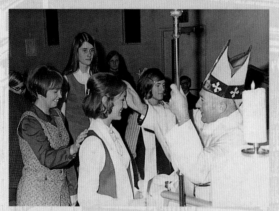

Bishop Breitenbeck confirming students

Tens of thousands of people have since walked through the doors to attend a Catholic faith inquiry class or talk with one of the Paulists about their questions, doubts, and faith. For many of them it was their entrance into the Catholic Church, as they were baptized and confirmed as adult converts. For many Catholics working in downtown Grand Rapids, the small chapel has been an ideal place to go for a few moments of reflection and prayer or to attend daily Mass.

When urban renewal came through downtown, the Center relocated in 1964 to its present site at 246 Ionia Avenue. A larger chapel and additional meeting space enabled the Center to expand its programs. An attractive brick façade was added in 1977 and the chapel interior was renovated in 1984. While the Center has never looked like a traditional church, for many, the intimacy of the liturgies has been a great assist to their faith life.

The life of the Center flowed out onto the streets of the city. Creative use of media and advertising were used to bring the message of faith to those outside a religious tradition. The Center offered book and film discussions and brought in speakers on issues of faith and culture. Outreach to separated and divorced Catholics and others on the margins of the church became another ministry of the Center. Vatican II inspired courses on church renewal, the Paulists and Center members engaged in ecumenical dialogue, and members actively joined the efforts for peace in the 1960s and '70s. They continue to work for peace and justice in Habitat for Humanity, the Heartside neighborhood, and a mission in Honduras.

From its beginning the unique mission of the Center in spreading the faith attracted the attention and support of lay Catholics. Even while remaining members of their home parish, they helped spread news about the Center's programs and supported the physical and financial operation through the Paulist Guild and Men's Club. The Lay Advisory Board and later the Center Community Leadership Group provided the initiative as more people assumed responsibility for the Center in committees on education, peace and justice, and liturgy. Father Robert Cary, CSP, leads the pastoral staff.

The Center is in an ideal location for its members and the Paulist Fathers to continue the tradition of presenting Catholic faith and life for downtown workers, visitors, and faith seekers from all over the metropolitan area.

Holy Spirit
Grand Rapids

HOLY SPIRIT PARISH had a unique beginning on the northwest side of Grand Rapids. Under the name of St. Agnes, a small group met for weekend services at Rosedale Cemetery Chapel while plans for a parish church were discussed. When adequate acreage was made available on Lake Michigan Drive, the diocese made plans to change not only the parish location but also its name. On January 15, 1952, the Parish of the Holy Spirit was canonically established by Bishop Francis J. Haas, with Father Bernard Sikorski as its pastor.

By 1953, 101 families had gathered and had begun to develop plans for a building that would house not only the parish church but also the beginnings of a school. Classroom doors opened on September 9, 1953. The school had six grades. By the end of that year, parish registrations had risen to 260 families.

Each year brought growth in the parish. Construction was begun on a convent for the Felician Sisters who taught at Holy Spirit. By 1957 construction of a new church auditorium began, along with additional classrooms needed to accommodate the ever-growing school. On August 14, 1958, a fire of unknown origin destroyed half of the building which was to have been used for worship. Parishioners rallied in great numbers to clean the damaged area and prepare the still-under-construction space for weekend worship. Work was completed, and

on September 27, 1959, the new church auditorium was formally dedicated by Bishop Allen Babcock.

Through all the growth and trials the parish experienced, there was always the vision of a permanent worship space that would truly stand as the center of parish life. After years of hard work, sacrifice, and planning, the new parish church was dedicated on Pentecost Sunday, the Feast of the Holy Spirit, May 22, 1994.

Although the people of Holy Spirit Parish are proud of their church building, it is evident to all that the real church is the People of God. Father Sikorski's leadership was followed by that of Fathers Richard Lawie, Anthony Vainavicz, David LeBlanc, and Leonard Sudlik. Family registrations have risen to more than 1,500 families.

All who come to this place are invited to live the parish Mission Statement: "The Parish of the Holy Spirit is a Christ-centered community that is challenged by the Spirit to live and spread God's Word through ministry and outreach."

Immaculate Heart of Mary
Grand Rapids

THE END OF WORLD WAR II brought large numbers of veterans back home to Grand Rapids who soon married, began families, and built new homes. The southeast side of the city quickly grew, and a new Catholic parish was needed to serve the area's spiritual needs. The Bishop of Grand Rapids, the Most Reverend Francis J. Haas, contacted the Oblates of Mary Immaculate in Massachusetts to ask if their order would staff the new parish. The Oblates readily agreed and sent Father Charles Killgoar, O.M.I., to begin the task of building Immaculate Heart of Mary Parish.

Father Killgoar's energy and enthusiasm were contagious, and on April 3, 1949, a core of 120 families celebrated the first Mass in their new church. Ingenuity overcame limited financial resources with a rented trailer becoming a temporary rectory. Used pews were purchased to seat 300 and an organ was borrowed from O'Brien's Mortuary every weekend. Parishioners set to work in a fervor of parish socials and fund-raisers to build a school and

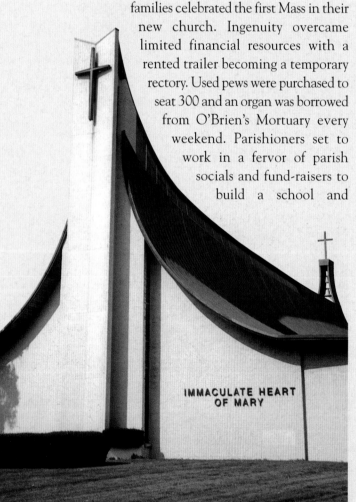

convent. The Dominican Sisters staffed the school, which opened in the fall of 1952 with 82 pupils. The cinder block church was brick-veneered and underwent redecorating and renovations as the parish continued to grow.

In 1966 a new, permanent church was opened which today serves over 1,300 families. A parish center, including a gymnasium, was built in 1981 and the school was expanded and remodeled in 1992. Yet the heart of Immaculate Heart of Mary Parish has never been its buildings, but its people. Countless parishioners are active in Christian service, which includes spiritual assistance within the parish, school support, and social endeavors that weave them into a vibrant community. They truly live out their Mission Statement: "...striving to be a Catholic community alive in our faith, our worship, and our service to others." Father Julian Reginato is the first diocesan priest to pastor the parish.

Our Lady of Aglona
Grand Rapids

I MMIGRANTS OF LATVIAN origin settled in the Grand Rapids area around 1949. One of the first Latvian Catholics to settle here was Vladislaus Gorsvans. On his initiative, a group of Latvian Catholics gathered in the chapel of the Cathedral of St. Andrew for a Mass celebrated by a visiting Latvian priest, Father Peter Bojars, from Chicago. Our Lady of Aglona was established in March 1951 with the arrival of Father Stanislaus Matiss, who came from Germany.

Bishop Joseph Rancans, a native Latvian bishop and a political refugee, arrived in Grand Rapids in 1951 at the invitation of Bishop Francis J. Haas. With the encouragement of such a native leader, the group of Latvian immigrants purchased a small church of their own in September 1954. When a highway project caused that church to be razed, another church (the present place of worship) on the corner of Broadway Avenue and First Street in Grand Rapids was purchased.

On December 2, 1969, Bishop Rancans died. The Latvian community suffered a great loss

because he had done so much to keep the small group of 90 to 100 people together. Because the group was so small, a full-time priest was not available after the death of Father Matiss in 1981. The Latvian community has had the services of retired priests: Fathers Eduard Statkus, Edwin Plewka, Edward Kubiak, and, presently, Eugene Golas.

In recent years, Dr. Zigfrids Zadvinskis, a retired Grand Rapids physician and chairman of the American Latvian Catholic Association, was able to assist in the project that made it possible to exhume the body of Bishop Joseph Rancans so that it could be laid to rest on Latvian soil as he had requested. The Latvians from the Grand Rapids area, with government assistance, raised funds to help pay for the exhumation, transfer, and reburial.

The faith and culture of the Latvian community is kept vibrant as they gather for the weekly liturgy and several annual social events.

Church razed by highway project. Demolition permit issued June 8, 1961

Our Lady of Sorrows
Grand Rapids

ITALIAN IMMIGRANTS began arriving in Grand Rapids as early as the 1880s. By the turn of the century, the diocese began to plan for an Italian parish in the city. In 1908 Father, later Msgr. Salvatore Cianci, was recruited from Rome to come to Grand Rapids and lead the Italian community. Father Cianci said the first Mass for the Italian congregation on September 20, 1908, in the basement of St. Andrew's Cathedral.

The congregation worshipped at St. Andrew's until a temporary church and school building was built in 1921 at the current location on the corner of Hall Street and Sheldon Avenue. The school opened in 1922 under the direction of the Dominican Sisters.

After many years of service to the Italian community, Msgr. Cianci died in 1953. Msgr. Joseph Shaw served as the parish administrator for the next two years. In 1954 the Dominican Sisters at the school were replaced by the Consolata Missionary Sisters from Italy. In 1955 the Consolata Fathers took over the duties of parish priest. The first Consolata pastor, Father Efrem Davanzo, oversaw the construction of a new church in 1957 and a new rectory in 1958.

As population patterns changed, the parochial school was closed in 1970. The Consolata Fathers left the parish in 1988, replaced by diocesan priests, with Father Theodore J. Kozlowski as the current pastor.

Our Lady of Sorrows has always incorporated Italian customs into its worship. For many years, from the 1920s to the 1960s, large processions were held through the streets of the "Little Italy" neighborhood. Italian language Masses were offered as late as 1988.

Procession through neighborhood streets in 1950s.

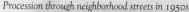

Salvatore C. Lucchese

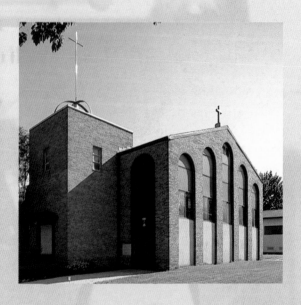

Sacred Heart of Jesus
Grand Rapids

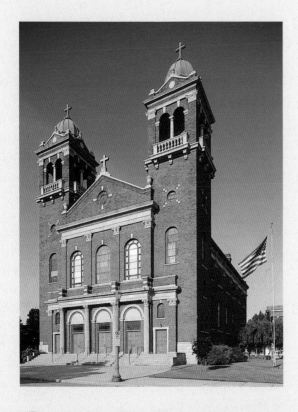

Sacred Heart of Jesus Parish owes its origins to the settlement of Polish immigrants in the southwest part of Grand Rapids in the late 1800s, many of whom worked in the local gypsum mines. It was the third such Polish-speaking community of faith in the city. The founding parish priest, Father Ladislaus Krakowski, and his fledgling community were a courageous and creative lot.

A sign of life and vitality in any parish is the sacrament of baptism. The first baptisms took place in June 1904. But it was on Thanksgiving Day in 1904 when Bishop Henry Joseph Richter presided over the dedication of the school, convent and church complex on Valley Avenue. Shortly thereafter, the School Sisters of Notre Dame of Milwaukee arrived to staff the school, which opened in January 1905 with seven grades. The priest's house was completed in February 1906, and a new expanded convent was opened in December 1908. Because of the growth and development on that side of the city, "running out of room" was the order of the day. The school had

to be expanded in 1918. By 1921 there were 650 children enrolled in the school. With 800 children in 1925, an addition was made to the school again, with a "bungalow" structure which would serve until the late 1950s.

In 1920 a new church building was started. The first Mass was celebrated in the basement in January 1921, and on Christmas Eve 1923 the first Mass was celebrated on the main floor of the structure.

Despite the Depression, which began in 1929, the parish grew. Great sacrifices were undertaken to pay off the new church building, built in the style of the Major Basilica of St. Paul-outside-the-Walls in Rome. No new construction was undertaken until the "bungalow school" was replaced by a two-story brick and glass building in 1959. The old school building on Valley Avenue was turned into a gymnasium that same year. All of this brick-and-mortar growth was made possible by the efforts and financial sacrifices of the parish populace.

As years have gone by, the complexion of the parish has changed. The older generations have yielded their leadership to the new ones, who know more of the New World than the Old. Under the pastoral leadership of Father Edward A. Hankiewicz, the parish today is a diverse community of faith and culture unified around a traditional approach to liturgy and social practice. The commitment to gospel values – and the expression of the same – is as vibrant as when the parish first started.

St. Alphonsus
Grand Rapids

S T. ALPHONSUS PARISH was founded in 1888 to serve Catholics in the northeast portion of Grand Rapids. Prior to 1888 this area had been part of St. Andrew's Parish. The parish and neighboring St. John's Home were established with a bequest to the diocese from John Clancy. Bishop Henry Joseph Richter invited the Redemptorist Fathers to administer the parish, and they continue to lead St. Alphonsus Parish to this day.

Masses were said in the orphanage and Finn's Hall until a combination church and school building was completed in 1889. Mass was celebrated on the second floor of this building until 1909. The school opened on September 2, 1889, with the Dominican Sisters in charge.

With the congregation and school both outgrowing their respective locations, plans for a new church were developed in 1905. The new church (the same one that is currently in use) was consecrated on December 22, 1909. An addition to the school was built in 1914.

As the parish grew, the church was improved and remodeled and another addition was made to the school in 1957. The 1889 and 1914 portions of the school were replaced with a modern school structure in 1964. At that time St. Alphonsus had the largest enrollment of any parochial school in the diocese. Major renovations and repairs were made to the church in 1978.

St. Alphonsus is particularly proud of its many young men and women who have been ordained to the priesthood or entered religious life. St. Alphonsus has also had very active organizations for its parish men and women. The parish has been involved in many outreach projects, lately transforming its convent into low-cost housing and operating a clinic out of the church basement. Father Thomas Donaldson CSsR is pastor.

St. Anthony of Padua
Grand Rapids

IN 1906 Bishop Henry Joseph Richter granted permission to establish a new church in Grand Rapids to minister to the predominantly German families who lived about two miles away from St. Mary's or St. James. Construction began in August of 1906 on Richmond Street N.W. Four months later the church-school was opened. On opening day over 200 children were enrolled at the school. Mass was held in the auditorium for the 164 registered families.

In 1909 the Conventual Franciscan Friars accepted the responsibility of shepherding the parish that had been pastored by diocesan priests for the first two years. In 1914 construction began on a new church to accommodate the growing community. The basement was the first phase of the project. World War I was going on and funds were lacking, so the project did not advance past the first phase. The parish celebrated religious services in the basement for 43 years.

In 1956 Bishop Allen J. Babcock changed the boundaries of St. Anthony of Padua Parish and, in January of 1957, more acres were purchased at 2510 Richmond N.W. In subsequent years, eight more acres were acquired. Building began in August of 1958 for a gymnasium and parish hall.

In October of 1959 the first Mass was celebrated in the new gym-church. In September 1962 the transition was completed with the opening of the newly constructed school. By 1966, the old buildings at Richmond and Broadway had been sold.

For 34 years, the people of St. Anthony celebrated Mass in the gym-church. In June 1993 construction of the new church and administration building began. (Until then the administrative offices had been in the Friary.) The first Mass was offered in the new church on April 10, 1994. The building project was to be completed in phases. On June 26, 1994, the Most Reverend Robert J. Rose, Bishop of Grand Rapids, dedicated and blessed the new church. Spiritual growth is flourishing in the parish of 1200 registered families, which has grown from 800 families over the last six years. Father Edmund Goldbach OFM Conv. is pastor.

St. Anthony of Padua Parish continues to grow with the expansion of its education center and a schoolyard nature area.

St. Francis Xavier
Grand Rapids

THE SITE for St. Francis Xavier Parish was purchased in 1906 by Father John Schmitt, rector of St. Andrew's Cathedral. On September 7, 1914, Bishop Henry Joseph Richter blessed the combination church-school building which had been constructed on the site, and St. Francis Xavier Parish began. The parish was served by priests from the Cathedral until Father Thomas Reid was appointed the first resident pastor in 1917. The Sisters of Mercy taught in the school.

Father John McAllister became pastor in 1923. He began the parish bulletin, "Folks and Facts," and he described St. Francis as "the parish with a soul." A gymnasium was constructed in 1929, a school addition in 1938, and a convent in 1941.

Succeeding pastors were Father, later Msgr., John McNeil in 1943, Msgr. Robert Bogg in 1950, and Father, later Msgr. Francis Schultz in 1953. During this time, major portions of the parish were separated from St. Francis to become the daughter parishes of St. John Vianney and Immaculate Heart of Mary.

Msgr. Schultz directed the construction of the current church, completed in 1960. When this new church was completed, St. Francis Xavier was one of the largest parishes in the diocese. Msgr. Schultz also thought this church could someday become a new cathedral for the diocese. Additions and renovations were also made to the school in 1956 and 1963.

Since the retirement of Msgr. Schultz, succeeding pastors were Fathers Casimir Zawacki (1969-1970), John Najdowski (1970-1977), David LeBlanc (1977-1980), John Wisneski (1980-1987), Charles Antekeier (1987-2000), and José Quintana (2000-present). A perpetual adoration chapel was established in 1993.

St. Isidore
Grand Rapids

IN 1891 the concentration of Polish workers' families in the northeast section of Grand Rapids led a group of men, under the direction of Father Ponganis of St. Adalbert's, to raise $1,000 to buy land for a church on the corner of Diamond Avenue and Flat Street. Six years later, in 1897, Bishop Henry Joseph Richter blessed the cornerstone.

Records show that the parish was first referred to as St. Stanislaus, but in 1900 the bishop declared it to be St. Isidore's. Thus both saints are depicted in stained glass windows above the main altar.

By 1910, with over 450 families, the parish needed a new church. Five days before the blessing of the cornerstone, Father Matkowski, who had been the spiritual and physical force in this new parish for 13 years, died. In 1913 the first Mass was celebrated in the basement of the new church. When the upper portion was completed, Bishop Michael J. Gallagher consecrated the church on March 22, 1917. During the 40-year pastorate of Father Joseph S. Pietrasik, the parish grew spiritually and financially. Before his death in 1952, Father Pietrasik was instrumental in fostering the vocations of over 30 priests and 100 nuns.

Under the direction of Father Theodore Liebek, a much-needed convent was constructed in 1955 and a new rectory in 1957. St. Isidore's School, built in 1926 and recently renovated, houses preschool, kindergarten, and first through eighth grades.

The Pope John Paul II Eucharistic Adoration Chapel, housed in the school since August 15, 1994, provides around-the-clock adoration of the Blessed Sacrament for the faithful.

Under the spiritual leadership of Father Donald E. Lomasiewicz since 1987, St. Isidore's celebrated its Centennial Jubilee in 1997 with the publication of *The Grand Rapids St. Isidore's Story*, written by the late Dr. Eduard Adam Skendzel.

Although St. Mary's Parish was founded on the west side of Grand Rapids in 1855, the Irish Catholics of the West Side did not feel comfortable in that German parish. These English-speaking Irish Catholics became the founders of St. James Parish. The first ministry to the Irish Catholics was a mission of St. Andrew's Parish called the "Eddington Church." Father B. J. Wermers of St. Andrew's purchased the land for St. James on Bridge Street in 1867. His successor at St. Andrew's, Father James Pulcher, organized the parish in 1868, and plans were begun for a church in 1869.

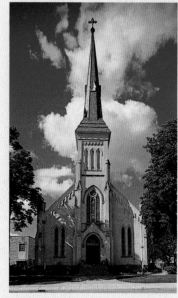

St. James Church, the building currently in use, was dedicated on July 21, 1872, and Father Pulcher became the parish's first pastor. A school was opened on September 1, 1886, with the School Sisters of Notre Dame in charge. Fathers Gustave Limpens and Robert Brown succeeded Father Pulcher as pastor.

A new school was built in 1922 during the pastorate of Msgr. Edward A. Lefebvre at a cost of $180,000. The Depression soon hit the parish and this debt became unmanageable. The next pastor, Father T. Raymond Dark, was able to restructure and reduce the debt. It was retired by his successor, Msgr. Raymond Baker, in 1944.

The church has been renovated over the years to meet contemporary liturgical requirements. The parish has worked to adapt to changes in its neighborhood. It has also focused on community outreach, founding the West Side, now City-Wide, Food Drive among other activities. Father Steven D. Cron is pastor.

St. Joseph the Worker
Grand Rapids

ST. JOSEPH THE WORKER PARISH was established in 1887. This was the fifth Roman Catholic church in Grand Rapids.

Father Henry Frencken presided over the church from 1887 through 1906. He was brought from Belgium to run the only Dutch-language church in the nation. Father Frencken was known as "the beggar" because he was always trying to get money for the parish. The church was a one-story, brick building, 74 x 42 feet with a foundation 18 feet deep. It took several years to build because the parishioners were the builders. Here is a chronology of the parish:

1889 School built and run by the Sisters of Mercy.
1891 Quarters built for the priest.
1903 Convent built.
1928 Priest appointed by diocese to reflect ethnic group.
1930 First baptism. Children were of Dutch, German, Irish, and Polish descent.
1938 First graduating class administered by Father Edward Alt.

1940 Italians joined the church.
1943 Church burned. For nine years church was held in the fellowship hall.
1948 First Hispanic baptism.
1950 First Hispanic wedding.
1952 Church rebuilt with materials salvaged from the fire.
1970 School closed because of low enrollment.
1988 Fire in the sanctuary.

St. Joseph the Worker Parish has been the only predominantly Hispanic parish in the diocese. Since 1994 the church has seen enormous growth. Membership has increased from 75 registered members to over 400. Liturgy services have also increased from two to four services a weekend, with the Sunday 10:00 a.m. Mass full to overflowing. In contrast to these positives, the church continues to struggle financially.

The goal of the future is to build a new church and provide continuous religious services for the Hispanic community. Father Pedro V. García is pastor.

St. Jude
Grand Rapids

ST. JUDE'S PARISH began in 1946 with a few people celebrating Mass in the chapel of the Michigan Veterans' Facility. Within a year, the faith community numbered over 100 families and moved to a section of land just off Plainfield Avenue where two Quonset huts served as a church and social hall.

In 1952 an ambitious young priest was assigned to the fast-growing parish. Father Charles Brophy's insight and innovation were to play a key role in the spiritual and physical development of St. Jude's. Within three years, the pastor had secured a pristine 36-acre parcel of land as a permanent setting for the now 238-family parish. A family center where Masses could be held was built, and a school and convent were added, but all the fundraising and anticipation centered on promises of a magnificent new church.

The liturgical movement in the early 1960s indicated widespread changes ahead for the Catholic Church. Centuries-old traditions were giving way to new concepts such as celebrating Mass in English rather than in Latin. Father

Brophy decided that the new structure would be a prototype of this modern process. He reasoned: "...Architecture is intended to establish living bonds between the conditions of contemporary man and his faith...."

St. Jude's Church was completed in 1964. Its design made viable an approach to worship that would be reinforced two years later in the decisions of Vatican Council II. The altar faced the congregation, a radical concept at the time.

In June of 2000, after 10 years of study, planning, and fundraising, the parish broke ground for an addition to the church and school consisting of five classrooms, a family center, and a new reception area-office complex.

In the year 2001 the parish, under the leadership of Father Thomas S. Vesbit, consists of 1,500 families who are proud of their past and hopeful for their future with their strong commitment to spirituality, hospitality, and stewardship.

St. Mary
Grand Rapids

The interior of the church is dominated by 27 magnificent stained glass windows depicting the life of the Blessed Virgin Mary, along with the life of Jesus. The windows surrounding the sanctuary portray biblical stories.

The parish established a school, and in 1891 property was secured and a school building was erected. A rectory and later a convent were also constructed. The school closed in 1990 and the building was razed in 2000.

The present parish family is ongoing, loving, nurturing, and welcoming. While St. Mary's is no longer the small German parish on the West Side, it continues to be a stable, influential presence in its neighborhood, in the city of Grand Rapids, and in the diocese. Although the parish no longer has a school, it continues to grow and at present has 660 families in its membership, with Father Dick Host as pastor. St. Mary's Parish is a member of the Steepletown Ministry and shares religious and social activities with the parishes of St. James and St. Adalbert.

THE ROOTS OF ST. MARY'S PARISH date back to the establishment of a Catholic community on the west bank of the Grand River in 1833 by Father Frederic Baraga. This mission was later moved across the river to become St. Andrew's Parish.

About the year 1855, German Catholics sought a parish of their own on Grand Rapids' West Side. With the help of Father M. M. Marco, the first church was opened in 1857 in a modest structure. In 1873 Father Ehrenstrasser, then pastor, oversaw the design and construction of the Gothic-style church that now dominates the West Side skyline. Its tower was completed in 1884 and is over 200 feet high. The four beautiful bells in the tower were purchased in December of 1877. The largest, called "St. Simon," weighs 3,741 pounds.

St. Paul the Apostle
Grand Rapids

THE STORY of St. Paul the Apostle Parish begins in 1962 when Msgr. Bryant, the pastor of St. Stephen's Parish, authorized the building of an annex on Burton Street on land purchased from the Ridgemoor Golf Course. The facility included a chapel, a hall, and four classrooms. St. Stephen's Annex was under the supervision of Father William McKnight, then associate pastor at St. Stephen's. A school also opened in 1962. Sisters Gregory Ann and Marie Bernadette administered and taught while residing at St. Stephen's convent.

During these early years, priests from Aquinas College (particularly Spanish professor Father Valentin Rodriguez) and Marywood assisted with Sunday liturgies and sacraments.

On June 18, 1965, in recognition of the growing population in the Burton and Breton areas, the quasi-parish was officially renamed St. Paul the Apostle and given the full status of parish. Msgr. William Powers, a retired military chaplain, was appointed pastor. A white house on the parish's western property border was purchased to house the parish office. A house at the corner of Burton and Woodlawn was purchased with help from Peter Wege. That house was used as the pastor's residence for 15 years.

After Msgr. Powers retired in 1969, Father Denis Nash was able to repay the debt owed St. Stephen's Parish and the diocese.

Father Ernest Bernott came to St. Paul's in 1972. The school enrolled 99 students at this time. With a dedicated school board, Father Bernott approved the addition of a junior high program and enrollment doubled in just four years.

In 1979, after several years of service at St. Robert of Newminster Parish, Father John McGee began eight years of ministry at St. Paul's. During Father McGee's tenure, the rectory and the old parish center (now school library and preschool-Sunday nursery) were constructed.

In 1987 Msgr. John Giammona, former military chaplain in Vietnam and chancellor of the diocese, accepted the pastorate of St. Paul's. During his years, the parish continued to see new housing developments begin in this area. A new church was needed to replace the original chapel. On October 20, 1991, Bishop Robert J. Rose dedicated the present church and renovated areas.

Father Louis Stasker, a former Sulpician seminary rector and pastor in Muskegon, came to St. Paul the Apostle as its sixth pastor in 1994. During the last few years the parish has grown to 950 families. Parish needs and programs have also grown. In the spring of 1997, the parish expanded the parish offices and meeting spaces and added a free standing food pantry. Father Stasker was succeeded in 2000 by Msgr. Ernest Schneider.

What began as an "annex" has developed into an important presence in southeast Grand Rapids.

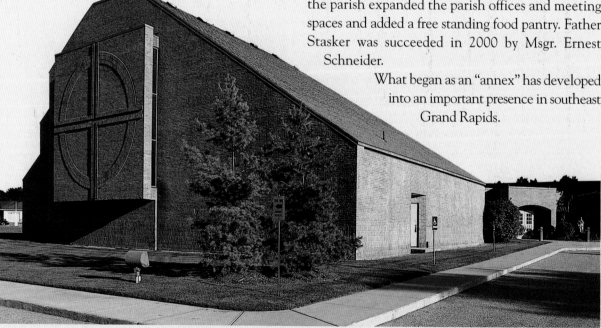

SS. Peter and Paul
Grand Rapids

LOUIS GALINIS AND ANTHONY CHIPLIS were the first Lithuanian Catholics to arrive in Grand Rapids, about 1885. As more and more Lithuanians came to the city and settled on the northwest side, Bishop Henry Joseph Richter decided that a national parish should be established.

On August 1, 1902, a church committee was formed. The committee purchased eight lots on the northeast corner of Myrtle Street and Quarry Avenue N.W. In December 1904 Father Wenceslaus V. Matulaitis was appointed first pastor of the new parish. Between 1906 and 1912, the parish grew from 70 to 500 families, reflecting the patterns of immigration to the city.

The parish school opened on September 14, 1907, with an enrollment of 86 pupils. By 1912 there were 300. The Grand Rapids Dominican Sisters staffed the school until 1928, when they were followed by the Sisters of St. Francis of the Providence of God of Pittsburgh, Pennsylvania, who were able to provide teachers of Lithuanian descent.

The parish bought 10 acres on Preston Avenue N.W. for a cemetery, which was consecrated on July 11, 1915. A new church was completed and dedicated by Bishop Edward D. Kelly on February 24, 1924. Father Joseph A. Lipkus was appointed pastor in 1925 and served in that capacity for 36 years. The present school was completed in September 1964.

Each July since 1941 the parish has sponsored the St. Anne's Novena, a devotion which attracts participants from around the diocese. Arrival of additional Lithuanian families after World War II briefly slowed but did not stop the inevitable "Americanization" of the parish. A significant portion of its aging and increasingly transient neighborhood fell to freeway construction in the early 1960s. SS. Peter and Paul today has a membership of both urban and suburban families who find it an ever-challenging but comfortable church home. Father Dennis W. Morrow is pastor

Frank Bieszka

The people of God with Bishop Rose on the 75th anniversary of the dedication of the church, February 24, 1999.

St. Thomas the Apostle
Grand Rapids

FOUNDED IN 1924 by 75 families under the leadership of Father Aloysius M. Fitzpatrick, St. Thomas the Apostle Parish today is a Catholic faith community of 900 families. Located on the east side of Grand Rapids just off Fulton Street and bordering Aquinas College, the parish complex has grown from the original church-school building to encompass a beautiful Romanesque church, school, gymnasium, rectory, and newly constructed ministry center. Originally staffed by Dominican Sisters with an enrollment of 63, the school today serves some 300 students with a talented lay faculty in greatly expanded facilities and programs.

Lay Catholic leadership and activity has been a hallmark of St. Thomas Parish throughout the course of its 75-year history. During the Second World War, the parish was recognized for support of its servicemen and women through a youth publication named "The Prop Wash". Also noteworthy in later years were theatrical productions by parishioners. The parish has administered a refugee resettlement program and has donated land for the Mercy Respite Center. More recently, St. Thomas has become notable for its extensive lay ministry and leadership formation, Christian service outreach activities, and worship planning and experience.

Framing the life of the parish is its mission statement: "The people of St. Thomas the Apostle Catholic Church are centered in Jesus Christ and guided by the Holy Spirit. We are committed to providing a spiritual home for God's family and to nurture one another through the Sacraments and our shared faith."

Succeeding Father Fitzpatrick in guiding the parish were Father Robert W. Bogg, Father Joseph F. Drew, Msgr. Raymond J. Sweeney, Father Frederick J. Voss, Msgr. Walter F. Jude, Father James C. Cusack, and Father Donald J. Heydens. Father James A. Chelich is pastor at the present time.

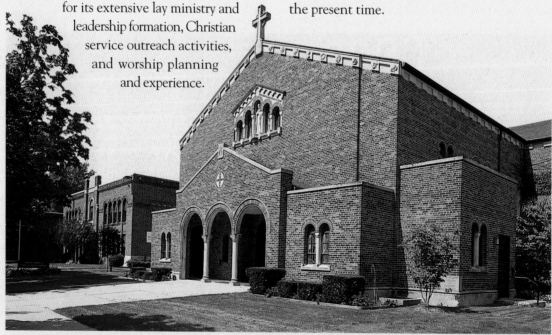

St. Pius X
Grandville

T HE FIRST MASS of the newly founded St. Pius X Parish was celebrated in the Grand Theatre in downtown Grandville on March 23, 1953, by Father John Hoogterp. On April 12, 1953, Bishop Francis J. Haas appointed Father John McDuffee to be the first pastor. Father McDuffee served until 1959. Succeeding pastors have been Msgr. Walter Grill (1959-1968), Father John McGee (1968-1973), Father Edmund Farrell (1973-1979), Msgr. Herman Zerfas (1979-1980), Father Michael Danner (1980-1989), Msgr. John Najdowski (1989-1998), and Father George Darling (1998-present).

Groundbreaking for the original church took place in January 1956. An elementary school was built and opened in 1961 with 105 students in grades four through seven. A religious education program was developed and continued to operate after the school closed in 1969.

In 1975 Holy Redeemer Parish was established in Jenison as an outgrowth of St. Pius X Parish.

Groundbreaking for an addition connecting the original church and school building and incorporating new worship space took place on August 23, 1987. Within the next five to seven years, the old church space was converted to house the parish offices (which had been in the rectory), meeting rooms, and a media library.

Father Danner leads groundbreaking.

Plans are currently underway for a year-long celebration of the parish's 50th anniversary in 2003.

Our Lady of Guadalupe
Grant

L A CAPILLA DE NUESTRA SENORA de Guadalupe (the Chapel of Our Lady of Guadalupe) was built and dedicated in 1948 to serve the spiritual needs of Hispanic migrant farm workers and their families in the area. A kitchen and shelter were added in the 1990s.

The chapel is a daughter parish to St. Bartholomew's Parish in Newaygo, and the two parishes share a pastor. The current pastor is Father Loc Trinh.

St. Charles
Greenville

IN 1859 Father Henry Rievers of Parnell celebrated the first Mass in Greenville in the home of one of the five Catholic families then living there. In 1875 a small frame building was purchased and remodeled into a church dedicated to St. Charles Borromeo by the priest in charge, Father Charles G. Bolte of Ionia. In January 1914 Father Charles F. Bolte arrived as the first resident pastor of the parish of some 33 families. In 1934 a mission-style church was built.

In September 1994 the church, expanded in 1976, was struck by lightning and burned to the ground. The parishioners spent two and a half years planning and building the current church, which was dedicated by Bishop Robert J. Rose. From the ashes of the fire, the parish experienced a resurrection of new vitality and energy, which led them to strategic planning beginning in the fall of 1998.

A school, established in the 1920s, closed soon thereafter. In 1947 the current school opened and today has an enrollment of approximately 125 students in grades K-8. Religious education offers programs for graders Pre-K through 8, with a very active high school youth ministry.

Approximately 40 different groups are active in ministries of education, service, and worship. In addition to the usual parish activities, St. Charles boasts a very active Knights of Columbus Council, a solid contingent of Cursillistas, weekly day-long adoration of the Blessed Sacrament, group spiritual direction, Morning Prayer from the Liturgy of the Hours, involvement in an ecumenical food pantry, and a strong stewardship program of time, talent, and treasure.

St. Charles Parish, with its pastor Father G. Fredrick Brucker, currently has about 660 families, with many summer visitors from the surrounding lakes.

St. Gregory
Hart

ST. GREGORY'S PARISH in Hart began as a mission of St. Joseph in Weare in 1908. Father Francis Emmerich of Weare recognized the need for a Catholic church in the small, growing village of Hart. Five lots were donated to the church, and on September 9, 1908, Bishop Henry Joseph Richter blessed the cornerstone of St. Gregory's Church. Exactly one year later, the bishop returned to dedicate the completed church. At that time, the congregation numbered 30 families.

St. Gregory's was a mission of Weare until 1936, with Mass being said in Hart twice a month on Sundays. In 1936 Father Edward O'Hara was appointed the first resident pastor of St. Gregory's, and the mission became a parish. At that time, St. Joseph, Elbridge, was assigned as a mission of Hart. The new parish soon acquired a rectory and a parish cemetery.

Under the leadership of Father Charles Popell, St. Gregory's School opened in 1950. The school was taught by Dominican Sisters from Grand Rapids until it closed in 1968. The building was converted into a parish center in 1975.

By 1981 St. Gregory's Church was in need of major renovation and repair, and a decision was made to build a new church. The new church was built during the pastorate of Father Thomas McKinney and was completed in 1985.

In 1950 St. Gregory's became the mother parish of a new congregation, Our Lady of Fatima in Shelby. In 1954 St. Gregory's became one of the first centers for ministry to migrant workers. A Spanish-speaking priest from Mexico said Mass and ministered to the area migrant workers and their families. In 1994 the parish renewed its role in Hispanic ministry, led by the pastor, Father Ronald Schneider, and Sister Guadalupe Moreno.

St. Margaret
Harvard

ESTABLISHED IN 1893, St. Margaret of Scotland Church and Cemetery were blessed on October 4, 1894, by Bishop Henry Joseph Richter. At the time, there were 33 families. During succeeding years, St. Margaret has been a mission of Big Rapids, Carson City, Maple Valley, Sand Lake, and currently Greenville. At different times, St. Margaret had Mass once a month or more often, sometimes on Sundays, sometimes on a weekday, depending on weather and travel conditions. Currently, Mass is celebrated at 5:00 p.m. every Saturday and on the eve of holy days. Stations of the Cross are held during Lent, and the rosary is recited in October and May.

The church building remained essentially the same until the summer of 1990, when an 800-square-foot expansion, to accommodate 55 additional seats and a cry room, was added to the side of the church. A new parish hall, including three restrooms, a first for St. Margaret, was added to the north side of the church. The new addition was dedicated on November 24, 1990, by Bishop Robert J. Rose, a frequent visitor to St. Margaret's while he was a teacher at St. Joseph Seminary in Grand Rapids (1956-1971).

Native son Father John Otterbacher was ordained for Glenmary on February 28, 1953. Now retired, he occasionally visits.

St. Margaret's Mission currently has 68 families, with a surge of summer visitors from the surrounding lakes. In the summer, there are frequent bake sales and a parish picnic. In the winter, there are a Christmas party, a Lenten "Soup Supper," and other gatherings. The education commission recently began a home-based religious education program for parishioners.

Friendly St. Margaret's Mission Parish is probably one of the best-kept secrets of northern Kent County.

Christ the King
Hesperia

CHRIST THE KING PARISH in Hesperia traces its beginnings to St. Leo's Church in Volney, Newaygo County. There, following World War II, local Catholic families sought to establish a church in Hesperia. Father Edward Kubiak, administrator of the Brunswick, Fremont, and Hesperia congregations, presented a proposal to the diocese. In April 1947 Bishop Francis J. Haas approved the request for construction of a church as a mission of St. Michael, Brunswick.

The land was donated by Edward LeFevre and a committee was formed, including Edward and Neil LeFevre, Louis Biegalle, Orval Hyatt, Clement Kraus, Rudolph Messner, Rudolph Murn, Martin Nolan, Leo Osborne, Henry Senecal, Gerald and Vern Wilcox, and Carlo Yob. In August 1947 the cornerstone was blessed by Msgr. Daniel Hyland. The Altar Society was inaugurated the same year.

On August 24, 1948, Father Edward Kubiak celebrated the first Mass in the new church. Later, Msgr. Robert Bogg,

Alfreda Lesnikowski, 104 years old, with her daughter, Vervaleria Poholski.

chancellor of the diocese, officially dedicated Christ the King at a Labor Day Mass.

On September 6, 1956, construction of a grade school was completed at St. Michael, Brunswick and blessed by Msgr. Gerard Guzikowski. In August 1957 a portion of the West Hesperia Cemetery was obtained for members of Christ the King.

The church was modernized and expanded in 1973 under the guidance of Father John Giammona. In 1983, with the leadership of Father William Reitz, a parish council was established. In 1986, during the pastorate of Father Joseph Malewitz, a social hall was completed, and in 1990, while Father Isidro Gargantiel was pastor, a bell tower was erected.

Father Donn Tufts, who came to the parish in 1993, has initiated a variety of new programs, including the Rite of Christian Initiation of Adults. Today Christ the King Parish numbers 150 families, among them a special member, 104-year-old Alfreda Lesnikowski.

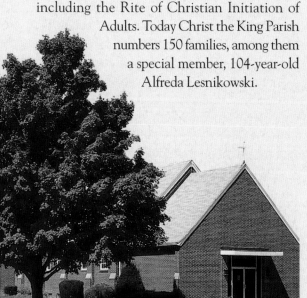

Our Lady of the Lake
Holland

SEEDS OF THE CATHOLIC CHURCH sown along the shore of Black Lake in the 1670s by missionary pioneer Father Jacques Marquette took root in the hearts of Odawa Indians there. Some 170 years later, Dutch immigrants arrived to find that many of the 300 Native American villagers were practicing Catholics, converted to Christianity through Father Marquette's work and preaching.

Bishop Rose anoints the new altar, assisted by Father William Duncan, pastor, October 1998.

Early Catholics established the first church, St. Francis de Sales, in 1903. Because those early seeds of Catholicism grew rapidly throughout the final century of the millennium, members of this vibrant faith community again crossed the waters of the Black River, as founders of a daughter parish on the north side of the river—Our Lady of the Lake. Now, at the dawn of the new millennium, some 1300 families gather there to celebrate their faith.

In April 1979 the formal establishment of a new Holland parish was announced by Bishop Joseph M. Breitenbeck. Our Lady of the Lake Church was dedicated in October 1982 with a procession of some 900 people from Waukazoo School, the temporary worship site, to the new church. Between 1982 and 1993 the parish grew from 245 to over 800 families.

Between March 1993 and August 1995, a Mission & Ministry 2000 Joint Pastoral Plan was developed in cooperation with St. Francis de Sales Parish to accommodate the growing needs of the Holland-Zeeland Catholic community. August 1998 saw the groundbreaking for a 50,000-square-foot Corpus Christi Center to serve as a school and center for faith formation for the two churches.

Meanwhile, in May 1997, a major expansion and renovation of the church was begun, under the leadership of Father William Duncan. It doubled the size of the sanctuary and included a Blessed Sacrament Chapel, a Daily Mass Chapel, and a Reconciliation Chapel. It enlarged and renovated the gathering space, offices, classrooms, nursery, and Father Nash Hall.

The renovated church was dedicated in October of 1998, and Corpus Christi Center opened in September of 1999.

St. Francis de Sales
Holland

THE CATHOLIC FAITH in the Holland area has nurtured countless and diverse men and women since the 1670s, when Father Jacques Marquette introduced Catholicism to the Odawa Indians camped along the lowlands of Lake Macatawa. These Native Americans remained in the area practicing the Catholic faith until shortly after the Dutch settlers arrived in 1847.

Initially the growth of Catholicism in the newly established Holland community was modest, with only six Catholic families by 1879. During the late 1800s and early 1900s, the Catholic population swelled with parishioners representing a variety of European ancestries, including people of Dutch, French, Scottish, Irish, Italian, and Polish descent.

Since the 1940s, the parish has been further enriched by the arrival of Hispanics settling in West Michigan for the same reasons as the early Europeans - an abundance of jobs in the area. With the Vietnam War and the fall of Saigon in 1975, the Vietnamese community of St. Francis has steadily grown and contributes another important dimension to the parish.

On December 12, 1995, a fire destroyed St. Francis de Sales Church. Over the following two years, the parish experienced the love of God through an ecumenical spirit as neighboring churches, representing numerous denominations, provided their own worship spaces for weekly Masses.

Early in their history, St. Francis parishioners recognized and embraced their multicultural history. This appreciation of diversity is best illustrated by the parish mission statement, which confirms: "We believe the various cultures within our community are gifts from God and rather than assimilate them we seek to be enriched by them." St. Francis de Sales treasures its diversity and considers it to be a reflection of the richness of the Creator. Father Stephen S. Dudek is pastor.

Christ the King
Howard City

FATHER RAYMOND BRUCK was the founding pastor of a Catholic church in Howard City in the 1970s. A nucleus of 19 people met to discuss the feasibility of starting a church. The first Mass was held in a Masonic Hall on July 25, 1970. Next, a Free Methodist church was purchased for $5,000. Later, St. Apollonia Church in Morley joined with Christ the King to build a new church and rectory. Membership soared.

Father Louis Anderson was pastor from 1979 to 1982. While here, he finished his doctorate degree. Groundbreaking for a new fellowship hall was begun. Father Phillip Witkowski was pastor from 1982 to 1990. He instituted renewal programs, a yearly family festival, fish fries during Lent, and youth retreats. A parking lot was paved and extended. A carillon was installed, and Our Lady's Grotto was built.

Father William Zink, pastor from 1990 to 1995, started a golf league and a ski club, named the "Holy Duffers" and the "Holy Kristies" respectively. He organized groups to work with Habitat for Humanity. A reception was held for his silver jubilee in 1993.

Father Phong Pham joined Christ the King from 1995 to 1999. A happy and dedicated priest who greatly increased our membership, Father Pham encouraged the people of Christ the King and the people of St. Francis de Sales, Lakeview, to work together. Youth programs were greatly enhanced, and the music programs flourished.

In 1999 Father Phillip Sliwinski became pastor, joining the parish with hopes and ideas for today's church. His work is just beginning.

Christ the King Parish's spirit is manifest in its mission statement, which reads: "The mission of the parish family of Christ the King is to be an instrument of God through the Holy Spirit in our speaking, acting, and sharing love and life with one another and our community."

St. John the Baptist
Hubbardston

FATHER GEORGE GODEZ visited Hubbardston from Westphalia as early as 1852. During his once-a-month appearances he would say Mass in the home of John Cowman. A church was built in 1853, and the congregation was known as St. John the Baptist at Fish Creek. A new, larger church (the one currently in use) was built in 1868 under the leadership of Father Charles G. Bolte of Corunna.

The first resident pastor, Father William DeBever, was appointed in 1869, and the first rectory was completed in 1871. A Catholic school was established in 1883 with lay teachers, and later that year Dominican Sisters from Racine, Wisconsin, arrived to teach in the school. The Racine Dominicans remained in Hubbardston for 90 years, the last one leaving

in 1973. As the years went by, the church saw the construction of a rectory in 1907, a school in 1916, and a convent in 1927.

Father Eugene Fox was appointed pastor in 1938 and remained pastor of Hubbardston until he retired from active ministry in 1985. He remained in residence in the parish until his death in 1992. The parish high school closed in 1963, and the grade school was closed in 1968. A CCD program was organized at that time.

Since the retirement of Father Fox, the parish has shared a pastor with St. Mary's Parish in Carson City. St. Mary's, Carson City, and St. Joseph's, Pewamo, are daughter parishes of Hubbardston, being formed from territory formerly included in the Hubbardston parish.

SS. Peter and Paul

Ionia

IN THE MID-1800S, Father George Godez came from Westphalia to offer Mass with a small Catholic community in Ionia. Later a priest came from Corunna. In about 1860, 15 families were worshipping at the home of Peter Hackett. They established a cemetery and then built a small frame church and a rectory on an acre of land donated by Peter Hackett. The church was known as St. Peter's. In 1863 Father Charles G. Bolte became the first resident pastor of the parish.

In 1871 the parish opened a grade school for about 60 students, with a convent upstairs for three Immaculate Heart of Mary Sisters. On January 1, 1882, the present church of SS. Peter and Paul was dedicated. The original church became the school. Then, in 1904, the present "Academy" was dedicated and high school grades were added. The transept wings were added to the church in 1916. A new rectory was completed in 1951, and a north wing was added to the school in 1961.

Today the school serves students from pre-K through grade 8. The 1951 rectory has been converted into a convent for Dominican Sisters and the pastor lives in a home in the neighborhood.

The story of these buildings reflects the story of the people's faith. Volumes of sacramental and funeral records offer a glimpse into their joys and sorrows on the way to the Kingdom. The journey goes on. Over these many years, the parish has grown to about 800 families and, like its Founder, has "progressed steadily in wisdom and age and grace." (Luke 2:52) The current pastor is Father Melvin E. Fox.

St. Bernard
Irons

Msgr. Walter Jude with his three sisters: Sister Helen, Sister Donata and Sister Emeliana

IN 1894 Irons was a station on the Chicago & Western Michigan (later Pere Marquette) Railroad. The town was founded about 1909. Because of the railroad stop, it was decided that Irons would be a good location for St. Bernard's Church.

Early parishioners in the area were predominantly of Lithuanian and Bohemian origin. Father Ignatius Kelmelis was the first priest, coming from Scottville.

In the early 1900s two lots and a small wooden hotel building, to be remodeled into a church, were purchased. The mission counted 21 families and Mass was celebrated about once a month.

In 1948 Father Benedict Marciulionis was appointed the first resident pastor. A little house was bought and used for a rectory, and a larger cinder block church was built. The original building was demolished.

Father Albert Bernott, the second pastor, built a new rectory in 1954. A third and larger church was built on the existing foundations under the direction of Father Joseph Reitz in 1963. The parish at that time joined the Manistee Catholic School system.

Vatican II brought more changes. Sanctuary and appointments were updated, the cement block church walls were bricked, and a steel bell tower was erected. A year-round, large Christmas shrine was built. Msgr. Walter Jude was pastor.

St. John Cantius, Free Soil, became a mission of St. Bernard's in 1999.

A Labor Day Festival has become a tradition at the parish and draws visitors from a large area each year. Father Thomas C. Niedzwiecki is pastor.

Holy Redeemer
Jenison

HOLY REDEEMER PARISH of Jenison had its beginnings on April 3, 1975, with the appointment of Father Norman Droski as its first pastor. Approximately nine acres of land had already been purchased as a building site, about which Father Droski writes: "I remember driving to the site of the future parish. I could not find it as I passed hayfield after hayfield in the township."

The new Holy Redeemer Parish celebrated its first Mass in the Jenison High School auditorium on April 20, 1975, and continued to worship there for three years until the initial part of the church was completed in 1978.

Father Thomas G. Simons became the second pastor in 1984. By this time, the parish had grown from the initial 310 families to 660 families. Soon plans were in the works to expand the parish facilities. The Phase II building addition, completed in 1987, added the Emmaus Chapel and classrooms, and enlarged the parish center.

Under Father Denis P. Nash, pastor from 1991 to 2000, Holy Redeemer Parish continued to grow and thrive. The parish now numbers some 850 families. The facilities have grown and changed too, with the enclosure of the entryway and the installation of beautiful stained glass windows. The Phase III building addition, recently completed, added classrooms, a gymnasium/family center, and a music rehearsal room. Father Richard J. Lawie is the current pastor.

St. Mary Magdalen
Kentwood

I N JUNE OF 1956, Bishop Allen J. Babcock took a young priest, Father John Breitenstein, out to a 17-acre field on 52nd Street in Paris Township (now Kentwood), to a tract located on the north side of the street halfway between Kalamazoo and Eastern Avenues. There he instructed the priest to found a new parish, St. Mary Magdalen. The first Mass was said in the Bowen Roll-arena, a skating rink at the corner of 52nd and Division, for 125 families.

A year later, in July of 1957, parishioners attended Mass in their own church, a V-shaped structure located on the east side of the property. It eventually came to serve as a church on weekends and a CCD facility for five Dominican Sisters from Media, Pennsylvania, who came to the parish in September 1962. Father Breitenstein's original intention had been to build a Catholic school, but when he failed to find sisters to staff the school, he signed a contract with these Dominican Sisters, specialists in teaching religion to public school children.

The present church, a semi-circular structure seating over 800 people, was completed in January 1965. An addition to the church, which included a combination school of religion and parish center, was dedicated on May 25, 1969. The building program was an indication

of the swift growth of the parish community, which by then had grown from the original 125 families to almost 900 families. At present the parish ministers to about 1,500 families. A major renovation of the church proper was completed in September 1985.

Father Breitenstein, who retired in April, 1971 because of ill health, was followed by Fathers William Reitz (1971-1977), John Giammona (1977-1982), James Kowalski (1982-1988), Michael McKenna (1988-1994), and the present pastor, Father Louis Anderson.

St. Edward
Lake Odessa

ON DECEMBER 8, 1945, Bishop Francis J. Haas assigned Father Donald Farrell the task of organizing a new parish in Lake Odessa. The parish would serve the Catholic population of Lake Odessa, Clarksville, Sunfield, Woodland, Woodbury, and Nashville (until 1972). The site for the first church and pastor's residence was the upstairs of the former A & P store. Father Farrell and 42 parishioners celebrated the first Mass at St. Edward's on December 30, 1945.

In the summer of 1947, a three-acre site was purchased on the corner of M-50 and Washington Boulevard. Construction of the church began on May 1, 1949, and on September 17, 1950, 200 parishioners gathered for the first Mass in the church. In January 1972, after numerous bingo games (played on the beach of Jordan Lake) and chicken dinners, the debt was paid. The burning of the mortgage was a cause of great excitement and joy for this small community. Three years later, the parish celebrated its 25th anniversary with an afternoon Mass followed by a dinner and dance at the community center (now the Odessa Township Offices).

By the spring of 1988, the church was remodeled to its present form. A new steeple and bell chimes were added to the church in the summer of 1996. In October 1997 ground was broken for a new parish family center, and on December 12 of the following year Bishop Robert J. Rose blessed and dedicated the facility. Since that time, the center has become the home for religious education classes, a latchkey program, the Altar Society's annual bazaar, funeral luncheons, wedding receptions, and a variety of parish functions. In the spring of 2000, the church basement was remodeled and made available for parish use. On September 17, 2000, the parish gathered to celebrate its 50th anniversary.

St. Edward's has grown from 42 people to nearly 400 each Sunday. Yet the mission of the parish remains the same: to celebrate our Catholic faith in Jesus Christ through sacraments, religious education, fellowship, and community outreach. St. Edward's strives to be the center of Catholicism in the Lakewood area.

St. Francis de Sales

Lakeview

LAKEVIEW is first named in the National Catholic Directory in 1892 as a mission of St. Clara's Church at Maple Valley, presently the mission parish known as Coral. During the early years, responsibility for the spiritual needs of Catholics in the Lakeview area was handled by priests from Big Rapids and Maple Valley.

In 1915 Lakeview Catholics were asked to pledge money to pay off the balance of a land contract. Nothing more was done until 1936, when Father Linus M. Schrems, pastor at Greenville, inquired of the chancery office about property in Lakeview that was owned by the diocese. It was not until 1945 that Father James H. Moloney, pastor at Sand Lake, received a loan of $5,000 to begin construction of a church at Lakeview. St. Andrew's Cathedral put up $2,000 and Grand Rapids' St. Isidore's Parish $3,000, with the money to be repaid in three years.

After the loans were repaid, two members of the parish asked Bishop Francis J. Haas for permission to build a church. He approved the request, and planning began for a church on the corner of Richardson and Fifth Streets. Fundraising also got underway in earnest, with bingo games and a food booth at School Section Lake.

At first Lakeview shared its priests with St. Mary's, Sand Lake, and St. Clara's, Coral. Priests from the seminary in Grand Rapids alternated with Father Jerome Winikaitis of Sand Lake. One of those priests was Father Robert J. Rose, later Bishop of Grand Rapids. Mass was held in the basement of the church for 15 years while the parish raised money to finish the structure. Finally, on Sunday, February 23, 1964, Father Winikaitis celebrated the first Mass in the newly completed church. Father Philip Sliwinski is the current pastor.

St. Mary of the Woods
Lakewood Club

IN 1915 a group of Chicago resorters in the Fox Lake-Lakewood Club area gathered to form a Catholic community of worship. The Lakewood resort development was a popular summer resort from 1915 to 1930. There was a real need for a church during the summer months.

In 1915 a prominent Catholic from Chicago was able to persuade Bishop Michael J. Gallagher to send a priest. A small typical country church holding 70 to 100 people was built in 1916 at a cost of $2,000. Priests mostly from Muskegon and Montague served the church during the summer months.

In 1941 the old church burned. Within a month, a new church was built by donations from Catholic, Protestant, and Jewish resorters.

For years, the Lakewood area was pretty much abandoned. Most of the old summer cottages deteriorated and the area became overgrown with trees. Recently, the population has increased, with new homes, better roads, and an improved park area being built.

Named a parish in 1963 with Father Walter Marek as administrator, St. Mary of the Woods received Father John LaGoe in 1970 as its first resident pastor. In 1971 a hall designed for meetings and religious education was built across the street from the church. The church was renovated in 1984, and the hall was enlarged in 1986 with the addition of offices and a kitchen. In 1988 a new rectory was built, mainly with the help and labor of the parishioners. The current pastor is Father Paul T. Johnson.

St. Mary of the Woods has grown from 50 families in 1963 to 140 registered families at present. For over 20 years a parish festival has been held in August. It is the prayer of St. Mary of the Woods Parish that its tradition of friendliness and welcome will be felt for many years to come.

St. Mary
Lowell

THE CITY OF LOWELL nestles in the Flat River Valley just southeast of Grand Rapids. Although the city was settled in the 1830s, Mass was celebrated in the homes of parishioners until the first church was built in 1879. Its construction was initiated by Father James Savage, pastor of St. Patrick's in Parnell. The church, located on the corner of Lincoln Lake Avenue and Chatham Street near downtown Lowell, cost $3,300 to build.

Father Savage dedicated the new church in June 1879 to the "service of almighty God and in honor of the ever-glorious and Immaculate Virgin Mary." The parish feast day, September 8, is the feast of the Birth of Mary.

St. Mary's Parish was a mission parish served by various area priests for 50 years until Father Robert Bogg was named as its first pastor in October 1927.

In the fall of 1953, after almost a decade of discussion and fundraising, St. Mary's School opened. The school served as an important focus of parish life for 40 years. Since the school's closing in 1995, the building on Amity Street has been used for parish functions.

In 1963 Father Marciulionis purchased property adjacent to the school for a new church. Father Thomas Schiller was assigned to St. Mary's in 1978 to oversee the construction of the church, which took two years. The church with its attached rectory, located next to the school, was dedicated on April 20, 1980.

Several items from the original church, such as a stained glass window, a crucifix, the Stations of the Cross, and the cornerstone, were incorporated into the new building. With Father George J. Fekete as pastor, the story of St. Mary Parish continues to be written today. Its members work, celebrate, and sometimes struggle together to nurture a vital Catholic presence in Lowell.

St. Simon
Ludington

THE EARLY SETTLERS in the Ludington area were primarily of French descent, but as the lumber industry grew, people of many nationalities arrived, with a heavy concentration of Scandinavian, German, and Irish settlers. There was a large number of Catholics among them, and their spiritual needs at first were administered by traveling priests who came by horseback from Muskegon.

In 1868 the Catholics in Pere Marquette Village, later renamed Ludington, were formed into St. Simon Parish, the name given it by the Right Reverend Caspar Henry Borgess, Bishop of Detroit.

On land donated by a lumber company owned by Protestants, the first Catholic church in Mason County, St. Simon's, was constructed in 1872.

The parish's first assigned pastor was Father Charles DeCeuninck, who came to St. Simon's

in 1876. The first church, made of lumber and shingles, was located on the north side of Foster Street, the site later occupied by the brick home of the parish janitor. That house still stands.

Father Robert Brown, who was pastor at St. Simon from 1889 to 1893, urged construction of a parish school, and in 1891 an eight-grade elementary school opened. A high school was begun in 1903 with the addition of a ninth grade. The first high school graduating class was in 1907.

As the parish grew, a larger church was needed, and in 1902 a brick church with twin steeples and bell towers was constructed at a cost of $20,000, much of the money being donated by two prominent St. Simon's families, the Danahers and the Cartiers. In 1913 the construction of a two-story elementary and high school building was completed.

In June 1957, a fire set by children playing with matches and dropping them through a basement window swept through the sanctuary and sacristies, causing considerable damage. The church was repaired and repainted and continued to serve the parish until 1969.

In 1967 a new pastor took over the duties at St. Simon's and immediately launched a fundraising campaign to build a church in an area closer to the population center. The first Mass was celebrated in the new church on Christmas Eve 1969. The current pastor is Father Kenneth Schichtel.

St. Stanislaus
Ludington

POLISH FAMILIES in Ludington purchased property on Fifth Street for a new parish in 1897. The Rosary Society was formed in 1899. Bishop Henry Joseph Richter appointed Father Joseph Pietrasik to build a combination church-school building in 1900. Area lumber and brickyards donated materials and parishioners donated labor. The building was constructed for a total cost of $365.

On May 9, 1901, Bishop Richter blessed the new St. Stanislaus Church. The first Mass was said on September 2, 1901, and the first baptism (of Theresa Sniegowski) and funeral (of Martha Janowiak) soon followed. The first seminarian from the parish was the future bishop of Marquette, Thomas Noa.

St. Stanislaus' rectory was built in 1907 and the school opened in 1909, operating until 1967. Our Lady of Fatima Grotto was built in 1947. A new church was completed on July 22, 1955, at a cost of $160,000.

St. Ignatius
Luther

IN 1891 the priests from Big Rapids began to visit Luther on a regular basis. In 1895 there were about 10 Catholic families in the area. In 1903 the mission was transferred to St. Philip Neri Parish in Reed City, and the priest visited from there once a month.

The congregation in Luther purchased the old brick town hall to use as a church in 1916. They named it St. Ignatius Church. At that time there were about 20 families in the mission. Luther remained a mission of Reed City for 45 years except for one year when it was attended from Free Soil. In 1948 the mission was transferred to St. Bernard's Parish, Irons.

Under the leadership of Father Albert Bernott, a new church was constructed and the first Mass was celebrated on Christmas Day 1952. The church, blessed on October 18, 1953, was built with much donated labor. It was valued at $40,000 but only cost $15,000 to build.

In 1972 St. Ignatius was temporarily closed and merged with St. Ann's Parish in Baldwin. Since 1973, St. Ignatius has been a mission of St. Ann's.

THE FIRST CATHOLIC CHURCH in Marion was probably built in 1888. Priests came from St. Ann's in Cadillac to minister at the mission in Marion. In 1895 Marion was one of eight missions being served from Cadillac.

Bishop Henry Joseph Richter dedicated St. Agnes Church on July 21, 1908. The church was named in honor of Agnes Kerwin, the daughter of W. W. Kerwin of Chicago, who donated much of the construction cost.

St. Agnes remained a mission of St. Ann's until 1950, when St. Stephen's in Lake City became a parish. St. Agnes was a mission of St. Stephen's until 1972. In 1972 Bishop Joseph M. Breitenbeck established St. Agnes as a parish. Father Melvin Fox became the first pastor. Succeeding pastors have been Fathers Delvin Tilmann, James Chelich, Rock Badgerow, and Joseph Fix.

In 1958, under the leadership of Father Edmund Farrell of Lake City, the Marion congregation built a new church. Many parishioners donated labor, materials, and financial help. John Vokes, Dr. Douglas Youngman, Anthony Hartlep, and Emil Badovinac were parish leaders during the construction. The first marriage in the new church took place November 22, 1958, between Tom Wilson and Sandra Case. The congregation doubled in size during Father Farrell's pastorate.

The church interior was renovated in 1983, and Bishop Breitenbeck consecrated the church the following year. The downstairs portion of the building was renovated in 1985. Folding wall dividers were installed for classrooms.

The parish is especially proud of one of its young men who became a priest, Father John LaGoe. The congregation currently numbers over 100 families. In addition to charitable activities, the parish enjoys potluck dinners, a yearly pancake breakfast, monthly get-togethers, card parties, and canoe trips.

Between 1830 and 1840 Irish settlers moved into the wilderness west of Grand Rapids. Their immediate needs were the sacraments, a church, and a priest. Father Viszoczky met their needs riding circuit from St. Andrew's. The area's first Mass was celebrated in Patrick Prendergast's cabin in 1845. The year 1852 saw the construction of a church in which a Belgian priest, Father Van Paemel, offered Mass.

At Easter 1872 Detroit Bishop Caspar Henry Borgess dedicated the second church, which stood until it burned in 1898. The current statue of Mary in the parish social center alone survived. Seven itinerant priests served at St. Mary's, including Father Thomas O'Connor.

Legend says Father O'Connor claimed that he set fire to the church because it was old and dilapidated. It is also reported that he ended the brawling of the Irish clans in the parish, dismissing the women one Sunday morning and locking the church on the men for a good dressing-down.

During construction of a new church under Father O'Connor, a furious wind pushed the east wall two inches out of plumb. It was left as it was. Photos as early as 1945 show reinforcing rods stretching across the nave supporting the walls and the windstorm story. During the night of August 10, 1979, another furious wind toppled the steeple, leading to the tearing down of the church. At its demolition it became obvious that the roof barely rested upon the east wall.

Father Timothy O'Connell was appointed first resident pastor in 1923, coming to the "new" and current rectory built in 1909–later substantially renovated in 1996.

The congregation of St. Mary's has grown from 41 families (40 Irish and one German) in 1898 to a polyglot 400 today. Over the years a parish center, an outdoor shrine, and an expanded cemetery have been added. In 1983, under Father Terrence Stewart, a new house for the people of God at Marne was dedicated by Bishop Joseph M. Breitenbeck.

St. Mary
Miriam

SURROUNDED by fertile farmland and the parish cemetery, St. Mary's Church in Miriam stands as a testament to the faith and perseverance of our early German settlers. Located at 9041 W. Krupp Road in Otisco Township, Ionia County, the church stands on land given to Bishop LeFevere of the Detroit Diocese in 1860 by John Albert and Peter Kemp. The present church was erected in 1871. Father Charles Bolte of Ionia directed the construction and served as pastor. In 1938 the church became part of the Grand Rapids Diocese. On May 29, 1971, the parish celebrated its centennial status with an outdoor concelebrated Mass and many other special events.

Today the congregation numbers 105 families. Mass is offered Sunday mornings at 9:30 and Wednesday evenings at 7:00. Monthly breakfasts, the ladies' Altar Rosary Society, and the men's Holy Name Society are some of the activities offered. As a parish family, the church hosts a country festival yearly during the second weekend of September. The parish's famous "barbecued chicken with all the trimmings" and cash raffle draw many visitors.

Parishioners take a special pride in their new activity center, constructed five years ago next to the church. A beautiful structure, it features ample room for all parish activities. In August of 1999, at the summer picnic, the congregation celebrated the burning of the mortgage.

St. Mary's shares support of a school, a religious education program, and a community food pantry with nearby sister parish St. Joseph's, Belding. Both churches also share a pastor. The current pastor is Father Troy Nevins.

Many religious vocations have come from this small country parish: two priests, seven nuns, and one deacon. God has blessed the parish in many ways. The parishioners of St. Mary's pray that their faith and commitment to others continue to grow and that they always follow God's way.

St. James
Montague

ONLY A YEAR after erecting their first church in Whitehall, parishioners of St. James Parish decided to move it closer to where most of them lived— on the other side of White Lake. And so, during the winter of 1876, skids were placed under the building. Teams of draft horses then pulled the wood frame church across the frozen lake and up the steep banks of the west shore. The church was skidded to a location south of downtown Montague, where it served the parish for the next 82 years.

Father Chris Rouech, pastor, baptizes.

In 1958 the parish built a new church and school complex at its current site, a 26-acre campus on Dowling Street.

These moves enabled St. James to provide a stable Catholic presence on both sides of White Lake for 125 years. During the summer months, the parish of more than 400 families swells as tourists and summer residents find a warm welcome at the Eucharist and other activities.

The parish is especially proud of its K-6 school, which opened in 1962, and its sponsorship of the White Lake Giving Tree. In 1999 the Giving Tree provided abundant packages of food and Christmas gifts to more than 175 families in the area. The parish also operates a community clothing closet which gives used clothes to anyone without question.

St. James has been a "mother parish" since its beginnings in 1875. At one time, as many as seven mission churches were served by the priests at St. James. Today St. John the Baptist Church in Oceana County's Claybanks Township is the only mission church still served by St. James – a partnership that has existed since 1882.

With new families being lured by the area's natural resources and the rejuvenation of industry in the twin cities of Whitehall and Montague, parish leaders are excited about the opportunities for continued growth and outreach for the church.

Our Lady of Grace
Muskegon

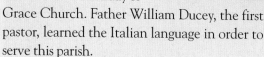

I N MUSKEGON during the early 1930s a group of faith-filled Italian Catholic families looking for a church redesigned a home on the corner of Jackson and Charles Streets. On April 20, 1924, the first Mass was offered at Our Lady of Grace Church. Father William Ducey, the first pastor, learned the Italian language in order to serve this parish.

The name of the parish – from the patron saint of Amaseno, Italy, "Nostra Signora di Grazia"– was suggested by Alessandro Lauretti. A painting of the patron, once the center of his altar of daily prayer, remains in the parish.

In 1937 Father Flynn was appointed to Our Lady of Grace and served there for 33 years. Under his leadership, the parish outgrew its home and built the current church on the corner of Marquette and Getty. The first Mass was celebrated in the new church on May 14, 1950.

In 1959 a school was added and a convent was built on the property. These buildings still serve the parish, although the school has been closed.

From 130 dedicated Italian families in 1924 to over 500 families of more than 36 nationalities today, Our Lady of Grace is known as a family-oriented, fun-loving, hard-working, friendly parish. Throughout the years, Our Lady of Grace has sponsored many diverse outreach ministries. The parish is recognized as a leader in serving others through its food pantry, holiday food baskets, Christmas Giving Tree, donations to LOVE, INC., Haiti Twinning Project, and work in Catholics Acting on Social Teachings (CAST). Father Michael P. Olson is pastor.

Visitors to Our Lady of Grace often comment on the enthusiastic participation in the Mass and the friendliness of the people who know it as "home," where the gospel message is taught and lived and all are welcomed.

St. Francis de Sales
Muskegon

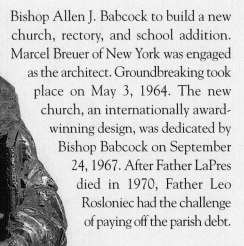

WHEN Bishop Francis J. Haas commissioned Father Joseph Ciesluk, on August 31, 1948, to open a new parish in southwest Muskegon, the new pastor wasted no time. On November 21, 1948, the first Mass for St. Francis de Sales Parish took place at Ruddiman Terrace Center, with 165 persons participating; in December the first infant baptism took place; and in October 1949, the parish broke ground for a new church on McCracken Avenue. In December Bishop Haas blessed the cornerstone. The first Mass was celebrated on May 14, 1950.

In September 1951 the parish, under the leadership of Father Julius Amman, started plans for a school. In September 1953 the Bernardine Franciscan Sisters began teaching in the catechetical program. On September 8, 1955, the parish school opened with 234 students in six grades, and in 1956 grades seven and eight were added.

Father Louis LaPres, third pastor, received permission from Bishop Allen J. Babcock to build a new church, rectory, and school addition. Marcel Breuer of New York was engaged as the architect. Groundbreaking took place on May 3, 1964. The new church, an internationally award-winning design, was dedicated by Bishop Babcock on September 24, 1967. After Father LaPres died in 1970, Father Leo Rosloniec had the challenge of paying off the parish debt.

The parish school joined the Muskegon Consolidated Catholic School system in September 1971. In November 1979 the former church was named "Wilma Hall," in honor of Sister Wilma Stembroski, longtime teacher. In June 1981 the Bernardine Sisters withdrew from the school.

During the pastorate of Father R. Louis Stasker the parish expanded the entryways to the church and added a chapel and family center. Under current pastor Father Thomas Simons, the parish undertook a strategic planning process, "Faith in Our Future," expanding parish staff, ministry, and services. The parish celebrated its 50th jubilee in 1998.

St. Jean Baptiste
Muskegon

IT WAS 117 YEARS AGO that Bishop Henry Joseph Richter of Grand Rapids presided at the laying of the cornerstone for a new church in the Muskegon area. His Excellency gave the church the name of St. Jean Baptiste.

On December 8, 1883, on the Feast of the Immaculate Conception, the first priest, Father LeTellier, celebrated Mass in the basement of the new church. Kneeling at the foot of the altar, the congregation sang the "Veni Creator" with much emotion. "We are at last home," the parishioners told the pastor. After 10 years of effort, the French Canadians had their own place to worship where hymns, prayers, and sermons could be said in French.

However, with the transfer of Father LeTellier in 1884 and the decline of the lumbering trade, the spirit of the French was dampened. How could they finish the upper portion of St. Jean Baptiste with no money?

It was then that a young priest from Montreal, Canada, Father J. Roch Magnan, came to St. Jean Baptiste. He found only an outline or sketch of the upper church. He knew he must work hard to bring the spirit back to the parish. He first took a census; there were 400 families. He then called upon the Oblate Fathers to conduct a retreat. Hope and confidence returned, and the money was raised to finish the church. It took five long years to accomplish this, but the church was finally completed in 1887.

The church is a brick veneer structure over wood frame throughout. It is planned along the Latin cross shape, as are the gothic cathedrals of Europe, and is on an east-west axis. The style is gothic, with pointed windows, a vaulted ceiling, and transept wings. When completed, the church cost upwards of $30,000.

The unique Stations of the Cross were donated by a Protestant lady, Mrs. M. Ryerson. The stained glass windows were made by a Chicago firm. The beautiful altars were hand-carved by Mr. Cedaire Blais. The wonderful statues were donated by friends, parishioners, and school children. Father J. Roch Magnan donated the statue of St. Jean Baptiste. Father James B. Wyse serves as pastor.

St. Joseph
Muskegon

T HE STORY of St. Joseph Catholic Church in Muskegon's Nelson Neighborhood is a 118-year-old story of the people of God. St. Joseph's is a parish of approximately 150 households. Financial failure, potential merger, and the fear of outright closure threatened Muskegon's smallest parish for the past several decades. Still, the parish entered the new millennium with a solid faith. However, the parishioners, after over a year of careful thought and prayer, recommended to Bishop Rose that the parish be closed and the old church razed.

In 1882 the German immigrants of Muskegon's St. Mary's Parish asked Bishop Henry Joseph Richter for a parish of their own where services could be held in their native tongue. With the bishop's consent, they purchased land at the corner

St. Joseph Parish closed March 25, 2001.

of Fifth Street and Monroe Avenue. There they laid the cornerstone for their new church on October 14, 1883. The first Mass was celebrated in St. Joseph's Church on Christmas Day 1883. The parish started with 40 families.

A school was built in 1885 with Dominican Sisters as the first teachers. A new brick school was built in 1917 and served the parish until 1969. St. Joseph's School had grades through high school from 1928 until 1953, when it consolidated with the Greater Muskegon Catholic Schools.

After the grade school consolidated with St. Michael's School in 1969, the building served the social needs of the Nelson Neighborhood until it was torn down in 1991. The former convent was converted into a parish family center in 1971. The last pastor was Father David L. Harpe.

St. Mary
Muskegon

ON JUNE 23, 1833, Father Frederic Baraga baptized 21 people in a tiny church overlooking Muskegon Lake on "Pigeon Hill." Built by Native Americans, this church was dedicated to St. Joseph by Father Baraga on April 20, 1834. It was later replaced by St. Mary's Church at a different location.

When the Native Americans ceded the land to the settlers, lumber mills were erected and laborers were needed. Unrest in Europe brought German people, the famine in Ireland brought the Irish, and French Canadians migrated to Michigan. By 1853 there were 400 inhabitants in Muskegon; by 1857 the number had grown to 2,000. By 1888, 47 lumber mills were in operation, and Muskegon was a prosperous community.

The Catholic people were served by missionary priests from Grand Rapids, but the growth of the population prompted Father Edward VanPaemel to instigate the building of a new church. With five-dollar donations and lumber from a mill owner whose wife was Catholic, a 20- by 30-foot building, without windows, was erected. Planks laid across shingle blocks served as pews. With various additions, this building served the community for 40 years. On June 2, 1889, the foundation for the "new" church, at the present location, was completed. On July 27, 1893, the statue of the Blessed Virgin Mary was raised into its niche in front of the church.

From these humble beginnings grew the daughter parishes of St. Joseph, St. Jean Baptiste, Our Lady of Grace, and Prince of Peace.

In 1893 St. Mary's had 300 families registered. In 1999 there were 357 families under the pastorate of Father Ernest J. Bernott. In the 167 years since Father Baraga baptized 21 people at Muskegon, the numbers have varied. Times and fortunes have changed, but St. Mary's faces the year 2000 strong in faith and ready to celebrate the great jubilee.

St. Michael
Muskegon

A SIGNIFICANT POLISH population developed in Muskegon in the early 1900s, and most of the Polish Catholics attended St. Mary's and St. Joseph's parishes. Father Casimir Skory of St. Adalbert's Parish in Grand Rapids assisted these pioneers in establishing their own parish. Father Francis Piaskowski united the Polish community for services at St. Jean Baptiste Church until the parish was established under its first pastor, Father Andrew Narloch, in 1909.

Father Narloch immediately purchased ground for the new parish site, and a combination church and school building was constructed in 1911. The school opened in 1913, staffed by the Sisters of Mercy. A new school was built in 1925 and again in 1959. The school is currently part of the Greater Muskegon Consolidated Schools.

Father Andrew Sikorski became pastor of St. Michael's in 1938. One of his first projects was the construction of the parish church in 1943. The church was consecrated on May 30, 1944. Father Sikorski served as pastor for 34 years until his retirement in 1972. After his retirement he continued to assist in the parish for many more years. He was succeeded as pastor by Fathers Edward Bielskas, Eugene Golas, and Thomas Hack.

Sacred Heart
Muskegon Heights

SACRED HEART PARISH, Muskegon Heights, was begun in 1915 by a group of Hungarian people who recognized the need for a Hungarian Catholic parish in their area in order to preserve ethnic rituals as they learned the "rights and ways of their adopted country." Bishop Edward D. Kelly purchased land in Muskegon Heights in 1916, and in 1919 assigned Father John J. Sonefeld as founding pastor.

Parishioners attended Mass in Schoenberg Hall, over a local meat market, until a temporary church could be set up in what is now the rectory basement. In 1924 the upper church was completed and blessed.

Sacred Heart's first school was blessed by Bishop Joseph G. Pinten in September 1940. It was staffed by Grand Rapids Dominican Sisters.

During his 28 years as pastor, from 1940 until his death on Ascension Day in 1968, Msgr. Albert A. Kehren led the rapidly growing parish. Adjacent buildings were purchased to serve as a convent and additional classrooms. In 1951 Bishop Francis J. Haas broke ground for Catholic Central High School, which opened in September 1953 with 775 students.

When a new church was dedicated by Bishop Allen J. Babcock in November 1957, the old church was remodeled as the priests' residence. In 1967 Bishop Babcock dedicated a new school building.

In the late 1960s, under the leadership of Msgr. James L. Jendrasiak, the parish remodeled the church sanctuary in accord with renewed liturgical practices.

In 1994 Sacred Heart Parish celebrated its 75th anniversary. As part of the celebration, a major renovation of the church began under the leadership of Father Charles Dautremont and a committee of 13 with the generosity of all the parishioners. Lay involvement on the school board and parish council, as well as in the various ministries, increased. At present the parish remains strong and vigorous. Father Norman P. Droski is pastor.

St. Thomas the Apostle
Muskegon Township

IN THE MID-1940S, the Joseph Smith family donated 2.5 acres of land to the Diocese of Grand Rapids in memory of their son Thomas. Thus, the parish of St. Thomas came to be.

Most of the Catholic churches in Muskegon were built because of an ethnic need in the area. The City of Muskegon alone had five parishes to serve Italian, Irish, French, Slovakian, and German communities. This was obviously necessary because of language differences in the early 20th century. St. Thomas was one of the first Catholic churches in Muskegon to develop  because of a geographical need. In 1948 two Franciscan priests took the task of bringing a church to East Muskegon—Fathers Rudolph Hornberger and Clementin Grosskopf.

The 20 families starting St. Thomas, along with Fathers Rudy and Clem, had a strong sense of purpose when they began building. They worked diligently, saving money and building what is now Founders' Hall so they could meet the needs of anxious parishioners. St. Thomas was on its way.

In 1962 the new church held its first Mass. The Franciscans continued to oversee St. Thomas, with Fathers Donatus Grunloh and Conan Mitchell taking residence. In 1986 the people of St. Thomas said farewell to the last Franciscan Fathers, Fathers Miro Wiese and Conan Mitchell, and welcomed their first diocesan priest, Father Ronald Schneider. Father Ron opened new doors for St. Thomas and spent eight years in the parish. He was transferred to Hart, Michigan, in 1994, and the current pastor, Father Philip Witkowski, took his place.

St. Thomas continues to grow and flourish as members live their Catholic faith as active Christians in both the parish and the community.

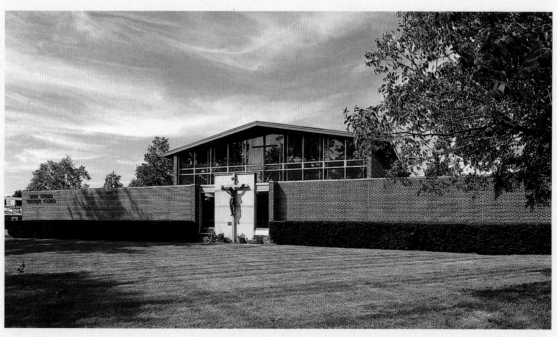

St. Bartholomew

Newaygo

THE ROOTS of Catholic faith and worship began in the early 1800s in the homes of Catholics living in Croton, Newaygo, Grant, Fremont, White Cloud, and Ensley. Missionary and diocesan priests, Sisters of Mercy, and Marywood Dominicans came from Detroit, Grand Rapids, Muskegon, Big Rapids, Manistee, and Traverse City to serve these people.

St. Mary's, a miniature white frame church built in Croton in the 1800s and the first Catholic church in Newaygo County, still stands today, together with its cemetery, on Locust Street about a mile north of Croton Road. In the 1970s its title and care were transferred to the Newaygo Historical Society.

The first St. Bartholomew's Church, which served Newaygo and Grant for nearly 60 years, was established, and a new church was dedicated by Bishop Henry Joseph Richter around the Feast of St. Bartholomew, August 21, 1902. This small, simple church is also still standing, high on the riverbank just north of Newaygo on Evergreen Road.

In 1948 Our Lady of Guadalupe Chapel was built a few miles south of Newaygo in Grant to serve Hispanic migrant families.

St. Bartholomew's present church was relocated on Brooks Road, and the new church was blessed and dedicated by Bishop Allen J. Babcock on Pentecost Sunday 1960. A family center and religious education classrooms were added in the mid-1980s. The current pastor is Father Loc Trinh.

Prince of Peace
North Muskegon

IN AUGUST 1960 a parcel of land on Dykstra Road was purchased by the diocese as a site for a possible future parish. In 1974 five couples on the north side of Muskegon began to meet with diocesan officials to form a new parish. After much consideration, Bishop Joseph M. Breitenbeck established the parish on November 5, 1975, and appointed Father Bernard Schafer the first pastor.

The parish began meeting in Laketon Junior High School. Mass was said there and at St. Alban's Episcopal Church. The parish family chose the name Prince of Peace for their parish in February 1976. Plans were soon begun to construct a church. The first Mass in the new church was held on Christmas Eve 1978. The church was dedicated on April 29, 1979.

Over the past 20 years, Fathers Melvin Fox and Robert Hart have succeeded Father Schafer as pastor. During this time the parish has continued to grow as a faith community.

St. Anne
Paris

S t. Anne's Parish in Paris was founded in 1888 when a settlement of about 30 families, mostly Irish Catholics, wished to have their own church. St. Anne's was a mission of St. Mary's Parish in Big Rapids, and Father Thomas Dalton came from there once a month to say Mass in a little log house. In 1903 St. Philip Neri Parish in Reed City received a resident pastor, and St. Anne's has been a mission of that parish since that time.

Bishop Henry Joseph Richter blessed St. Anne's Church on August 24, 1893. The building had been constructed by the men of the parish. In 1920 the church was enlarged by 18 feet and a basement, belfry, steeple, and vestibule were added. At that time, a new bell was also donated, blessed, and installed.

In the early days, the priest would come by train to Paris on Saturday night and have supper in the homes of various parishioners. He would then go to the church to hear confessions. The priest slept in the sacristy and offered Mass on Sunday morning.

Over the years, St. Anne's continued to improve its church building and to grow as a community. The parish celebrated its centennial in 1988.

St. Patrick
Parnell

S T. PATRICK PARISH was founded by Irish immigrants who settled in the townships of Grattan, Ada, Vergennes, and Cannon in the early 1840s. By June of 1844, Father Andreas Viszoczky was coming regularly to say Mass in area homes. On December 7, 1844, 29 families pledged money to build a small church. The church was dedicated in the next year, but it was outgrown by 1859. A second church was built during the pastorate of Father Henry Rievers. It was destroyed by fire in 1868. A third church was completed by 1871, but it was also destroyed by fire in 1876. The fourth church, the one currently in use, was completed in 1878. The current fieldstone rectory was built by Father John Troy in 1910.

Over the years, St. Patrick became one of the larger rural parishes in the diocese. A school was opened by Father James Crumley in 1893. Father Crumley also is credited with naming the community "Parnell" in 1889. A larger school was built in 1905 by Father James Byrne. This school included a high school from 1920 to 1963. The current school was built in 1963 during the pastorate of Father Edmund Farrell.

St. Patrick Parish is well known for its large, historic church. From 1989 to 1993, Fathers Julian Reginato and Wayne Wheeler led the parish through a complete restoration of the church and rectory. St. Patrick is also known for its chicken dinner festival, which dates back to the 1860s.

St. Patrick Parish celebrated its sesquicentennial in 1994. A number of descendents of the Irish founders still remain in the parish, and many new families are moving into the parish as well. In 2000 the parish, led by Father Ronald Hutchinson, built a parish center to help continue its mission in the Parnell area.

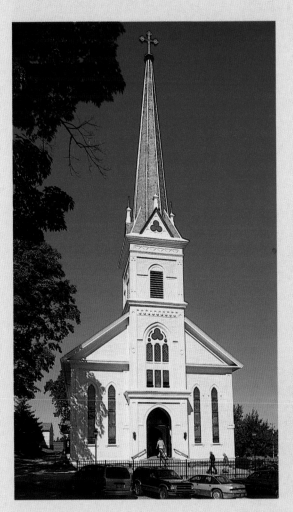

St. Vincent de Paul
Pentwater

S T. VINCENT DE PAUL CATHOLIC CHURCH was built in Pentwater between 1868 and 1870. The church's location at 637 W. Sixth Street is the original $50 site purchased from Charles Mears in 1867. Initially a mission church, St. Vincent's was served by priests who trekked from Wright, Muskegon, Ludington, and Manistee to celebrate Mass.

In 1882 Father Louis Baroux, pastor of St. James, Montague, became the first priest to regularly offer Mass at St. Vincent's on the third Sunday of each month. At the time there were 25 Catholic families in the area – 15 English, five French, three German, and two Belgian. By 1883 or 1884 about 20 children were attending catechism classes. During Father Frederick L. Ruessman's pastorate (1890-1895), Mass was being celebrated on two Sundays of each month.

A disastrous fire in March 1900 destroyed Pentwater's furniture factory, the principal area

employer, and it was not rebuilt. By 1902 only nine families were left at St. Vincent's. In that same year, Father Francis Emmerich was appointed as the first resident pastor of St. Joseph's, Weare. St. Vincent's then became a mission of St. Joseph's, beginning a linkage that still exists today.

In 1907 St. Vincent's Church was renovated, and the steeple and bell were added. The church was enlarged in 1938 by adding a new sanctuary and double sacristies. Father Lawrence Quaderer directed the redecoration of the church in 1949. In 1961 a meeting hall, kitchen, and restrooms were added.

Led by Father Charles Brown, St. Vincent's continues to grow as a faith community enriched by the presence of many new parishioners who have settled in the area in their retirement. The community is enriched by many seasonal members and vacationers as well.

St. Joseph
Pewamo

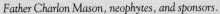

THE CORNERSTONE of St. Joseph's Church, Pewamo, was officially dedicated in 1903. Since then there have been numerous changes, but the parish maintains its "small country church" flavor, rich in history and tradition. Many of the parishioners have been lifelong members of this parish, and their presence is a rich blessing.

St. Joseph's Parish mission statement reads: "We, the parishioners of St. Joseph's, Pewamo, believe in working together because together we can accomplish more. We strive to be a loving, caring parish, building on our strength of family values. We desire to be a good example to others, with our lives grounded in the values and truths of our Catholic faith. Guided by the wisdom of the Holy Spirit and empowered by our love for the Lord and one another, we reach out to others in Christian love and service."

This mission statement rings true in many aspects of parish life at St. Joseph's. While the parish is comprised of fewer than 400 families, together they have achieved many important goals. St. Joseph's has maintained a strong Catholic school since 1913 and has implemented several programs and events designed to enrich and renew the parish and the broader community. Among these programs are the Rite of Christian Initiation of Adults (RCIA) and pre-Cana classes, religious education programming, Altar Society, Knights of Columbus, and the popular summer festival. As a parish united in Christ's love and example of service, St. Joseph's hopes to witness to God's presence in the Pewamo community.

Living in a culture where families are in crisis, the parish is proud of its strong commitment to family values, and prays that every member may realize his or her value and potential and may be assured of the full support of the parish family.

Father Charlon Mason, neophytes, and sponsors.

St. Patrick
Portland

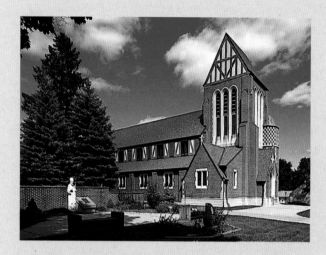

ORGANIZED as a mission in 1878 under the direction of Father Charles G. Bolte, the church was named in honor of St. Patrick by Mary (McCormack) Manning in 1879. Mary was a teenage immigrant from Ireland who left her homeland to come alone to the "land of religious freedom." Upon her arrival in New York, after earning her first week's pay of one dollar, she offered a Mass of thanksgiving at St. Patrick's Church in New York City. Eventually she married Daniel Manning, and the two settled in Portland, Michigan. Mary raised the most money for the new church, thus "winning" the privilege of naming it. Mary's great-great-granddaughter, Sarah West, is currently a student at St. Patrick's School.

Many improvements were made for the church by Father H. C. Koenig. However, it was in 1899 that St. Patrick's Church was formally organized under Father Matthias Auer, its first permanent pastor of 60 families of Irish and German heritage. A rectory was built in 1899 and a school, staffed by the Sisters of St. Joseph of the Nazareth Academy from Kalamazoo, in 1906.

A second church was built in 1926; it is still in use today. In 1938 St. Patrick's Church became a part of the Diocese of Grand Rapids. Under Msgr. Louis Flohe, a new, larger school was built in 1951, with new additions in 1961. By the early 1970s the parish had grown to over 1,000 families under the leadership of Father Joseph Malewitz. He saw to the completion of a new rectory in 1972. Father Donald Weber had

the sanctuary of the church remodeled in 1976 to meet the standards established by Vatican Council II. The "Father Flohe Foundation" was initiated by Father Richard VanLente in 1988 with the intent to fund the educational programs for the parish and to ensure their continuity.

Father Julian Reginato called upon parishioners in 1990 to donate sufficient funds to remodel the exterior of the church building and the grounds. The first phase of renovation of the interior of the church started during the summer of 1997 and was completed under the direction of the associate pastor, Father Troy A. Nevins.

The current pastor of over 1,200 families is Father Charles D. Hall. Father Hall has set in motion a strategic planning process for the present and future needs of the growing parish family. The rectory building continues to serve as the parish administration building and now also houses the youth and family ministry programs. As of July 1999, Father Hall and Associate Pastor Father Peter Vu reside in a house on Grape Street. With the addition of a DK class in September 1999, the school now instructs students through grade 12.

At the stroke of midnight on December 31, 1999, first grader Naomi Steffes won the honor to begin the ringing of the bells as Father Hall processed down the aisle to greet people for Mass, beginning the ceremony with the sign of the cross. Together, all reaffirmed their belief "In the name of the Father, and of the Son, and of the Holy Spirit." After Mass there was a parish social and the signing of a "Great Jubilee Year of 2000" scroll.

St. Catherine
Ravenna

ST. CATHERINE'S PARISH of Ravenna was established by Father Thomas Whalen of St. Mary's Church in Muskegon at the request of Bishop Henry Joseph Richter. The church was dedicated on October 25, 1908. The priests of St. Mary's, Muskegon, continued to shepherd the parish until 1933, when a rectory was built and Father John Sydlowski became the first resident priest.

In 1936 Father Stanislaus Betka was appointed to the parish. Under his leadership, St. Catherine's grade school and convent, the first to be established in east Muskegon County, were built. They were dedicated on September 2, 1951. The school was staffed by the Sisters of Charity of Mount St. Joseph of Ohio. In September 1954 they were replaced by the Dominican Sisters of Grand Rapids. Presently Sister Peter Mary Korson administers the school.

A parish hall was built in 1955, and in March 1964 ground was broken for a new church. It was dedicated by Bishop Allen J. Babcock on March 28, 1965.

In June 1976 Father Betka retired and Father James P. Yager was appointed pastor. During his pastorate the parish received a donation of a house to be used as a rectory. The move was made on December 3, 1992. The old rectory was renovated and is currently used as a kindergarten classroom.

Father Yager retired in 1992, and the parish was served by several interim pastors until Bishop Robert J. Rose appointed Father John F. Porter as pastor. He arrived on February 3, 1993.

More recently, Sister Jeannette Chiasson, O.P., and Sister Joan Foley, O.P., serve as Pastoral Associate and Director of Religious Education respectively, both for St. Catherine's, Ravenna, and for St. Francis Xavier, Conklin.

In January 1998 the church underwent an extensive renovation, bringing it up to date liturgically and making it handicapped accessible.

St. Philip Neri
Reed City

P RIESTS began to visit Reed City from Big Rapids in 1876, and by 1883 the community had a resident pastor, Father Theophilus Nyssen. He was followed by Father Louis Baroux. The congregation returned to mission status in 1888 and was served from St. Mary's, Big Rapids, until 1903. When Father Anthony Schumacher was appointed resident pastor in 1903, he was also assigned four missions – Paris, Evart, Baldwin, and Luther – and a station at Nirvana.

The first church of St. Philip Neri was outgrown and replaced in 1922 when Father Joseph Henige was pastor. Father Edward

Chmielewski led the people in constructing a school in 1948. Classes had already started in 1947 in the church basement, taught by the School Sisters of Notre Dame. The new school opened in November 1948.

Father (later Monsignor) Victor Gallagher was appointed pastor in 1957 and was also appointed diocesan CCD director. St Pius X Convent was opened in Reed City to serve as a home for the Victory Noll Sisters who worked in CCD programs throughout the diocese. When the parish built a new church in 1961, the old church became a Religious Education Resource Center under the direction of Msgr. Gallagher and the Victory Noll Sisters.

St. Philip's School closed in 1970 and was later sold to the public school district. By 1971 Reed City had only one mission remaining, St. Anne's in Paris. With the partition of the diocese in 1971, the CCD center was relocated to Grand Rapids, and the Religious Education Resource Center was sold in 1973. The present pastor is Father Daniel C. Aerts.

ST. MICHAEL'S CHURCH, Wheatland, was a German-speaking community in 1862 when early settlers took advantage of the Homestead Act to clear the land and take residence. It is hard to determine how long people lived in the area before a priest came to minister to them. Several priests either from the Detroit Diocese or the newly established Grand Rapids Diocese visited and offered the sacraments between 1871 and 1888.

The parish was established in 1871, and a church was built at the corner of M-20 and 50th Avenue in 1886. By 1925 the church, the rectory, the combined first school and convent building, and land for a cemetery were all in place.

The present convent was built in 1949 and the current school in 1961. The parish has been blessed with the presence of the Mercy Sisters of the Detroit Province since the parish school first opened its doors in the fall of 1904. Sister Bertha and Sister Amata, although in retirement, continue to teach on a part-time basis in the school, which today numbers over 150 students in pre-school through sixth grade. The present church was dedicated on September 7, 1975. On July 14, 1996, Bishop Robert J. Rose dedicated the new parish center, kitchen area, and cafeteria.

On March 30, 1998, over 300 community members gathered at the church to dedicate the new facility of God's Helping Hands of Mecosta County. Four churches joined with St. Michael's Church to expand the work of the former St. Vincent dePaul Society. The new facility is situated on the southeast corner of the parish property and now is sponsored ecumenically by nine churches. GHH has received state recognition for its innovative ministry to the poor and marginalized.

St. Michael's Parish also has significant involvement in the diocesan Haiti project, Habitat for Humanity, Help Pregnancies, and other community outreach programs.

Under the guidance of Father William F. Zink, St. Michael's is committed to total stewardship. To quote from its mission statement: "We believe that everything we possess is from God. We believe that a first portion of what we receive should be shared with the community. We believe that coming together in worship publicly acknowledges who God is and who we are."

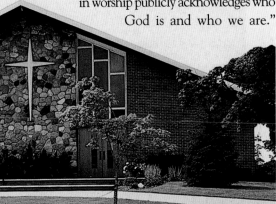

Louis and Mae Buron, 56-year members of St. Anthony.

ST. ANTHONY'S PARISH began in Robinson Township in 1910. Fathers Henry Maus and Daniel Hyland from St. Patrick's, Grand Haven, helped the people build a church on donated land. With the help of a grant from the Catholic Church Extension Society, the church was completed in 1913 and dedicated by Bishop Henry Joseph Richter in 1915. The small congregation remained a mission of Grand Haven until 1930.

In 1930 St. Anthony's became a mission of St. Mary's Parish, Spring Lake. This arrangement continued until 1955. Father Theodore Liebek of Spring Lake encouraged the establishment of the Altar Society in 1946; he also supervised a major remodeling of the church in 1952. In 1954 when St. Mary's School opened, St. Anthony's purchased a bus to transport students from Robinson to Spring Lake and also to Muskegon Catholic Central High School.

St. Anthony's Mission was transferred back to the administration of Grand Haven in 1955. St. Anthony's students attended St. Patrick's School until it closed in 1969. They later participated in a joint religious education program. A parish council was established in 1970, with Stanley Stolarz serving as general chairperson. The church was again redecorated in 1974 and in the early 1990s.

Our Lady of Consolation
Rockford

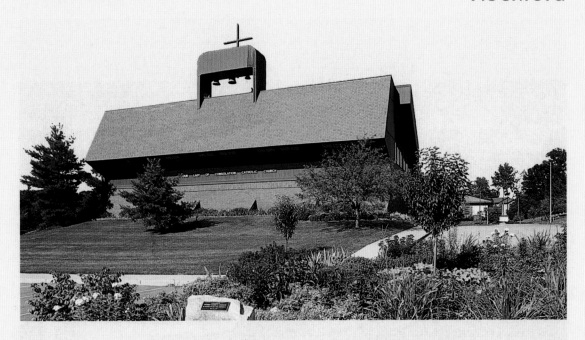

ESTABLISHED IN 1972, Our Lady of Consolation Parish in Rockford is a relatively young parish, and like a youngster, the church is experiencing tremendous growth.

Our Lady of Consolation had humble beginnings. In 1962 a 23-acre site overlooking the city of Rockford was purchased. Groundbreaking ceremonies were held in 1966 for a building known as the "Annex," in which services were held and which later became the school gymnasium. The Annex was a mission of Assumption Parish in Belmont, under the direction of Msgr. Joseph Podhajski. It served 134 families. A school opened in 1967 for 85 students.

In 1968 the mission and school were dedicated by Bishop Allen J. Babcock. The church was named Our Lady of Consolation as a tribute to the Consolata Missionary Sisters who staffed the school. The church became an official parish on March 28, 1972, and Father James Cusack was appointed the first pastor.

During Father Cusack's pastorate, the parish grew to 275 families, and a family center and rectory were constructed. Father Paul Milanowski became pastor in 1978. A new church was built in 1984, and the Annex became part of the school.

Bishop Joseph McKinney was pastor from 1985 to 1998. During this time, a new family center was built, the parish grounds became home to the North Kent Service Center to serve the needy, and Bishop Hills, an assisted living residence for the elderly, was constructed.

Parish life at Our Lady of Consolation is notable because of the many ministries and service organizations. The parish also hosts many choirs and bible study groups. Father Thomas Page became pastor in 1998. With a parish community of over 1,400 families, the parish has begun its most ambitious building campaign yet, with plans for the church to double in size by 2002.

Our Lady of the Assumption
Rothbury

THE CREATION of Our Lady of the Assumption took many circuitous turns before the community became a full-fledged parish.

St. Michael's of Muskegon annual report for 1925 actually listed Elbridge and Rothbury as missions of the Muskegon parish for the first time. The parish was called St. Mary's of Rothbury. At that time it had three Bohemian, fourteen Polish, and five Slovak families for a total of 22. Services were held once a month in the township hall. In 1925 several acres of land were donated to the parish for a church building and cemetery.

By 1927 services were being held twice a month, and in 1930 the mission church was named Our Lady of the Assumption. At this time the mission was transferred from St. Michael's, Muskegon, to St. James, Montague, with Father Max Ostrowski as the pastor.

In 1957 land was donated by Mr. George Storm for its current site on the north side of Winston Road just west of U.S. 31. The building was designed by Humbrecht Associates of Fort Wayne, Indiana, and parishioners did the decorating and landscaping. The building cost was approximately $75,000. A private blessing of the church of Our Lady of the Assumption took place on Father's Day in 1958, with Father Andrew P. Sikorski officiating.

The church was made a diocesan parish on July 9, 1969, with St. John the Baptist, Claybanks, as its mission. This date also marked the appointment of its first pastor, Father Albert Watson. In 1973 the parish celebrated its golden jubilee with an outdoor Mass. Improvements were made to the church between 1995 and 1998 when enhanced lighting, a handicapped accessible restroom, and a new carillon bell system were installed.

Mary Queen of the Apostles
Sand Lake

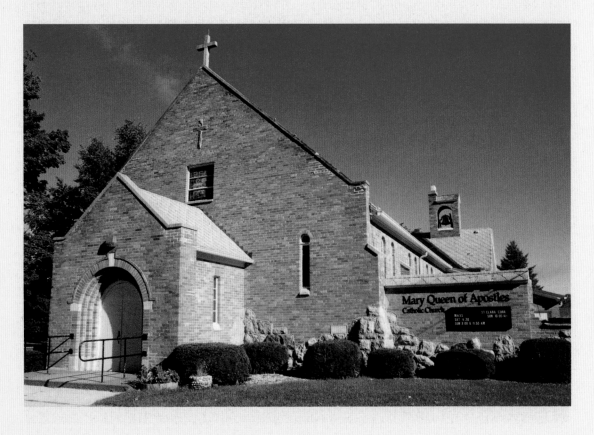

ST. MARY'S, Sand Lake, has its origin with the early settlers of this area in the 1860s. They were affiliated with others of common faith from St. Mary's in Grand Rapids, St. Patrick's in Parnell, St. Mary's in Carson City, and, as their mother church, St. Mary's in Big Rapids.

Before the first church was built, Mass and other services were held in homes of the families. The priest would come by train from Big Rapids about once a month. He would stay at the home of one of the parishioners, hold Mass, and return by train on Monday morning.

A schoolhouse was converted into the first church and used until 1923. In 1917 property was purchased, and in 1923 a basement was built and used for services. Parishioners still tell of their relatives working their team of horses to shovel and scoop out the hard clay at the site.

Father Sebastian VanGessel, who previously served the parish from Big Rapids, became the first pastor in 1923.

Completion of the church began in 1923 with many men of the parish contributing to the construction. Even the stonework that can be seen in the front of the church was contributed by two brothers. The first Mass was celebrated in the new church on August 6, 1933. There were 45 families registered at that time. Today St. Mary's – renamed Mary Queen of Apostles – is a faith-filled community of over 400 families under the pastoral leadership of Father Joseph W. Kenshol.

THE FIRST THOUGHTS of a Catholic parish in Saranac came in March of 1951 when Father John F. Grzybowski was the pastor of St. Mary's Parish in Lowell. The Simpsons, among others, were instrumental in St. Anthony's establishment. Margaret Simpson wrote a letter to Bishop Francis J. Haas asking if he thought it would ever be possible to have a Catholic Church in Saranac. She explained that there were about 17 Catholic families in the area.

In May of 1951 Oliver Simpson, Margaret's father, sold their home to the church to be used as a Catholic chapel. On November 25, 1951, the first Mass was said, with 75 people attending. After various moves to different buildings, ground was broken for a new church on April 28, 1957. Mass was held in the lower level until March 21, 1965, when the church proper was finished.

In the 1950s, 1960s, and 1970s, many dinners were served to pay for the church. Some dinners were held at the Morrison Lake Pavilion and others at the Youth Building on the Ionia Free Fair grounds. St. Anthony also held a Dinner/Festival at St. Robert in Ada. In October 1971, the church debt was paid off. Proceeds from bingo paid off the rectory debt in March 1976. A church organ was bought the same year.

In February 1982, church bells were purchased. In the fall of 1984 a shrine to Mary was built according to plans by Jan Yaw. Every year there is a May Crowning Ceremony.

In 1991, renovation was done to the church proper. On March 10, 1991, Most Rev. Robert Rose sealed the corner stone as part of the 40-year celebration. In 1998, a campaign began for renovation and an addition of a new hall. The parish's annual chicken barbecue dinners, dinner dance, and building fund donations contribute to the financial growth of St. Anthony's Parish.

Active councils include the Pastoral, Finance, Women's Guild, and Knights of Columbus. The parish is grateful to the pioneers and present parishioners of St. Anthony, "The Parish with a Heart." Father Norbert Leyrita is the current pastor.

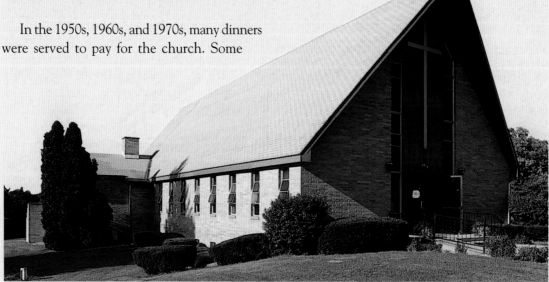

St. Jerome
Scottville

S<small>T. J</small>EROME'S C<small>HURCH</small> began in 1910 on one acre of land purchased for $1,100 on the corner of W. State Street and Reinberg Avenue in Scottville. The building of the church was entrusted to the pastor of St. Simon's Church, Ludington, Father Dennis Malone. On the eleventh day of May 1912, the cornerstone was laid by Bishop Henry Joseph Richter. On October 3, 1912, the front half of the church was blessed by Bishop Richter and placed under the patronage of St. Jerome. Mass was celebrated for the first time by Father Felix Vogt. The church bell was rung for the first time during midnight Mass on Christmas Eve 1913.

The first census showed 20 families registered. The Holy Sacrifice of the Mass was offered once a month on Sunday and once or twice a month on weekdays by the priests of St. Simon's. Sunday School, vespers, and benediction were held every Sunday.

St. Helena's Society was organized and the first meeting was held on October 23, 1910, with 14 members. They committed themselves to the work of raising money for the church and fostering the spiritual development of the parishioners.

Under the direction of Father William Hoogterp, the St. Jerome Guild was established. The purpose of this group was to bond the young, single, and married women of the parish into a Catholic Child Study Club. The guild functioned from 1953 to 1973.

The Men's Club was formed during the 1950s under the direction of Father Edward Kubiak and, following an inactive period, was revived by Father Joseph Battersby.

St. Peter's Church, Riverton Township, which was St. Jerome's mission church, joined St. Jerome's Parish when their church burned in the 1940s.

During the 1940s and 1950s extensive remodeling was done to the church. Between 1986 and 1988 the interior was renovated according to the reforms of Vatican Council II. The church celebrated its 75th anniversary on July 26, 1988. As of the year 2000, approximately 150 families are registered at St. Jerome's.

Our Lady of Fatima
Shelby

Father Joseph Alksnis received the appointment and wrote his first letter to the bishop in March 1952 concerning his residence in Shelby. In April 1952 Father Alksnis met with contractors about constructing a church with a basement, to seat 300 people. The diocesan building committee approved plans for the Shelby church minus a proposed free standing bell tower. On September 15, 1952, ground was broken for the new church.

IN SEPTEMBER 1950 a delegation of eight men met with Bishop Francis J. Haas about having a resident pastor in their midst. A year later, in September 1951, the building committee of Our Lady of Fatima met with Bishop Haas about purchasing land for a church. On December 8, 1951, a site of two and one-half acres was purchased from the Henry family for $1,200. The land was situated just beyond the Shelby village limits on U.S. 31. Bishop Haas was ready to send Shelby a resident pastor.

The basement structure was completed in time for Christmas services that year. The upper structure was complete enough to use by Palm Sunday 1954. The building cost $75,000 to build. Under Father John F. Vallier, a free standing carillon bell tower was completed during the fall of 2000. The present pastor is Father Mark F. Bauer.

Holy Family
Sparta

I N 1947 Bishop Francis J. Haas appointed Father T. Vincent McKenna pastor of what was to be Holy Family Parish in Sparta. Father McKenna found an enthusiastic group of Catholic families waiting to help him establish the new parish, and the first Mass was celebrated on July 6, 1947, in the Sparta Township Hall.

A residence on Centennial Street was purchased in December of that year to serve as the parish rectory. Almost immediately a Holy Name Society and an Altar Society were formed, and they began numerous fundraisers which eventually allowed the parish to break ground in September 1948 for a church which was to cost $30,000 and seat 220.

Catechism classes for children were introduced in 1950, and the following year a youth group was formed.

In 1954 Msgr. Joseph Walen, diocesan director of Catholic charities and editor of the *Western Michigan Catholic* newspaper, was named the second pastor of Holy Family. The parish continued to grow, and in 1959 work began on a new church and rectory complex which is still in use. The first Mass in the new church was celebrated by Msgr. Walen on August 15, 1963.

By 1985 the parish had increased to nearly 500 families, and again a point had been reached where the facilities were no longer capable of meeting the needs of its members. In 1987 construction of a new religious education center, social hall, and enlarged entryway to the church began under the leadership of Father Martin S. Kurylowicz. The debt was paid off in 1998, considerably ahead of schedule. Father Philip A. Shangraw serves as pastor.

St. Mary
Spring Lake

CHARLES ALLEN and his wife Catherine settled at Mill Point in 1850 in a home at 110 W. Savidge Street. Father Rievers would visit once or twice a year and say Mass in their home, using an old bureau for the altar. The vestments, altar stone, chalices, and other necessities were carried in his saddlebags.

The small Catholic community was later given a lot at 208 North Division by Hunter Savidge. They made an appeal to Bishop Caspar Henry Borgess in Detroit for permission to build a church and have their own pastor. St. Mary's was dedicated in the autumn of 1866. The area's name of Mill Point was officially changed to Spring Lake on February 27, 1867.

Father Takken, an elderly Belgian priest, was the first resident pastor. After Father Takken left the parish, St. Mary's was once again dependent upon the visits of missionaries. Father Van Paemel and Father Murphy were two of the first.

After the establishment of the Grand Rapids Diocese in 1882, Father Michael Dalton was appointed, and the parochial residence was moved to St. Patrick's in Grand Haven. Property was purchased on the corner of Savidge and Prospect Streets. The new church was erected at a cost of $25,000 and dedicated on June 18, 1924, by Bishop Edward D. Kelly. It seated 250.

In 1953, with the permission of Bishop Francis J. Haas, a professional consultant was hired to organize a fundraising campaign to raise $100,000 to build a school. The parish raised $118,000 and on August 9, 1953, groundbreaking ceremonies were held. Additional property was purchased east of the school for a convent and playground in 1953 for $16,500.

Three Pallottine teaching sisters and one housekeeping sister arrived from Huntington, West Virginia, on August 24, 1954, and Mass was celebrated at the convent for the first time on September 7, 1954. School began on September 8, 1954, with 150 students. The convent and school were formally blessed on October 8, 1954, by Bishop Allen J. Babcock.

In 1958, a development fund was begun for a new church and an addition to the school. New classrooms were ready in the fall of 1962. Property was purchased on Savidge Street east of the rectory. Construction of the new church on that property began in the spring of 1966 under the direction of Msgr. Kupinski and was completed for Easter services on March 26, 1967. A chapel was built, housing over 200 statues of the Blessed Mother. In 1995 under the direction of current pastor Father Anthony C. Vainavicz, the church was renovated: a choir area was added, the Madonna Chapel became the Eucharistic Chapel, and old confessionals became shrine areas. In the fall of 2000 the Pieta was relocated in front of the church. In January 2001, an 18 rank pipe organ was added to the church.

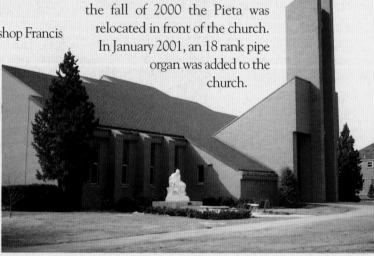

St. Bernadette of Lourdes
Stanton

On December 10, 1889, two lots were purchased by Bishop Caspar Henry Borgess of Detroit for a mission at Stanton. From 1879 to 1961, Stanton was served by priests from Miriam, Greenville, Big Rapids, and Carson City. In 1889 the mission was named for the first time as St. Apollonia.

The church building in Stanton was remodeled in 1911, and a bell was donated by the Neff family. The church was struck by lightning the next year, but it was quickly repaired.

In 1961 Father Edwin Thome was assigned as a resident priest to serve the missions of Sheridan, Stanton, Six Lakes, Edmore, and Vestaburg. The territory was divided into two mission centers: Stanton and Edmore. St. James Mission House in Edmore was purchased to serve as a rectory, education center, and chapel.

Also in 1961, plans were begun for a new church in Stanton because St. Apollonia's Church was too small. A new church was constructed and was dedicated in 1963. Its name was changed at that time to St. Bernadette of Lourdes.

Father Thome was transferred in 1969. He was succeeded by Fathers James Bozung, Eugene Alvesteffer, William Zink, Fredrick Brucker, Louis Baudone, Donn Tufts, Isidro Gargantiel, and Vincent Bryce, O.P.

St. Bernadette's gained parish status in 1974, sharing a priest with St. Margaret Mary Parish in Edmore. In 1975 a rectory was built in Edmore and St. James Mission House was sold. St. Bernadette's built a parish center with classrooms, office, kitchen, and gymnasium in 1977.

Throughout the last two decades, many improvements and renovations were made to the church and parish center, including an organ, stained glass windows, and air conditioning. Today St. Bernadette of Lourdes Parish continues the long history of Catholic presence in Stanton under the pastoral ministry of Father Vincent Bryce, OP.

Sacred Heart
Victory Township

VICTORY TOWNSHIP was formed in 1868 and named to commemorate the Union victory in the Civil War. In 1895, Father Laurence Hayden of St. Simon's Church in Ludington said Mass in John Sladick's home once a month for a dozen families.

Sacred Heart Church was built in 1900 and dedicated by Bishop Henry Joseph Richter. The church became a mission of the newly formed St. Stanislaus Parish in Ludington in 1901. The mission was transferred to St. Simon's in 1908. From 1925 to 1952, Sacred Heart was a mission of St. Jerome, Scottville. The church was a mission of St. Mary's, Custer, from 1952 to 1964.

In 1964 Bishop Allen J. Babcock established Sacred Heart as a parish, and Father Thomas Neis was appointed the first pastor. The parish became a mission again in 1980. Sacred Heart has since been a mission again of St. Stanislaus (1980-1984, 1993-present) and St. Simon's (1984-1993).

Father John Ruba (native son) and Father Dennis O'Donnell (current pastor) show a then and now look at their buggies.

St. Joseph
Weare

Emmerich. A German-born immigrant, Father Emmerich served as pastor for St. Joseph's and the mission parish of St. Vincent's, Pentwater, until his death in 1944. Under his leadership the parish built a new and much larger brick church for the growing population. Father Emmerich also oversaw the building of a parish school which opened in 1904 and was run by the Dominican Sisters from Marywood. Father Emmerich's influence was also felt throughout the surrounding area, as he built churches in Hart and Riverton.

CATHOLIC IMMIGRANTS primarily from Belgium, the Netherlands, and Germany first settled the area of Weare Township in northern Oceana County. These faithful people were served by priests who came from as far away as Ludington, Montague, Muskegon, and Detroit.

To meet the needs of a growing parish and community, a hall was built in 1953. A religious education addition and kitchen facilities were added in 1979. An ox roast was begun in 1949 to raise funds to build the hall and continues bringing families and friends together today.

The first church building for St. Joseph's was built in 1883. In 1902 the parish celebrated the appointment of its first pastor, Father Francis

Father Pedro Garcia began a Spanish Mass in 1974 to serve the growing number of Hispanic residents and farm workers in the area.

Today St. Joseph's Church continues to serve the needs of an agricultural community dedicated to celebrating and living their faith, ever connected to their roots of family and faith. Father Charles Brown is the current pastor.

St. Joseph
White Cloud

ST. JOSEPH'S CHURCH, White Cloud, celebrated 100 years in July 1992. At that time, Msgr. Ted Sniegowski was resident pastor. Bishop Robert J. Rose came for the celebration, which was followed by dinner in the basement of the church. The crowded conditions may have been a factor in the parish's decision to undertake a building program. Already St. Joseph's had a building fund and was holding summer festivals to raise money.

In 1993 Msgr. Sniegowski retired and Father John Au was appointed pastor, staying until 1997. With no resident priest, Father Richard Van Lente from All Saints, Fremont, became the parish administrator. Father Ray Bruck, a retired priest, became pastoral assistant.

At that time St. Joseph's had plans for a new church on a new site. Preliminary figures quickly showed that the parish could not raise that kind of money. Instead, they set out to build a parish hall on their current site.

All members of the parish pulled together to make the new hall a reality. Tim Frisbie took over the building plans. Cooks for the parish Dorothea Smith, Ann Frisbie, Joanne Campbell, and Mary Eggleston visited nearby kitchens and soon had plans for the hall. Cindy Wendlowsky, Director of Religious Education, assessed classroom needs. Others who helped make the new hall possible were Tony Frisbie, Chris Feldpausch, and Mary Bleiler.

In December 1999 Bishop Rose approved the hiring of an architect. The building cost was anticipated at $565,000. St. Joseph's feast day, March 19, 1999, was groundbreaking day. Exactly six months later, on September 19, 1999, the new hall was dedicated. The air-conditioned hall has a large meeting room seating 300 people, six classrooms, and a modern kitchen.

St. Joseph's summer festival, which includes a barbecued turkey and beef dinner and a silent auction, is always a successful fundraiser. In addition, three-year pledges will help to pay off the cost of the building over the next 10 years.

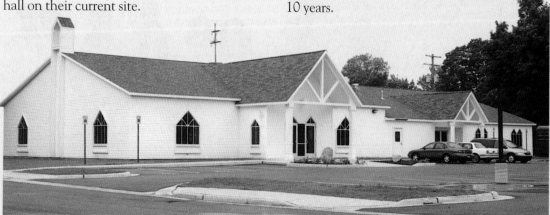

St. Joseph
Wright Township

I N THE SUMMER OF 1844, Henry and Mary Omlor Host left Ohio with their family for a new life in the recently opened Territory of Michigan. They settled in Wright Township, where they were soon followed by Mary's two sisters and their families, Anthony and Catherine Omlor Armock and Jacob and Margaret Omlor Finkler.

Other German Catholic families came to the area and started praying in each other's homes. They included: Frank and Mary Hoffman Robach, Jacob and Mary Omlor May, Francis and Mary Gerber Fritz, Joseph and Elizabeth Gerber Dietrich, Marcus and Josephine Hoffman Alt, Adolph and Mary Kaltz Rasch, George and Genevefa Knauf, Michael and Elizabeth Huter Schoenborn, Joseph and Elizabeth Brown Bauer, George and Mary Fritz Zahm, Joseph and Mary Frisch Kluting, Peter and Barbara Ruffung Lothschutz, Peter and Catherine Hust Miller, Jacob and Barbara Omlor Brown, John and Mary May Umlor, John and Margaret Finkler Dohm, Anthony and Mary Heitz Klein, and Joseph and Mary May Heitz.

Once a month, Father Andreas Viszoczky came to celebrate Mass in their homes until a church could be built. That first church was built in 1853. In 1869 Henry Host, Jacob Finkler, and Jacob May donated four acres of land for a second wood frame church under the direction of Father Rhode.

The first baptism was that of Helen Braun, daughter of Jacob and Barbara Braun. The first marriage was that of George Knauf and Geneveve Ritz on September 30, 1855.

A decision was made to tear down the old church and build again. In 1974 Bishop Joseph M. Breitenbeck came to dedicate the new church. In the year 2000, with Father Leo Rosloniec as pastor, renovations to expand the church building are ongoing. The parish continues to be committed to its faith and family traditions.

Holy Name of Jesus
Wyoming

ON JULY 26, 1908, Bishop Henry Joseph Richter dedicated Holy Name Church on property donated by Mrs. Donna DeBoer. Father Thomas Reid was named its first pastor. The first church building served as church, school, and convent. However, because of the growth of the parish, Father James P. Flannery found it necessary to build a larger temporary church. Much of the work on this building was done by parishioners who volunteered their time and labor.

In 1960 the present church was built and consecrated. The priests who led this successful effort were Fathers Joseph Delehanty and Louis VanBergen.

The parish mission statement speaks of the goals and aspirations of the people of Holy Name of Jesus. It states: "Holy Name of Jesus is a parish committed to the mission of Jesus Christ. We are called upon by the Holy Spirit to share our unique gifts, to spread the Good News, to develop and build the Body of Christ. We seek this through Eucharist, prayer, education, and Christian service."

The people of Holy Name opened their hearts and their parish to the Vietnamese community of Our Lady of LaVang in 1987 and now invite their Hispanic brothers and sisters to join in building up the Body of Christ.

The renewed church building of Holy Name of Jesus is a symbol of a people reborn in the Holy Spirit. Under the leadership of Father Donald E. Weber, the parish celebrates its 100th anniversary as a faith community conscious of the Spirit's blessing in the past and confident of God's presence in the future.

Our Lady of LaVang
Wyoming

IN THE FALL OF 1975, some of the Vietnamese began to enter the state of Michigan as refugees. The Vietnamese Catholic families occasionally met each other while attending Mass at the local churches. They exchanged addresses and telephone numbers to form a small network.

By the end of 1976, this first group of Vietnamese Catholics initiated the idea of inviting some of the Vietnamese priests from the Chicago and Detroit areas to occasionally visit Grand Rapids and say Mass in Vietnamese.

After Easter 1980, when Father Ngo-Chau-Minh's term expired in Grand Rapids, the diocese named Msgr. Herman Zerfas as director of the Vietnamese Apostolate. During this time, Msgr. Zerfas contacted and invited Father Peter Hoang Xuan Nghiem to join the Vietnamese community in Grand Rapids from a refugee camp in Hong Kong.

On June 5, 1980, Father Peter officially accepted the responsibility of directing the Vietnamese Apostolate. On July 1, 1983, Father Peter was reassigned to be the associate pastor at St. James Parish in Grand Rapids, and Father John Au-Duong-Truong took his place as director of the Vietnamese Apostolate; he remained director until July 1, 1988. Father John Au-Duong-Truong was then reassigned as associate pastor elsewhere, and Father Peter was renominated as the director.

On August 15, 1993, Bishop Robert J. Rose officially assigned Father Peter as pastor of the Vietnamese Catholic congregation at Holy Name of Jesus Church, retaining at the same time his title as director of the Vietnamese Apostolate in the diocese.

On February 9, 1997, while participating in the Tet celebration with his "Vietnamese Catholic children," Bishop Rose officially named the Vietnamese Catholic congregation Our Lady of LaVang.

After nearly a decade of searching, with the advice of the diocese, the community purchased its own church from Beverly Reformed Church. They moved into the new church on October 30, 1998. This church was then deemed the official operating institution of Our Lady of LaVang Parish. On Thanksgiving 1998, the first Mass was celebrated in the church; it was devoted to the Vietnamese martyrs. From that date, the parish conducted a regular schedule of liturgies and other parish events.

From a small group simply referred to as the Vietnamese Catholic Community, the Vietnamese Catholics had become the Vietnamese Apostolate and finally Our Lady of LaVang Parish. Over the years their worship site had changed seven times: St. Alphonsus, St. John Vianney, St. Joseph Center, St. James, Our Lady of Aglona, St. Francis Xavier, and Holy Name of Jesus had all in turn taken the fledgling parish under their wing. Finally the community had a worship space that was truly its own.

On Sunday, June 27, 1999, Bishop Rose dedicated a new church for Our Lady of LaVang Parish. It was the first church to be established specifically for Vietnamese in this diocese.

St. Dominic
Wyoming

B Y 1942 Bishop Joseph C. Plagens saw the need for a new parish in the area of Wyoming now served by St. Dominic's Parish. Property was purchased at 3860 South Division Avenue, and Father Francis Schultz established St. John Vianney Parish. Later, St. John Vianney moved to its present site, but the Division Avenue property was retained and served as a mission church of St. John Vianney with one or two Masses being celebrated there weekly.

With continued growth in the Wyoming area, Bishop Joseph M. Breitenbeck established St. Dominic's Parish on January 17, 1974. Father Robert J. Maternoski was assigned as the first pastor. The parish was located on the Division Avenue site formerly occupied by St. John Vianney.

Plans were made to build a new church on the site in 1976. At the same time, however, the parish had an opportunity to purchase its current church on Bellevue S.W. from the First Assembly of God congregation, which was building a larger church. The Bellevue church was purchased in 1976, and the parish took possession of the property in 1978.

Pastors succeeding Father Maternoski have been Fathers William Walters (1974-1977), Eugene Alvesteffer (1977-1986), Denis Nash (1986-1990), Thomas DeYoung (1990-1996), and Charles Dautremont (1996-present).

St. John Vianney
Wyoming

S T. JOHN VIANNEY PARISH was established in 1942 at 3860 South Division Avenue for a nucleus of 57 families. The first Mass was celebrated on August 2, 1942.

Because growth in the area necessitated finding a new location, land was purchased on Clyde Park Avenue S.W. in 1949. A church and school were built, with the first Mass celebrated on Christmas Eve 1951. The school, grades two through eight, was staffed by the Felician Sisters and opened in January 1952.

The parish built a convent on Clyde Park at Floyd Street and a rectory at Bellevue Street. In 1953 five classrooms and a cafeteria were added to the school. A larger convent was built on Floyd Street and the original convent was sold. In 1961 the parish added five more classrooms.

By 1963 membership in the parish had grown to 1,250 families, with over 800 children in the school. Our Lady of Lourdes Shrine was added in 1959, the church was enlarged, and more classrooms were added. In 1982 the Monsignor Schultz Activity Center was completed. The large convent became the Caring Place day care and preschool center, the church was remodeled, and landscaping of the grounds was completed.

Father John Klonowski with Altar Society members c. 1950.

Over the years, renovations continued. In 1997 the parish offices moved to the Caring Place; Faith Formation moved to the former parish office space; and a new library, computer lab, and science room transformed what was once the "cold lunch room."

Membership has remained fairly constant and is now about 1,550 families. Lay staff has increased, but clergy have decreased. By 1998 there was one priest instead of three or four, and no nuns were teaching in the school. The parish is served now by dedicated lay ministers and staff who assist the pastor, Father Larry King. St. John Vianney Parish remains a vibrant, caring community, able to change and respond to the challenges of the next century.

BIBLIOGRAPHY

American Catholic. Charles R. Morris. New York: Random House, 1997.

American Catholics: A History of the Roman Catholic Community in the United States. James Hennesey, S.J. New York: Oxford University Press, 1981.

By Her Fruits… Sister Mary Joseph Lynch-Sister of Mercy. Sister Mary Lucy McDonald, RSM. Farmington Hills, Michigan, Sisters of Mercy, 1981.

Catholic and American: A Popular History. Michael F. Perko, S.J. Huntington, Indiana: Our Sunday Visitor, Inc., 1989.

The Catholic Church in Detroit 1701-1888. George Paré. Detroit: The Gabriel Richard Press, 1951.

The Catholic Church in the Grand River Valley 1833-1950. John W. McGee. Lansing, Michigan: Franklin Dekleine Company, 1950.

The Diary of Bishop Frederic Baraga. Regis M. Walling and Rev. N. Daniel Rupp, eds. Detroit: Wayne State University Press, 1990.

The First One Hundred Years: The Basilica of St. Adalbert 1881-1981. Philip Jung. Greenville, Michigan: Greenville Printing Co., 1981.

Fr. Marquette's Journal. Michigan Department of State. 1990.

Friderici Irenaei Baraga. vol. 1. Congregatio De Causis Sanctorum. Rome: Tipografica "Leberit", 1998.

Gathered at the River: Grand Rapids, Michigan, and Its People of Faith. James D. Bratt and Christopher H. Meehan. Grand Rapids, Michigan: William B. Eerdmans Publishing Company, 1993.

The Grand Rapids St. Isidore's Story. Eduard Adams Skendzel. Grand Rapids, Michigan: Littleshield Press, 1999.

History of the Archdiocese of Cincinnati 1821-1921. Rev. John H. Lamott, S.T.D. New York and Cincinnati: Frederik Pustet Company, Inc., 1921.

Holy Trinity Parish Alpine 1848-1998. Donna O'Conner. Grand Rapids, Michigan: West Michigan Printing, Inc., 1999.

In God's Own Time, St. Francis deSales Parish, Muskegon, Michigan. Mona L. Schwind, O.P. Grand Rapids, Michigan: West Michigan Printing, Inc., 1997.

Jacques Marquette, S.J. 1637-1675. Joseph P. Donnelly, S.J. Chicago: Loyola University Press, 1968.

The Jesuit Relations and Allied Documents. Edna Kenton, ed. New York: Albert and Charles Boni, 1925.

"The North Dorr Church Property Dispute." Earl Boyea, *Michigan Historical Review*, vol.16, no. 2, Fall 1990, pp.75-90.

Memoirs of Mother Mary Aquinata Fiegler, O.P. Sr. Mary Philomena Kildee, O.P. GrandRapids, Michigan: The James Bayne Company, 1928.

Michigan. Bruce Catton. New York: W. W. Norton and Co., 1984.

Michigan: A History of the Wolverine State. Willis F. Dunbar. Grand Rapids, Michigan: William B. Eerdmans Publishing Co., 1970.

Period Pieces: An Account of the Grand Rapids Dominicans 1853-1966. Mona L. Schwind, O.P. Grand Rapids, Michigan: West Michigan Printing, Inc., 1991.

A Priest in Public Service: Francis J. Haas and the New Deal. Thomas E. Blantz, C.S.C. Notre Dame, Indiana: University of Notre Dame Press, 1982.

The Sacred Heart Story 1904-1979. Eduard Adams Skendzel. Grand Rapids, Michigan: Foremost Press Inc., 1981.

Seasons of Grace: A History of the Catholic Archdiocese of Detroit. Leslie Woodcock Tentler. Detroit: Wayne State University Press, 1990.

A Short History of American Catholicism. Martin E. Marty. Allen, Texas: Thomas More Publishing, 1995.

These Very Stones Cry Out. Fr. Patrick T. Cawley, ed. Boyne City, Michigan: Harbor House Publishers, 1999.

Other Selected Parish Histories
   125 Years of Faith 1856-1981, St. Mary's Church, Muskegon, Michigan.
   Golden Jubilee Memories of St. Mary's Church, Grand Rapids, Mi. 1857-1907.s
   St. James Parish, Grand Rapids, Michigan 1870-1945
   St. Mary's Parish, Big Rapids, Michigan 1873-1973.

PHOTO AND ILLUSTRATION CREDITS
FOR DIOCESAN HISTORY

Illustrations -- cover design; all chapter heading illustrations; Midnight Mass, p. 14; Father Andreas Viszoczky with children, p. 26; and the arted maps on pp. 12, 43, 48, 85, 132 and 147 -- © Margaret Leiber.

Unless otherwise indicated, all photos are the property of the Grand Rapids Diocese.